PRENTICE HALL LITERATURE

PENGUIN EDITION

Teaching Resources

Unit 1
Fiction and Nonfiction

Grade Eight

PEARSON

Prentice Hall

Upper Saddle River, New Jersey
Boston, Massachusetts

Copyright © by Pearson Education, Inc., publishing as Pearson Prentice Hall, Boston, Massachusetts 02116. All rights reserved. Printed in the United States of America. This publication is protected by copyright, and permission should be obtained from the publisher prior to any prohibited reproduction, storage in a retrieval system, or transmission in any form or by any means, electronic, mechanical, photocopying, recording, or likewise. The publisher hereby grants permission to reproduce these pages, in part or in whole, for classroom use only, the number not to exceed the number of students in each class. Notice of copyright must appear on all copies. For information regarding permission(s), write to: Rights and Permissions Department, One Lake Street, Upper Saddle River, New Jersey 07458.

Pearson Prentice Hall™ is a trademark of Pearson Education, Inc.
Pearson® is a registered trademark of Pearson plc.
Prentice Hall® is a registered trademark of Pearson Education, Inc.

ISBN 0-13-134197-9

4 5 6 7 8 9 10   10 09 08 07

Contents

Part 1 Make Predictions

from *The Baker Heater League* by Patricia and Fredrick McKissack
"The 11:59" by Patricia C. McKissack

"A Retrieved Reformation" by O. Henry

"Raymond's Run" by Toni Cade Bambara

Part 2 Author's Purpose

"The American Dream" by Martin Luther King, Jr.

"Up the Slide" by Jack London

"A Glow in the Dark" from *Woodsong* by Gary Paulsen

Vocabulary Warm-up Word Lists

Study these words from the selections. Then, complete the activities.

Word List A

communication [kuh myoo nuh KAY shun] *adj.* designed to help people stay in touch.
  News moves quickly through the modern <u>communication</u> chain of instant messaging.

courtesy [KUR tuh see] *n.* polite behavior
  Show <u>courtesy</u> to other movie-goers by keeping cell phones turned off.

customary [KUHS tuh mair ee] *adj.* usual; happening regularly by custom
  It is <u>customary</u> to give couples something gold on their fiftieth anniversary.

individual [in duh VIJ oo uhl] *adj.* separate; specific to one person
  One chef cannot possibly handle the <u>individual</u> requests of every diner.

loyalty [LOY uhl tee] *n.* being faithful and true to beliefs, ideas, or people
  We showed <u>loyalty</u> to the team by cheering it on throughout a losing season.

performance [per FAWR muhns] *n.* action that has been completed
  My <u>performance</u> on the test was great, thanks to all my study and review.

powerful [POW er fuhl] *adj.* having great strength
  The <u>powerful</u> jaws of an alligator can easily snap a floating log in half.

shattering [SHAT uh ring] *v.* breaking into small pieces
  I was shocked to see the baseball <u>shattering</u> the window.

Word List B

competing [kuhm PEET ing] *v.* taking part in a contest
  We were nervous about <u>competing</u> against the top team in hockey.

erupted [i RUHP tid] *v.* broke out suddenly
  The crowd <u>erupted</u> into applause and screams as the band took the stage.

exploits [EK sployts] *n.* brave or notable deeds
  Sir Edmund Hillary's <u>exploits</u> include being the first to reach the top of Mt. Everest.

hostile [HAHS tuhl] *adj.* unfriendly or angry
  Police on horseback kept the <u>hostile</u> crowd from becoming violent.

legacy [LEG uh see] *n.* something handed down from one generation to the next
  Firefighters killed in the line of duty leave a <u>legacy</u> of courage that inspires others.

predicted [pri DIK tid] *v.* told in advance
  As <u>predicted</u>, the race for governor was a very close one.

scoffed [SKAHFD] *v.* rudely made fun of
  The tall teenager <u>scoffed</u> at the idea that she couldn't dunk a basketball.

storyteller [STAW ree tel er] *n.* someone who tells stories aloud
  The <u>storyteller</u> used finger puppets as he told a fairy tale to the children.

Name _____ Date _____

from The Baker Heater League by Patricia C. and Fredrick McKissack
"The 11:59" by Patricia C. McKissack
Vocabulary Warm-up Exercises

Exercise A *Fill in each blank in the paragraph below with an appropriate word from Word List A. Use each word only once.*

On the worst possible day, all of Gina's normal [1] _____ systems were down. She wanted to give Ben the [2] _____ of a return call, but the phones were dead. Even her [3] _____ new computer wasn't working. The [4] _____ of all the household gadgets was harmed by the workers installing the new cable lines. Only Gina's [5] _____ to Meg kept her from walking over to Meg's house to use the phone. Ben had not invited Meg to his party, and Gina knew that this was [6] _____ her friend's feelings. Meg's quirky [7] _____ way of dressing and acting always seemed to mean she was left out. In her [8] _____ way of dealing gently with Meg, Gina would never reveal her excitement about the party.

Exercise B *Decide whether each statement below is true or false. Circle* T *or* F. *Then, explain your answer.*

1. A <u>hostile</u> environment can help make visitors feel comfortable right away.
   T / F _____

2. The <u>exploits</u> of most folk tale heroes are told in a way that stretches the truth and improves their <u>legacy</u>.
   T / F _____

3. In the 1950s many <u>scoffed</u> at the idea that people would walk on the moon.
   T / F _____

4. A great <u>storyteller</u> usually reads from a book when sharing a favorite tale.
   T / F _____

5. Some scientists in the 1990s <u>predicted</u> that computers would crash on January 1, 2000.
   T / F _____

6. Swimmers <u>competing</u> in a race take time to see where other racers are.
   T / F _____

7. A pimple has <u>erupted</u> when you can feel it but not see it.
   T / F _____

Unit 1 Resources: Fiction and Nonfiction
© Pearson Education, Inc., publishing as Pearson Prentice Hall. All rights reserved.

2

from The Baker Heater League by Patricia C. and Fredrick McKissack
"The 11:59" by Patricia C. McKissack
Reading Warm-up A

Read the following passage. Pay special attention to the underlined words. Then, read it again, and complete the activities. Use a separate sheet of paper for your written answers.

Shortly after my grandfather stopped working as a ticket salesman for the railroad, he died. He had spent 40 years on the job. His <u>powerful</u> frame seemed to shrink when he no longer had to open the ticket window at the <u>customary</u> time of 5:00 A.M. I watched the light leave his eyes, his joyful spirit fade away, until one day he didn't wake up at all. I was saddened by Grandpa's death. I wanted to understand what had happened. I wondered if missing the job and all the daily <u>communication</u> opportunities had killed him. Had my grandfather simply become too lonely to live? Thoughts like these were <u>shattering</u> my sleep each night. I decided to try to find some answers to my questions.

As I talked with Grandpa's buddies from the railroad, I did not find the answers I was seeking. I did discover many wonderful things about my grandfather, however. I heard stories of Grandpa's <u>courtesy</u> at all times, even when the rudest people would holler at him about ticket prices or schedules. I was touched to learn that Grandpa's <u>individual</u> efforts to help disabled people board trains led to better access for all who needed help.

Most importantly, I learned from every person what <u>loyalty</u> to a job really means. It means taking pride in yourself and in your own efforts. For example, few of Grandpa's buddies ever missed more than a week of work each year. All gave their time, talents, and best efforts to their work. This was especially true of my grandfather. I hope that someday my own job <u>performance</u> will make my grandchildren proud of me and my efforts. I know now that daily excellence is what I will try to achieve in my life and in my work.

1. Underline a phrase that tells how Grandpa's <u>powerful</u> body changed. Then, write what *powerful* means.

2. Circle the time that would have been <u>customary</u> for Grandpa to be working. Then, explain what *customary* means.

3. Circle a word that describes how life feels without <u>communication</u> opportunities. Then, describe your favorite *communication* channels.

4. Circle the words that name what was <u>shattering</u> the writer's sleep. Explain what *shattering* means.

5. Underline the words that describe a good example of Grandpa's <u>courtesy</u>. Give two other examples of *courtesy*.

6. Write a sentence about another time when someone's <u>individual</u> efforts made a difference.

7. Underline the writer's definition of job <u>loyalty</u>. Then, write your own definition.

8. Circle the words that describe the writer's job <u>performance</u> goals. Tell what *performance* means.

from The Baker Heater League by Patricia C. and Fredrick McKissack
"The 11:59" by Patricia C. McKissack
Reading Warm-up B

Read the following passage. Pay special attention to the underlined words. Then, read it again, and complete the activities. Use a separate sheet of paper for your written answers.

Even before railways crisscrossed the United States, there were lots of exciting stories about the <u>exploits</u> of early railroad workers. These were the workers who laid the tracks from coast to coast. Their <u>legacy</u> is one of back-breaking work in the face of great hardships. Nothing stopped them—not <u>hostile</u> Indians, not mighty rivers, not even mountains of solid rock. Many of the railroad workers came from China and Ireland and other nations. They were determined to succeed in their new home.

The people who paid for the tracks, planned the routes, and found the workers had the same "can do" attitude. They <u>scoffed</u> at anyone who said the idea of a Transcontinental Railroad was nothing but a crazy dream. These folks came up with solutions to every problem.

It was during the Civil War that work to span the nation with rails began in earnest. The two coasts of the United States were joined by rail on May 10, 1869. That is the day when two crews who had been <u>competing</u> to lay the most track the most quickly met in Utah. From the East came the Union Pacific crew. From the West came the workers of the Central Pacific. On that final day, a huge spurt of energy <u>erupted</u> from the crews, producing a record 10 miles of track in 12 hours!

If you were to read the speeches given to celebrate the completion of the Transcontinental Railroad, you might think that everyone had <u>predicted</u> success. Many took credit for it. Still, when you hear a good <u>storyteller</u> recount the heroic deeds and efforts of railroad workers who beat all the odds, it is clear who the real heroes were.

1. Underline the words that describe the workers' <u>legacy</u>. Then, explain what *legacy* means.

2. Write a sentence to tell why natural obstacles could have been viewed as more *hostile* than any people.

3. Circle words that tell what the railroad planners <u>scoffed</u> at. Then, write a sentence about something you have *scoffed* at.

4. Underline words that describe what the crews were <u>competing</u> to do. Write about a sport in which *competing* involves speed and distance.

5. Circle the words that describe what the workers did when they <u>erupted</u> at full force. Why is *spurt* a good word to use in the same sentence as *erupted*?

6. Had everyone <u>predicted</u> success for the railroad? Explain your answer.

7. Underline the words in the final sentence that describe <u>exploits</u>. Then, write a sentence telling why a good <u>storyteller</u> tells about people's *exploits*.

Patricia C. McKissack
Listening and Viewing

Segment 1: Meet Patricia C. McKissack
- How does Patricia and Fredrick McKissack's writing collaboration allow them to write many more books than if they wrote independently? What do you think the benefits of writing with a coauthor might be?

_____

_____

_____

Segment 2: Fiction and Nonfiction
- How does Patricia C. McKissack make her fictional stories "real"? Why do you think Patricia C. McKissack uses the phrase "ticktock" repeatedly in "The 11:59"?

_____

_____

_____

Segment 3: The Writing Process
- How do Patricia and Fredrick McKissack divide the steps in the writing process? Which of these steps do you think is the most important and why?

_____

_____

_____

Segment 4: The Rewards of Writing
- What advice does Patricia C. McKissack give students about how they should approach writing? In what ways do you agree with her?

_____

_____

_____

_____

Name _____ Date _____

Learning About Fiction and Nonfiction

Literature may be either **fiction** or **nonfiction.** The following chart compares and contrasts these two types of literature.

Characteristics	Fiction	Nonfiction
Overall Features	Fiction is prose that tells an imaginary story about people, animals, or other **characters.** Each character has particular **traits,** or qualities, that can affect the story. The story's sequence of events is its **plot,** which begins with a **conflict,** or problem, and ends with a **resolution,** or conclusion. The **setting** is the time and place when events in the story occur. The story's **theme** is its message about life.	Nonfiction is prose that deals only with real people, events, or ideas. Nonfiction works present facts or discuss ideas. Nonfiction works reflect the **author's style,** or use of language, including dialect, rhythm, and organization. The overall feeling of the writing is its **mood** or **atmosphere.**
Perspective	A story can be told from **first-person point of view,** the perspective of a character in the story; or from **third-person point of view,** the perspective of a narrator outside the story.	Nonfiction works are written from the perspective or **point of view** of the author, who is a real person.
Sample Forms	short stories, novellas, novels	speeches, editorials, articles, research papers, biographies
Author's Purpose	to entertain	to persuade, inform, or entertain

DIRECTIONS: *Read each item. Decide whether it is a work of fiction or nonfiction, and then write* fiction *or* nonfiction *on the line provided.*

_____ 1. a piece of literature that tells about a ten-foot-tall lumberjack

_____ 2. a piece of literature that presents facts about "man-eating" plants

_____ 3. a piece of literature that urges readers to collect and use rainwater

_____ 4. a piece of literature that tells about the childhood of a famous real-life artist

_____ 5. a piece of literature about a kangaroo who misplaces her pocket

"The 11:59" by Patricia C. McKissack
Model Selection: Fiction

Fiction is prose that tells a story about characters or events from the author's imagination. The **characters** in a work of fiction are the people or animals who take part in the story's action. Characters have **traits,** or characteristics, that can affect the story's events. In "The 11:59," for example, Lester is a spellbinding storyteller. Through his stories, the reader learns about events that will happen to Lester later on.

A story's series of events is its **plot.** A plot usually begins with a problem, or **conflict;** and ends with a conclusion, or **resolution.** The plot of "The 11:59" hinges on the conflict between Lester's story about a mysterious train and the reality of his physical condition.

DIRECTIONS: *Read this passage from "The 11:59," and answer the questions that follow.*

Suddenly [Lester] felt a sharp pain in his chest. At exactly the same moment he heard the mournful sound of a train whistle, which the wind seemed to carry from some faraway place. Ignoring his pain, Lester looked at the old station. He knew nothing was scheduled to come in or out till early morning. Nervously he lit a match to check the time. 11:59!

"No," he said into the darkness. "I'm not ready. I've got plenty of living yet."

Fear quickened his stop. Reaching his small apartment, he hurried up the steps. His heart pounded in his ear, and his left arm tingled. He had an idea, and there wasn't a moment to waste. But his own words haunted him. Ain't no way to escape the final ride on the 11:59.

"But I'm gon' try!" Lester spent the rest of the night plotting his escape from fate.

1. What is Lester's **conflict**? _____

_____

2. What **character traits** is Lester shown to have in this passage? List two.

_____

3. How do these **character traits** set the rest of the story in motion? _____

_____

4. Tell what **resolution** ends Lester's conflict—and the story itself.

_____

from **The Baker Heater League** by Patricia and Fredrick McKissack
Model Selection: Nonfiction

Nonfiction is prose in which authors present people, events, and ideas from real life. Nonfiction works can report facts and present ideas. They also might present the author's opinions.

A work of nonfiction can sometimes refer to fictional, or imaginary, ideas. For example, *The Baker Heater League* describes some of the legends surrounding famous railroad men. Many details in these legends are fictional. However, it is a *fact* that Pullman porters liked to tell and retell these fanciful legends.

When deciding what kinds of facts and details to include in a nonfiction work, an author thinks about his or her **purpose.**

- To **persuade** readers, an author may use forceful facts and opinions.
- To **entertain** readers, an author may include amusing or unusual facts and details.
- To **inform** readers, an author may use a wide range of facts about a single topic.

DIRECTIONS: *Read this passage from* The Baker Heater League, *and answer the questions that follow.*

The real John Henry, believed to be a newly freed slave from North Carolina, joined the West Virginia steel-driving team hired to dig out the Big Bend Tunnel for the C. & O. Railroad, circa 1870. Many stories detail the life and adventures of this two hundred-pound, six-foot man who was so strong he could drive steel with a hammer in each hand. John Henry's death occurred after competing with a steam drill, winning and then dying.

1. What **real-life person** does this passage describe? _____

   What did this person do for a living? _____

2. List two **facts** from the passage.

   Fact 1: _____

   _____

   Fact 2: _____

   _____

3. Why do the authors include both facts and legends in *The Baker Heater League*? (*Hint*: What **purposes** do the authors have for writing the article?) _____

   _____

   _____

Name _____ Date _____

"The 11:59" by Patricia C. McKissack
from **The Baker Heater League** by Patricia and Fredrick McKissack
Selection Test A

Learning About Fiction and Nonfiction *Identify the letter of the choice that best answers the question.*

_____ 1. Which statement is true about **nonfiction**?
   A. It is told from the author's perspective.
   B. It includes only imaginary events.
   C. It includes only opinions.
   D. Its narrator is a character in the story.

_____ 2. Which of the following best defines the literary term **setting**?
   A. the early events of a story
   B. the point of view from which a story is told
   C. the author's reasons for writing a work
   D. the time and place of a story's action

_____ 3. Which of the following is a part of a story's **plot**?
   A. setting
   B. novella
   C. conflict
   D. narrator

_____ 4. Which of the following is an example of **nonfiction**?
   A. a short story
   B. a novel
   C. a fairy tale
   D. a textbook

_____ 5. In a nonfiction work, what is **atmosphere**?
   A. where the action takes place
   B. the overall feeling of the work
   C. the time period covered in the work
   D. the author's style

Critical Reading

_____ 6. Which phrase best describes Lester Simmons in "The 11:59"?
   A. superhuman character
   B. good storyteller
   C. retired train engineer
   D. superstitious fool

Unit 1 Resources: Fiction and Nonfiction

____ 7. What is the "11:59"?

    A. the Brotherhood of Sleeping Car Porters

    B. the time to tell stories of the old days

    C. the Death Train

    D. a passenger who tips poorly

____ 8. While locked in his apartment, Lester looks back over his life. Why does he do this?

    A. He is bored.

    B. He is looking for a new story idea.

    C. He is trying to remember what the 11:59 really is.

    D. He is preparing to die.

____ 9. Which event is the **resolution** of "The 11:59"?

    A. Lester hears the train whistle.

    B. Lester locks himself in his apartment.

    C. Lester meets his old friend Tip.

    D. Lester dies.

____ 10. What happens to Lester's watch at the end of "The 11:59"?

    A. It stops.

    B. It gets crushed.

    C. It gets stolen.

    D. It disappears.

____ 11. What message about death is conveyed in "The 11:59"?

    A. No one can escape death.

    B. Only cowards try to avoid death.

    C. Everyone dies at the same time.

    D. Dying is like a story.

____ 12. Who belonged to the Baker Heater League?

    A. heater repairmen

    B. train engineers

    C. sleeping car porters

    D. steel-drivers

____ 13. From whose **point of view** is *The Baker Heater League* told?

    A. Daddy Joe

    B. a retired railroad worker

    C. a member of the Baker Heater League

    D. the authors

____ **14.** Which sentence best describes the heroes of the railroad, such as Casey Jones and John Henry?

    A. They were fictional characters who never really existed.

    B. They had qualities the railroad workers valued.

    C. They were admired for their storytelling skills.

    D. They never had a chance to show their strength and bravery.

____ **15.** Why did the authors write *The Baker Heater League*?

    A. to entertain readers with a fictional story about railroad workers

    B. to teach readers the rules of the railroad

    C. to inform readers about early railroad workers

    D. to convince readers that railroad men are the best storytellers

Essay

16. In McKissack's story, Lester tells porters the entertaining story about the legend of "The 11:59." In a brief essay, explain how this story becomes, for Lester, a "real-life" experience.

17. In *The Baker Heater League*, the authors describe several heroes of the railroad. In an essay, identify and tell about one of these heroes. How did he become a hero? What special qualities does he have? How is he similar to or different from modern-day superheroes?

Name _____ Date _____

Selection Test B

Learning About Fiction and Nonfiction *Identify the letter of the choice that best completes the statement or answers the question.*

____ 1. Which statement best distinguishes **nonfiction** from fiction?
A. Nonfiction has only imaginary characters; fiction features real characters.
B. Nonfiction never includes the writer's opinions; works of fiction do express opinions.
C. Unlike fiction, the series of events in a nonfiction work make up its plot.
D. Nonfiction presents real people and events; fiction presents imaginary people and events.

____ 2. Which statement is true about **fiction**?
A. It can contain only real people.
B. It can contain imaginary events.
C. Its characters cannot express opinions.
D. It cannot contain any realistic details.

____ 3. Which of the following is the literary term for the concluding event in a **plot**?
A. novella
B. resolution
C. introduction
D. conflict

____ 4. From which **point of view** is a work of nonfiction told?
A. first-person point of view
B. third-person point of view
C. the author's point of view
D. the reader's point of view

____ 5. Which of the following groups contains one example of **fiction**?
A. essay, short story, biography
B. reference book, editorial, speech
C. autobiography, diary, letter
D. travel narrative, research paper, article

____ 6. Which of the following is an example of **nonfiction**?
A. a novella about a chimpanzee and the woman who raises him
B. an article about chimpanzees who use sign language
C. a story about a scientist who works with chimpanzees
D. a novel about a chimpanzee who "adopts" a human child

Critical Reading

____ 7. Which plot event best expresses the **conflict** in "The 11:59"?
A. Porters love to hear Lester tell stories about the "death train."
B. Lester hears the whistle of the 11:59 but isn't ready to die.
C. Lester dies of a heart attack when the 11:59 arrives.
D. Friends find Lester on the floor of his apartment.

___ 8. Which of the following is the **setting** of "The 11:59"?
A. St. Louis, the mid-1900s
B. the Brotherhood of Sleeping Car Porters, 1926
C. a Pullman car, the mid-1800s
D. the St. Louis Union Train Station, the shoeshine stand, 11:59

___ 9. In Patricia C. McKissack's story "The 11:59," who is Lester Simmons?
A. a larger-than-life railroad hero
B. an old friend of the narrator
C. a retired Pullman car porter
D. an engineer on the 11:59

___ 10. Which of Lester's **character traits** is illustrated in this passage from "The 11:59"?
In his creakiest voice, Lester drove home the point. "All us porters got to board that train one day. Ain't no way to escape the final ride on the 11:59."

A. his sense of humor
B. his pessimistic personality
C. his punctuality
D. his storytelling skills

___ 11. When Lester reviews his life, what does he decide?
A. that examining the past is a foolish thing to do
B. that he has no regrets and that he stands by his choices
C. that he only had good times and that his memories are all good
D. that he should have married Louise Henderson and had children

___ 12. Why does Patricia McKissack repeat the phrase *Ticktock, ticktock* near the end of "The 11:59"?
A. to build suspense and show the passing of time
B. to introduce some humor into the story
C. to emphasize to the reader that the Death Train has passed
D. to show that Lester is going insane

___ 13. Which of the following best expresses the **theme** of "The 11:59"?
A. You can't escape death no matter how hard you try.
B. Telling and listening to stories can save our lives.
C. Train travel is a passing way of life.
D. Everyone can be a hero in his or her own way.

___ 14. What was the Baker Heater League?
A. a brotherhood of storytelling railroad porters
B. a group of larger-than-life railroad heroes
C. a team of steel-drivers who worked for the railroad
D. a group of highly-skilled railroad engineers

___ **15.** In the McKissacks' *The Baker Heater League,* what is a Baker heater?
  A. a coal-burning train engine
  B. a heater used in Pullman cars
  C. a portable hot plate
  D. a pot-bellied stove

___ **16.** According to *The Baker Heater League,* why did the porters tell stories?
  A. to pass secret messages
  B. to entertain themselves
  C. to test younger porters
  D. to cover up their deep loneliness

___ **17.** How is Daddy Joe different from other railroad heroes the McKissacks describe?
  A. He is bigger and stronger.
  B. He is a real person.
  C. He is the subject of many songs and stories.
  D. He is the porters' very own hero.

___ **18.** The authors of *The Baker Heater League* write that pullman porters created Daddy Joe "in their own image." What do they mean by this?
  A. Daddy Joe's exaggerated feats and accomplishments actually happened.
  B. The porters were vain and prideful men.
  C. The porters gave Daddy Joe the qualities they most valued in themselves.
  D. Daddy Joe was so outlandish that he did not resemble an actual human being.

___ **19.** What makes *The Baker Heater League* a work of nonfiction?
  A. The authors describe their own personal experiences.
  B. It is set in a distant time and place.
  C. The authors provide facts about their subject.
  D. It contains legends about heroes.

___ **20.** What main **purpose** did the authors have for writing *The Baker Heater League*?
  A. to inform readers about Pullman car porters
  B. to express opinions about transportation
  C. to entertain readers with railroad "tall tales"
  D. to persuade readers to ride trains more often

Essay

21. *The Baker Heater League* is a work of nonfiction, but it refers to fictional legends and stories. In an essay, explain why you think the authors decided to include nonfactual information in a factual work. Use examples from the article to support your ideas.

22. In "The 11:59," the author uses the first half of the story to give important background information. In the second half of the story, she shows the unfolding of the story's plot. In an essay, do the following:

• explain what background information the author provides;
• identify the main plot events; and
• explain how the two parts of the story relate to each other.

Name _____

Unit 1: Fiction and Nonfiction
Part 1 Concept Map

Academic Vocabulary words you can use to discuss making predictions

_____
_____
_____
_____

Reading Skills and Strategies: Predictions

you can **predict** what will happen next

→ by

making informed guesses

and by →

reading ahead to **confirm or correct predictions**

(demonstrated in this selection)

Selection name: _____

(demonstrated in this selection)

Selection name: _____

Literary Analysis: Narratives

Narrative writing

has

a plot

and →

conflict

Reading Informational Materials: Consumer Documents: Maps and Schedules

When you read maps and schedules

use →

text aids and features

(demonstrated in this selection)

Selection name: _____

Basic Elements of Fiction and Nonfiction

- Characters
- Setting
- Plot
- Point of view
- Mood
- Author's Style

Types of Fiction and Nonfiction

- Short Stories
- Novels
- Essays
- Speeches
- Biographies

Comparing Literary Works: Narrative Structure

may or may not be chronological and use these devices:

→ foreshadowing

→ flashback

(demonstrated in these selections)

Selection names:
1. _____
2. _____

Part 1 Student Log

Complete this chart to track your assignments.

Writing	Extend Your Learning	Writing Workshop	Other Assignments

Unit 1: Fiction and Nonfiction
Part 1 Diagnostic Test 1

Read the selection. Then, answer the questions.

Basketball is among the most popular sports in the United States and has become increasingly popular around the world in recent years. The basic idea of the game is very simple. The object is to throw the ball through the opponents' basket while stopping them from scoring. Running with the ball without bouncing it is against the rules; the ball must be dribbled, shot, or passed to another player.

The ability to shoot accurately is one of the most important skills in basketball. For a lay-up shot, a player charges in under the basket and shoots the ball. The hook is an over-the-shoulder shot that allows a player to keep his body between the opponent and the ball. Very tall players sometimes dunk the ball by leaping high over the basket and slamming it through the hoop to score two points.

Watching professional athletes play basketball is fun, but playing it is even more fun. Whether it's cold and wet outside or a beautiful balmy day, you can probably find an indoor or outdoor court to play on. Even if no one is around to play with, you can have a good time practicing different shots all by yourself.

1. According to the selection, which type of shot allows a player to keep his body between the opponent and the ball?
   A. lay-up
   B. hook
   C. dunk
   D. slam

2. What is the main goal of a basketball team?
   A. to play the game in any weather
   B. to show how much fun the game of basketball can be and to encourage young people to play the game
   C. to dribble, shoot, and pass the ball
   D. to throw the ball through the opposing team's basket while stopping the other team from scoring

3. What is the writer's attitude toward the game of basketball?
   A. It is boring to watch but fun to play.
   B. It has many rules and is difficult to learn.
   C. It is a fun game to watch and play.
   D. It is the very best game in the world.

4. What advantage do tall basketball players have over shorter players?
   A. They are more likely to be professional athletes.
   B. They can dunk the ball into the basket.
   C. They can dribble and pass the ball better.
   D. They are better at hook shots.

5. At the beginning of the selection, the writer states that basketball is growing in popularity. Which of the following details provides the best explanation for why basketball is so popular?
   A. Running with the ball without bouncing it is illegal.
   B. Players must be able to shoot the ball accurately.
   C. Types of shots include the lay-up, hook, and dunk.
   D. One can always find a place to play basketball.

6. How many points does a team get for putting the ball through its opponent's hoop?
   A. one
   B. two
   C. four
   D. six

7. Which of the following methods of moving the ball is against the rules of basketball?
   A. running while holding the ball
   B. passing the ball to another player
   C. dribbling, or bouncing, the ball
   D. shooting the ball at a basket

Read the selection. Then, answer the questions.

Dragon myths have been told for thousands of years in various cultures throughout the world. Most people would be familiar with the fire-breathing dragon of European folklore. This huge, snakelike monster is almost invariably portrayed as a menace to society. Eventually, outraged citizens raise a clamor, and some valiant individual must step forward to battle the dreadful beast.

In medieval tales, it is usually a brave knight who volunteers to slay the dragon and frees the maiden it holds captive. Of course, the dragon has no intention of giving up without a fight. In the end, however, the knight's endeavor to vanquish his opponent is always successful. Despite its cunning and great physical strength, the wicked dragon is eventually slain, and his killer walks away with the treasure and the heart of the rescued maiden.

Unlike their European cousins, the dragons of Asia are usually portrayed as wise and friendly creatures. This kinder and gentler dragon seldom has wings and rarely breathes fire. Asian dragons can be distinguished by the number of toes they have. A three-toed dragon is Japanese; a four-toed dragon is Indonesian or Korean; and a five-toed dragon, or Lung, is Chinese.

8. Where can dragon myths be found?
   A. in Europe
   B. in Asia
   C. in both Europe and Asia
   D. throughout the world

9. How do European dragons contrast with Asian dragons?
   A. European dragons are fierce fire-breathing monsters, while Asian dragons are friendly and wise.
   B. European dragons are snake-like and have three toes, while Asian dragons have four or five toes.
   C. European dragons are misunderstood victims, while Asian dragons are secretly fierce in nature.
   D. Both European and Asian dragons are menaces to society and must be slain by brave knights.

10. According to the selection, in European legend, what does a knight receive as a reward for slaying the dragon?
    A. money from grateful villagers
    B. treasure and the rescued maiden
    C. fame and magical abilities
    D. great strength and valor

11. Which of the following is the best statement of the main idea of this selection?
   A. Myths about dragons can be found in almost all cultures throughout the world.
   B. Most of us are familiar with the fire-breathing dragon of European folklore.
   C. Despite its cunning and great physical strength, the wicked dragon is eventually slain.
   D. Asian dragons can be distinguished from one another by the number of toes they have.

12. What does the writer assume about the reader's knowledge of dragons?
   A. that the reader knows nothing about dragon legends
   B. that the reader knows how dragons look and behave
   C. that the reader is more familiar with European dragon legends
   D. that the reader is more familiar with Asian dragon legends

13. Which of the following is a conclusion one can draw about Asian dragon legends based on the selection?
   A. Asian dragons are actually just as fierce as European dragons.
   B. Asian dragons steal treasure and kidnap innocent maidens.
   C. Asian villagers do not want dragons living anywhere near them.
   D. Asian dragons are not usually attacked and slain by knights.

14. What makes the dragon a worthy opponent for the brave knight of European legends?
   A. It is an intelligent and friendly creature.
   B. It is an intelligent and dangerous creature.
   C. It likes to collect treasures and innocent young women.
   D. Its legends have been passed down for centuries.

15. From which country does a five-toed Asian dragon come?
   A. Japan
   B. Indonesia
   C. Korea
   D. China

"A Retrieved Reformation" by O. Henry

Vocabulary Warm-up Word Lists

Study these words from "A Retrieved Reformation." Then, complete the activities.

Word List A

active [AK tiv] *adj.* full of normal energy and activity
   After a long nap, the toddler had an <u>active</u> afternoon.

café [kaf AY] *n.* small restaurant
   During summer months, people can eat outdoors at the local <u>café</u>.

drugstore [DRUHG stor] *n.* store where medicines and other products are sold
   The local <u>drugstore</u> now sells all sorts of school supplies.

extremely [ek STREEM lee] *adv.* to a great extent or degree
   Candace was <u>extremely</u> excited to learn that she'd qualified for the finals.

flourishing [FLUR ish ing] *v.* succeeding
   The wilting plants began <u>flourishing</u> again as soon as they were watered.

inspection [in SPEK shun] *n.* very careful look at something
   An <u>inspection</u> of my locker finally turned up the source of the awful smell.

successful [suhk SES fuhl] *adj.* turning out as planned
   If our car wash is <u>successful</u>, we'll earn enough for the end-of-school trip.

typical [TIP uh kuhl] *adj.* showing the qualities and common traits of a group
   The <u>typical</u> teenager needs at least eight hours of sleep each night.

Word List B

anguish [ANG gwish] *n.* strong feelings of suffering or distress
   I can't imagine the <u>anguish</u> of losing a loved one in a tragedy.

burglary [BERG ler ee] *n.* act of breaking into a place and stealing things
   During the <u>burglary</u>, a silent alarm tipped off the police at the nearby station.

commotion [kuh MOH shun] *n.* great deal of noise and activity
   I could not study with all the <u>commotion</u> of the ball game outside my window.

similarity [sim uh LAR i tee] *n.* likeness; resemblance
   Have you noticed the <u>similarity</u> in the way your three uncles talk?

simultaneously [sy muhl TAY nee uhs lee] *adv.* at the same time
   It's hard to make a choice when several great movies come out <u>simultaneously</u>.

socially [SOH shuhl lee] *adv.* in friendly gatherings of people
   Middle school boys can be <u>socially</u> awkward at their first dance.

warden [WAR duhn] *n.* person in charge of a prison
   The <u>warden</u> was pleased to hear that so many inmates had enrolled for classes.

worthwhile [werth WYL] *adj.* useful and important
   The dull drive to the coast seemed <u>worthwhile</u> as we rode our first wave to shore.

Name _____ Date _____

Vocabulary Warm-up Exercises

Exercise A *Fill in each blank in the paragraph below with an appropriate word from Word List A. Use each word only once.*

I have a very [1] _____ imagination. A dream I had recently is the

perfect example of my mind at work. My dreams are always [2] _____

interesting. Upon close [3] _____, though, this one was really over the

top! The dream took place in a small town on the planet Venus. The town was highly

[4] _____ because of its famous [5] _____ that sold

medicines to heal any sickness. Truly, business was [6] _____ in

that space-age shop! Travelers from Earth also visited this town on Venus just to

eat in its famous [7] _____. The meals were prepared with all the

[8] _____ ingredients that have brought intergalactic fame to the foods

of Venus. Now, if only I could remember those recipes when I wake up!

Exercise B *Answer each question in a complete sentence. Use a word from Word List B to replace each underlined word or group of words without changing the meaning.*

1. What can people learn about you from the way you act <u>in groups of people</u>?

   _____

2. What punishment do you think <u>the act of stealing</u> deserves?

   _____

3. What type of personality should the <u>head of a prison</u> have?

   _____

4. When can lots of <u>noise and activity</u> be part of a fun celebration?

   _____

5. When have you felt <u>misery</u> over something that has happened?

   _____

6. What two things can you easily do <u>at the same time</u>?

   _____

7. When do you think your schoolwork is most <u>useful</u> for you?

   _____

8. With whom in your family do you share the most <u>likeness</u>?

   _____

Name _____ Date _____

"A Retrieved Reformation" by O. Henry
Reading Warm-up A

Read the following passage. Pay special attention to the underlined words. Then, read it again, and complete the activities. Use a separate sheet of paper for your written answers.

Search for Elmore, Arkansas, on a map or on the Internet and you come up with a big zero. However, Morrilton, Arkansas, proves to be an <u>extremely</u> interesting find. This small town was built in the 1870s. Morrilton seems to have the same features as the town of Elmore in "A Retrieved Reformation." Since O. Henry loved word games, to believe that he modeled his town after Morrilton is not unreasonable. Just reverse the syllables in "Morril"!

Pictures of Morrilton show a <u>typical</u> small town. Begun along the Little Rock and Fort Smith Railroad, the town quickly grew as a trade center. You can just imagine its main street back then. There would have been a row of red brick businesses, including a <u>drugstore</u>, food market, and bank. Things in Morrilton really began <u>flourishing</u> when a bridge to it was built across the Arkansas River. Tourists, shoppers, and farmers enjoyed visiting the charming town in the Ozark foothills. No doubt the <u>café</u> serving food on the main street has always been busy during summer months.

A closer <u>inspection</u> of Morrilton today reveals a <u>successful</u> small town. It even has a slogan: "Small City, No Limits." Travelers might stay in Morrilton while visiting the nearby Museum of Automobiles or the Petit Jean State Park. The park is great for <u>active</u> people. You can walk the trails or explore caves. Many beautiful things are found in the park, including a natural bridge and a 95-foot waterfall. There are also stunning views from the mountain for which the park is named. Legend says that a French girl fell in love with an American sailor. In order to come with him to his home, she disguised herself as a boy named Jean. The mountain ("Little Jean") is named for her.

1. Circle the words that tell what is an <u>extremely</u> interesting find. What makes something **extremely** interesting when you are searching for facts?

2. Underline words in the second paragraph that describe a <u>typical</u> small town. Then, write what **typical** means.

3. Write a sentence to explain why a <u>drugstore</u> would be found near a food market and a bank.

4. Underline the words that name people who came to Morrilton when it began <u>flourishing</u>. Tell what **flourishing** means.

5. Circle the word that tells what you find in a <u>café</u>. Why would a **café** be a good business to have during tourist months?

6. Circle the verb that tells what an <u>inspection</u> does. Why is the word *closer* used to describe an **inspection**?

7. Circle the words in the slogan that hint at the meaning of <u>successful</u>. Write a sentence to explain how this helps define **successful**.

8. Circle the words that show how people can be <u>active</u> at the park. Tell what **active** means.

Name _____   Date _____

"A Retrieved Reformation" by O. Henry
Reading Warm-up B

Read the following passage. Pay special attention to the underlined words. Then, read it again, and complete the activities. Use a separate sheet of paper for your written answers.

Early in the twentieth century, prisons began to be viewed in a different way. A movement began around the idea that time in jail could be made <u>worthwhile</u>. This would happen if each person left prison knowing that he or she would never commit a crime again. <u>Anguish</u> over spending "hard time" in jail would be replaced with feelings of progress toward a better life.

These ideas about prison reform began in Ireland. There, in the 1850s, Sir Walter Crofton suggested providing work and education to people in prison. He hoped this would help them understand how to fit in <u>socially</u> when they left prison. Instead of returning to old friends and criminal activities such as <u>burglary</u>, released prisoners would fit into mainstream society and find honest work.

Prisons had to change in many ways to meet these new goals. Early prisons were places of constant <u>commotion</u>. All the people in the prison were thrown together at all times. Nasty fights, bad feelings, and poor behavior were common. To change these patterns, the new prisons were designed so that each person had some space of his or her own.

<u>Simultaneously</u>, the jobs of people in charge at prisons changed. For example, the <u>warden</u> at a prison who was focused on reform efforts was expected to talk to each prisoner and figure out the best actions to take with that person. As the head of the prison, the warden set an example for all the other workers. Any <u>similarity</u> to the old system of "punish and control" was frowned upon. Instead, hopes were great that offering prisoners opportunities to learn and work hard would encourage them to change.

1. Underline the words that describe what people thought would make prison time <u>worthwhile</u>. Define *worthwhile*.

2. Circle the words that describe feelings very different from <u>anguish</u>. Then, explain what *anguish* means.

3. Circle the word in the following sentence that relates to the word <u>socially</u>. Write a sentence explaining how reformed prisoners needed to change *socially*.

4. Underline the two words that describe the opposite way of making a living from <u>burglary</u>. Then, write a sentence defining *burglary*.

5. Circle the words that describe the types of <u>commotion</u> that went on in old-style prisons. Write a sentence telling how you would feel if your life were full of *commotion*.

6. Circle two things that happened <u>simultaneously</u> in the prison system. Write about two events that have happened in your life *simultaneously*.

7. According to the passage, what is one responsibility of a prison <u>warden</u>?

8. Write a sentence, describing at least one <u>similarity</u> among prisoners throughout time.

"A Retrieved Reformation" by O. Henry
Reading: Make Predictions and Support Them

When you **make predictions** about a story, you make informed guesses about what will happen next based on story details and your own experience. You can **support your predictions** by finding clues in the story that hint at what will happen next.

As you read, **predict,** or make reasonable guesses about, what is going to happen. Keep track of your predictions and your support for them. Notice when the story includes details that could support predictions of more than one outcome. Some stories keep you guessing in order to hold your interest and build suspense.

These questions may help you predict what might happen next in a story:

- How would you describe the main character's personality?
- What is important to the main character?
- Does the main character think or speak about the future?
- Do other characters do or say things that hint at the future?
- Have you had experiences with people, places, or events that remind you of the ones in the story?

DIRECTIONS: *The following chart lists details from "A Retrieved Reformation." Use the questions above to make predictions based on those details as you read the story. Then, in the third column, write down what actually happens.*

Details From Story	Prediction	Actual Outcome (If Known)
1. Just out of prison, Jimmy looks "fondly" at his safe-cracking tools.		
2. Investigating a series of safecrackings, Ben Price recognizes them as Jimmy's work.		
3. In a new town, Jimmy makes eye contact with an attractive woman and "[becomes] another man."		
4. Jimmy works honestly for a year and is engaged to marry the woman. Ben Price arrives in town.		

Name _____ Date _____

Literary Analysis: Plot

Plot is the sequence of related events in a short story. As you read, identify the following parts of the story's plot:

- **Exposition:** the basic information about the characters and the situation
- **Conflict:** a struggle between two opposing forces in the story
- **Rising action:** the events in the story that increase the tension that readers feel
- **Climax:** the high point of the story, usually the point at which the eventual outcome is revealed
- **Falling action:** the events that follow the climax
- **Resolution:** the final outcome

A. DIRECTIONS: *The following six sentences describe the plot of "A Retrieved Reformation," but they are out of order. Write a number on the line before each part to indicate the order in which the event takes place in the story. Then, write the name of the plot part that the event represents. The parts of the plot are* exposition, conflict, rising action, climax, falling action, *and* resolution.

___ 1. _____ Ben Price pretends he does not know Jimmy and walks away.

___ 2. _____ Jimmy looks "fondly" at his safe-cracking tools.

___ 3. _____ A prison warden encourages Jimmy to "live straight."

___ 4. _____ Agatha is accidentally locked in a safe.

___ 5. _____ Ben Price, a detective, pursues Jimmy; Jimmy falls in love.

___ 6. _____ Jimmy cracks the safe to free Agatha.

B. DIRECTIONS: *Look at the sentences you labeled "rising action" and "falling action." On the lines below, write two details that describe the rising action of "A Retrieved Reformation" and two details that describe the falling action. The details might include events, actions, a conversation, or a character's thoughts.*

Rising action:

1. _____

2. _____

Falling action:

1. _____

2. _____

Name _____ Date _____

"A Retrieved Reformation" by O. Henry
Vocabulary Builder

Word List

virtuous	retribution	unobtrusively	anguish

A. DIRECTIONS: *Write the Word List word that answers each question. Use each vocabulary word only once.*

1. The safe cracker slipped out of the bank without being noticed. How did the burglars move? _____

2. In Elmore, Jimmy had a reputation for being honest, fair, and compassionate. What kind of person was he thought to be? _____

3. When Agatha is locked in the safe, her mother is extremely worried. What emotion is Agatha's mother feeling? _____

4. Ben Price is determined to see Jimmy Valentine punished for his crimes. What does Ben Price want? _____

B. DIRECTIONS: *On the line, write the letter of the word whose meaning is* opposite *that of the Word List word.*

____ 1. unobtrusively
    A. quietly   **B.** loudly   **C.** carefully   **D.** stealthily

____ 2. anguish
    A. relief   **B.** pain   **C.** torture   **D.** worry

____ 3. virtuous
    A. tireless   **B.** endangered   **C.** evil   **D.** truthful

____ 4. retribution
    A. punishment   **B.** collection   **C.** distribution   **D.** reward

"A Retrieved Reformation" by O. Henry
Support for Writing a New Ending

Plan a **new ending** to "A Retrieved Reformation" in which Ben Price arrests Jimmy Valentine. Use the following chart to come up with narration and dialogue you can use for your ending. In the second column, write your ideas about the characters' thoughts, feelings, actions, or dialogue. Base your responses on the personality traits described in the first column. As you write your new ending, remember the history that Ben Price and Jimmy Valentine share. Look for places in the story that indicate each man's thoughts and feelings about the other.

Characters' Personality Traits	Thoughts That Characters Might Have, Actions They Might Take, Things They Might Say
Jimmy is confident.	
Ben is confident.	
Jimmy is an expert safecracker.	
Ben is a good detective.	
Ben looks forward to his marriage but shows caution.	
Ben is curious about Ben's new life.	

In your new ending to "A Retrieved Reformation," remember to use the pronouns *he, she, him, her,* and *they* in reference to the characters; in your dialogue, match the characters' voice and personality.

"A Retrieved Reformation" by O. Henry
Support for Extend Your Learning

Research and Technology

Use the following chart as you gather information for an **oral report** on the life and works of O. Henry. In your Internet search, try to find out about events in O. Henry's life, how they influenced the characters and settings that often appear in his stories, and why he is considered a successful writer.

Events in O. Henry's Life That Influenced His Work	Settings and Characters in O. Henry's Stories	Reasons for O. Henry's Success as a Writer

Listening and Speaking

Answer the following questions in preparation for a **radio broadcast** of Jimmy Valentine's rescue of Agatha from the safe. You will be writing and giving the broadcast. Remember to use action verbs so that listeners will feel the characters' fear and anxiety, as well as their relief and happiness when Valentine succeeds in freeing the child.

1. What do the various characters say when Agatha becomes locked in the safe?

_____

2. What do the characters do? _____

_____

3. Does anyone notice the man (Ben Price) who is watching from afar?

_____

4. How do the characters react when Agatha is freed? _____

_____

5. How does Valentine act? _____

_____

Name _____ Date _____

Enrichment: Nineteenth-Century Science

When Jimmy Valentine was busy cracking bank safes, he did not have to worry about modern-day police **investigative techniques.** There was no Federal Bureau of Investigation, no scientific crime laboratories to identify evidence, and no organized method of fingerprinting.

William Herschel, a British official in India in the 1850s, was one of the first people to understand the importance of fingerprinting. He collected prints and eventually recognized that they could be used as a means of identification.

It is now widely understood that the small ridges on the tips of the fingers help us grasp and hold on to things. When we touch a surface, oils from our skin leave behind a print of the ridges—our fingerprint. Scientists eventually learned that every fingerprint is different, that everyone creates a unique pattern when leaving a fingerprint.

Police investigators came to understand the importance of this unique pattern. In 1892, Argentina became the first country to use fingerprinting as a standard police procedure. Soon, police forces in Europe and North America were collecting fingerprints at crime scenes. Today, the FBI fingerprint file contains millions of prints. The information is computerized and shared with state and local police agencies across the country.

In addition, all modern police agencies use forensic laboratories. (*Forensics* is the application of scientific knowledge to legal problems.) In these labs, scientists examine not only fingerprints but also footprints, hair, fibers, blood, and any other evidence left at a crime scene. They even trace the unique genetic prints in DNA (deoxyribonucleic acid) by examining a person's skin, body fluids, or hair.

DIRECTIONS: *Compare the task of Detective Price with the work of today's detectives, and compare Jimmy Valentine's fate with that of a modern safecracker.*

1. What modern forensic knowledge would have been useful to Ben Price in his investigation of the crime scenes in Richmond, Logansport, and Jefferson City?

   _____

   _____

2. Would Jimmy Valentine have worn gloves when he cracked safes? Why or why not?

   _____

   _____

3. What modern communication techniques would have helped Ben Price? Explain.

   _____

   _____

4. Would Jimmy Valentine be a successful safecracker today? Explain your answer.

   _____

   _____

"A Retrieved Reformation" by O. Henry
Selection Test A

Critical Reading *Identify the letter of the choice that best answers the question.*

____ 1. Which of Jimmy's actions gives a clue to his plans for continuing to crack safes?

    A. He goes to a restaurant to eat.

    B. He goes to his room to pick up his burglar's tools.

    C. He puts on fancy clothes.

    D. He drinks a seltzer and milk with Mike Dolan.

____ 2. Jimmy wears fancy clothes, eats well, and robs banks for quick money. What does this tell you about him?

    A. He wants to move to a big city.

    B. He likes "the good life."

    C. He wants to be famous.

    D. He grew up in poverty.

____ 3. Why is Ben Price interested in Jimmy Valentine?

    A. Ben Price wants Jimmy's safecracking tools.

    B. Ben Price wants to arrest Jimmy.

    C. Ben Price wants to be Jimmy's friend.

    D. Ben Price has known Jimmy from childhood.

____ 4. What can you predict that Jimmy will do when he notices Annabel coming out of the bank?

    A. He will find a way to meet her.

    B. He will ask her to be his partner in crime.

    C. He will use her friendship to get into the bank's safe.

    D. He will go ahead and rob the bank.

____ 5. Why does Jimmy Valentine decide to go into the shoe business?

    A. He likes fancy clothes.

    B. He wants to find an honest way to make a living.

    C. The prison warden warned him to stop cracking safes.

    D. He did not like the new safes.

____ 6. Jimmy meets Annabel, opens a business, and plans to marry. What are these parts of the story's plot called?

    A. falling action

    B. resolution

    C. exposition

    D. rising action

___ 7. Which event is part of Jimmy's old life in "A Retrieved Reformation"?
   A. Jimmy's shoe store is doing well.
   B. Jimmy and Annabel plan to marry.
   C. Jimmy has kept his safecracking tools.
   D. Jimmy has made friends in Elmore.

___ 8. What is the climax of "A Retrieved Reformation"?
   A. The little girl is locked in the safe.
   B. Ben price lets Jimmy go free.
   C. Jimmy has a chicken dinner.
   D. Jimmy meets Annabel.

___ 9. Which one of the following statements does *not* help you predict that Jimmy will open the safe?
   A. Annabel begs him to help.
   B. Agatha is terrified inside the dark safe.
   C. Mr. Adams is certain that no one nearby can do it.
   D. Mr. Adams is proud of his new safe.

___ 10. Which person most affects the surprise ending of "A Retrieved Reformation"?
   A. Annabel
   B. Mr. Adams
   C. Mike Dolan
   D. Ben Price

Vocabulary and Grammar

___ 11. Which word is the opposite of *unobtrusively*?
   A. quietly
   B. loudly
   C. sweetly
   D. happily

___ 12. Which sentence contains a proper noun?
   A. My parents are reading *Hamlet* in their book club.
   B. The boys like to read plays aloud.
   C. My sister is going to the theater tonight.
   D. He has a copy of the script for the new movie.

____ **13.** What does the word *anguish* mean in this sentence?

Annabel turned to Jimmy, her large eyes full of anguish, but not yet despairing.

    A. amusement

    B. illness

    C. anger

    D. suffering

____ **14.** In which sentence is a proper noun used correctly?

    A. My Sister is a year older than I am.

    B. She asked our Mother for help with homework.

    C. We saw a baseball game at Wrigley Field.

    D. I talked to sally after school.

Essay

15. What do you think Jimmy decides to do at the end of "A Retrieved Reformation"? Do you think he returns to Annabel and Mr. Adams to explain the truth about his criminal past? Does he take Annabel's rose and walk away? Write an essay telling what you predict Jimmy will do. Give reasons for your answer.

16. During the course of "A Retrieved Reformation," Jimmy Valentine changes his life and becomes Ralph Spencer. However, he keeps some of Jimmy Valentine's characteristics. In an essay, compare Jimmy Valentine and Ralph Spencer. How are they alike? How are they different?

"A Retrieved Reformation" by O. Henry
Selection Test B

Critical Reading *Identify the letter of the choice that best completes the statement or answers the question.*

____ 1. Which of Jimmy's actions gives a clue to his plans when he is released from prison?
   A. He goes to a restaurant and has a chicken dinner.
   B. He returns to his room and picks up his burglar's tools.
   C. He offers to give his friend his suitcase of tools.
   D. He drinks a seltzer and milk with Mike Dolan.

____ 2. Which of the prison warden's words to Jimmy help you predict the surprise ending?
   A. He says Jimmy is an "innocent" victim.
   B. He says Jimmy is "not a bad fellow at heart."
   C. He praises Jimmy for having friends in "high-toned society."
   D. He says the "mean old jury" had it in for Jimmy.

____ 3. What prediction is a reader likely to make after reading this line from "A Retrieved Reformation"?
   He opened this and gazed fondly at the finest set of burglar's tools in the East.
   A. Jimmy will sell his tools to Mike Dolan.
   B. Jimmy will probably put the tools away.
   C. Jimmy will keep the tools for sentimental reasons.
   D. Jimmy will use the tools again to crack a safe.

____ 4. What does this description of Jimmy after his release from prison tell you about his character?
   He was now dressed in tasteful and well-fitting clothes, and carried his dusted and cleaned suitcase in his hand.
   A. Jimmy is wearing a disguise so Ben Price won't find him.
   B. Jimmy is neat and likes to dress well.
   C. Jimmy wants to make people think he has changed.
   D. Jimmy does not want to be noticed.

____ 5. What characteristics make Jimmy Valentine a successful burglar?
   I.   He uses a special set of tools.
   II. He makes quick getaways.
   III. He works alone.
   IV. He is a good fighter.
   A. I, II, III   B. I, II, IV   C. I, III, IV   D. II, III, IV

____ 6. What is Ben Price's interest in Jimmy Valentine?
   I.   Ben Price is a burglar who wants Jimmy's tools.
   II. Ben Price has known Jimmy from childhood.
   III. Ben Price is a detective who has studied Jimmy's habits.
   IV. Ben Price believes Jimmy should not have been released from prison.
   A. I, II, III   B. II, III   C. I, II, IV   D. III, IV

___ 7. What is the best prediction you can make from the following sentence?
   Jimmy Valentine looked into her eyes, forgot what he was, and became another man.

   A. The young lady will have an effect on Jimmy's future.
   B. Jimmy will probably stay in Elmore for a short time.
   C. Jimmy will never rob another bank.
   D. The young lady is probably the banker's daughter.

___ 8. Why does Jimmy Valentine decide to go into the shoe business?
   A. He decides to give up crime and needs honest work.
   B. He has always liked fancy clothes and stylish shoes.
   C. The warden has warned him to stay away from burglary.
   D. The newer safes are nearly impossible to break into.

___ 9. Which situation is *not* a sign of Jimmy's changed life in "A Retrieved Reformation"?
   A. Jimmy's shoe store is flourishing.
   B. Jimmy is engaged to Annabel Adams.
   C. Jimmy has kept his suitcase of burglary tools.
   D. Jimmy has won the respect of the community.

___ 10. Jimmy meets Annabel, opens a shoe business, and plans to marry. These plot elements are examples of
   A. falling action.
   B. rising action.
   C. resolution.
   D. exposition.

___ 11. Which event would you say best describes the climax of "A Retrieved Reformation"?
   A. Jimmy meets Annabel.
   B. Jimmy gets out of prison.
   C. Agatha is locked in the safe.
   D. Ben Price lets Jimmy go free.

___ 12. Which sentences help you predict that Jimmy will open the safe?
   I. "There isn't a man nearer than Little Rock who can open that door."
   II. "Can't you *do* something Ralph—*try*, won't you?"
   III. The old banker sprang to the handle and tugged at it for a moment.
   IV. He looked at her with a queer, soft smile on his lips and in his keen eyes.
   A. I, II   B. I, II, III   C. I, II, IV   D. I, IV

___ 13. Which character determines the resolution of "A Retrieved Reformation"?
   A. Annabel
   B. Mr. Adams
   C. Mike Dolan
   D. Ben Price

Vocabulary and Grammar

____ **14.** The opposite of *unobtrusively* is
  A. quietly.
  B. illegible.
  C. unnoticeably.
  D. loudly.

____ **15.** If you are the victim of a crime, you might want
  A. admonition.
  B. coronation.
  C. retribution.
  D. celebration.

____ **16.** Which sentence contains a proper noun?
  A. We watched a baseball game at Wrigley Field.
  B. We saw a concert at the stadium.
  C. My family always spends the holiday out of town.
  D. She ate dinner at her favorite restaurant.

____ **17.** What does the word *anguish* mean in this sentence?
  Annabel turned to Jimmy, her large eyes full of anguish, but not yet despairing.

  A. anger
  B. suffering
  C. amusement
  D. illness

Essay

18. What do you think happens to Jimmy Valentine at the end of "A Retrieved Reformation"? Will he go back to his old ways, get married, or start a different life? Write an essay telling what you predict Jimmy will do, and give reasons based on examples from the story.

19. One way O. Henry keeps readers interested in Jimmy Valentine in "A Retrieved Reformation" is by creating a character with a distinct personality. He is real to readers because he makes both good and bad choices along the way. Write an essay in which you describe some of Jimmy's personal traits and the choices he makes, and explain how you think his personality traits affect those choices.

"**Raymond's Run**" by Toni Cade Bambara
Vocabulary Warm-up Word Lists

Study these words from "Raymond's Run." Then, complete the activities.

Word List A

energy [EN er jee] *n.* strength to be active
The racer used a final burst of <u>energy</u> to cross the finish line.

fantasy [FAN tuh see] *n.* something you imagine happening
The young girl had a <u>fantasy</u> of becoming President of the United States.

pageant [PAJ uhnt] *n.* well-planned presentation of a play or other performance
The students presented an elaborate Thanksgiving <u>pageant</u>.

prefer [pri FER] *v.* like something more than other things
I <u>prefer</u> to ride my bike instead of taking the bus or walking.

recipe [RES i pee] *n.* list of materials and instructions for making food
My favorite <u>recipe</u> for chicken was taught to me by my mother.

satin [SAT uhn] *adj.* made from a smooth fabric that is shiny on one side
The slippery <u>satin</u> ribbon kept coming untied.

strawberries [STRAW ber eez] *n.* small, red, juicy fruits
We couldn't resist picking the <u>strawberries</u> as soon as they ripened.

zoom [ZOOM] *v.* move quickly
I watched the cars <u>zoom</u> by on the freeway.

Word List B

chugging [CHUG ing] *v.* making a regular puffing sound while moving
Though I was out of breath, I kept <u>chugging</u> along to the finish line.

congratulate [kuhn GRACH uh layt] *v.* let others know you are pleased about their success
We lined up to <u>congratulate</u> the other team for winning.

gorilla [guh RIL uh] *n.* large, strong ape
They hoped to see a <u>gorilla</u> living in the wild in Africa.

hydrant [HYE druhnt] *n.* large, outdoor pipe supplying water to put out fires
You can't park in front of a fire <u>hydrant</u> in case it's needed in an emergency.

loudspeaker [LOWD speek er] *n.* device that makes sounds louder
Without a <u>loudspeaker</u>, it was impossible to hear the woman's soft voice.

periscope [PER uh skohp] *n.* instrument used in submarines to view the surface
The sailors raised the submarine's <u>periscope</u> to check the ship's location.

shoelaces [SHOO lays uhs] *n.* cords or strings that fasten shoes
Felicia always laces her <u>shoelaces</u> in unusual patterns.

tradition [truh DISH uhn] *n.* something handed down through time
It is a family <u>tradition</u> to make our own holiday candles.

"Raymond's Run" by Toni Cade Bambara
Vocabulary Warm-up Exercises

Exercise A *Fill in each blank in the paragraph below with an appropriate word from Word List A. Use each word only once.*

We are planning the school's spring [1] _____. Since everything will

be blooming, our theme is "A [2] _____ of Flowers." We need to write

skits, sell tickets, plan refreshments, and make decorations. We'll need lots of

[3] _____ to get it all ready in time! Since I [4] _____

jobs that are artistic, I'm working on decorations. We're going to create flowers out of

[5] _____ material so they'll shine under the lights. I have seen the

fabric at *Sew What?*, so I've offered to [6] _____ by the store tonight

to pick up some. The food team has decided to serve barbecue chicken. They hope

Principal Rivera will share the secret [7] _____ for his yummy sauce.

I think [8] _____ dipped in chocolate would make a great dessert.

Exercise B *Answer the questions with complete explanations.*

1. If something is done once, is it a <u>tradition</u>?
   _____

2. Would a <u>periscope</u> be helpful if you were traveling by car across the plains?
   _____

3. Why can't people use the water from a <u>hydrant</u> whenever they want?
   _____

4. Would a <u>gorilla</u> be able to live in your neighborhood?
   _____

5. Why do parents of toddlers prefer slip-on shoes to those with <u>shoelaces</u>?
   _____

6. When can a <u>loudspeaker</u> become annoying?
   _____

7. Why is it sometimes hard to <u>congratulate</u> someone who has defeated you?
   _____

8. Would a brand-new car be <u>chugging</u> up a hill?
   _____

Name _____ Date _____

"**Raymond's Run**" by Toni Cade Bambara
Reading Warm-up A

Read the following passage. Pay special attention to the underlined words. Then, read it again, and complete the activities. Use a separate sheet of paper for your written answers.

May Day is one of the world's oldest holidays. Since ancient times, people have gathered to welcome spring. The season's beautiful flowers and warm sun were celebrated, along with people's feelings of renewed <u>energy</u> for work and play. Over time, celebrations became bigger. Some villages would plan a special <u>pageant</u> that began the night of April 30. On this night, the villagers would put out their winter fires and go to the center of town. There, a new fire would be started. Bearing torches, the people would return home, singing and dancing.

Daytime celebrations usually included a maypole. A tall tree would be cut down and brought to the middle of the village. Colorful ribbons were tied to the trunk. They formed bright patterns as boys and girls danced around the pole, ribbons in hand. Legend said that your ribbon would wind around the ribbon of the person you would <u>prefer</u> to marry. Seasonal treats, such as fresh, juicy <u>strawberries</u>, were served.

May Day was a <u>fantasy</u> come true for flower lovers. Flowers were placed in doors and windows. People made bouquets for one another or filled baskets with blossoms and sweets to give away. One traditional May Day <u>recipe</u> used leftover oatmeal to make sweet oatcakes.

You can see that many modern spring celebrations come from the ancient May Day festivals. For example, the spring prom uses many of the same ideas. Young people dance together, perhaps hoping to find true love. Flowers are worn in lapels or at the wrist, and colorful <u>satin</u> ribbons are used in prom decorations. It is true that modern dancers seem to hop, jerk, and <u>zoom</u> across the dance floor instead of gently winding their way around a pole. Still, the true May Day feelings of young love, hope in a new season, and enjoyment of nature's beauty remain the same.

1. Underline the words naming what people need <u>energy</u> to do. Tell about something you do that requires *energy*.

2. Circle three words naming things that were part of the May Day <u>pageant</u> on April 30. Explain what a *pageant* is.

3. What type of people do you <u>prefer</u> to spend time with? Make a list of words used to describe your *prefer*red friends.

4. Circle the words that describe <u>strawberries</u>. Then, write your own sentence describing them.

5. Write a sentence explaining why May Day would be "a <u>fantasy</u> come true" for flower lovers.

6. Underline an ingredient that might be found in the <u>recipe</u> for sweet oatcakes. Then, write a sentence describing the food made from your favorite *recipe*.

7. Circle what is made of <u>satin</u>. Describe something else that could be made from *satin* material for the prom.

8. Underline the words that describe the opposite of <u>zoom</u>. Then, use *zoom* in your own sentence.

Name _____ Date _____

"**Raymond's Run**" by Toni Cade Bambara
Reading Warm-up B

Read the following passage. Pay special attention to the underlined words. Then, read it again, and complete the activities. Use a separate sheet of paper for your written answers.

Several of my friends thought I was crazy when I decided to start running cross-country, but I truly enjoy it. First, there are the amazing places you get to see while you run. Instead of dodging a fire <u>hydrant</u> here and masses of people there, you can run through the peaceful countryside. Second, I like the rhythm you get into during a long run. While you are smoothly <u>chugging</u> along, hearing nothing but your own breathing, your mind is free to roam.

One sports <u>tradition</u> that I adore is the annual Halloween cross-country track meet. To compete, you must wear a costume—the more elaborate, the better. The races are just for entertainment, but it is still a big accomplishment to win the events. Last year, I ran as a Greek god. I wore a toga over my shorts, a band of gold leaves around my head, and matching gold <u>shoelaces</u>. That costume barely slowed down my pace. However, one of the other competitors ran as a <u>gorilla</u> and nearly suffered a heat stroke under that hairy ape costume! He came in last, but I had to <u>congratulate</u> him for finishing at all.

This year I will not participate in the costumed meet. That weekend our school team is traveling to a nearby county to race against the state's top-ranked teams. Nevertheless, in the spirit of Halloween, I've decided to imagine I am a submarine captain while running. I can dream that I am gliding along beneath the ocean, which will help me stay cool while maintaining a steady speed. When I approach a hill, I will pretend that I have a <u>periscope</u> to peer through and see the other side. I have always found that hills are easier to conquer if you can just visualize yourself already on the downward slope.

I hope I will hear my name over the <u>loudspeaker</u> at the end of the race, when the winners are announced. Regardless, it is the fun of the run that counts.

1. Explain where a runner might be if he or she has to avoid a fire <u>hydrant</u>.

2. Underline the words that name what you might hear while <u>chugging</u> on a long distance run. Tell what *chugging* means.

3. Circle the words naming a sports <u>tradition</u>. Then, write a sentence about another sports *tradition* you know.

4. Explain why <u>shoelaces</u> would be especially important to a runner.

5. Underline the words used as a synonym for <u>gorilla</u>. Write a sentence describing what a *gorilla* costume would look like.

6. Explain why the writer would <u>congratulate</u> this last-place runner. Define *congratulate*.

7. Circle the words that name what the writer would like to see through an imaginary <u>periscope</u>. Write a sentence about a time when a *periscope* could be useful to you.

8. Underline the words naming what the writer hopes to hear over the <u>loudspeaker</u>. Then, explain what a *loudspeaker* does.

Name _____ Date _____

Reading: Make Predictions and Support Them

When you **make predictions** about a story, you make informed guesses about what will happen next based on story details and your own experience. You can **support your predictions** by finding clues in the story that hint at what will happen next.

As you read, try to **predict,** or make reasonable guesses, about what is going to happen. Keep track of your predictions and your support for them. Notice when the story includes details that could support predictions of more than one outcome. Some stories keep you guessing in order to hold your interest and build suspense.

These questions may help you predict what might happen next in a story:

- How would you describe the main character's personality?
- What is important to the main character?
- Does the main character think or speak about the future?
- Do other characters do or say things that hint at the future?

Have you had experiences with people, places, or events that remind you of the ones in the story?

DIRECTIONS: *The following chart lists details from "Raymond's Run." Use the questions above to make predictions based on those details as you read the story. Then, in the third column, write down what actually happens.*

Details From Story	Prediction	Actual Outcome (If Known)
1. Squeaky and Gretchen are good runners, and each girl is sure she is the one who will win the race.		
2. Mr. Pearson hints to Squeaky that she should let Gretchen win the race.		
3. Raymond climbs the fence to meet Squeaky after the race.		
4. After the race, Gretchen and Squeaky smile at each other.		

Name _____ Date _____

"Raymond's Run" by Toni Cade Bambara
Literary Analysis: Plot

Plot is the sequence of related events in a short story. As you read, identify the following parts of the story's plot:

- **Exposition:** the basic information about the characters and the situation
- **Conflict:** a struggle between two opposing forces in the story
- **Rising action:** the events in the story that increase the tension that readers feel
- **Climax:** the high point of the story, usually the point at which the eventual outcome is revealed
- **Falling action:** the events that follow the climax
- **Resolution:** the final outcome

A. DIRECTIONS: *The following six sentences describe the plot of "Raymond's Run," but they are out of order. Write a number on the line before each part to indicate the order in which the event takes place in the story. Then, write the name of the plot part that the event represents. The parts of the plot are* exposition, conflict, rising action, climax, falling action, *and* resolution.

____ 1. _____ Squeaky and Gretchen congratulate each other.

____ 2. _____ Squeaky looks after her older brother, and she anticipates a race.

____ 3. _____ Squeaky stands up for her brother and defends her reputation as the fastest runner in the neighborhood.

____ 4. _____ The race ends, and Raymond begins to climb the fence that separates him from the runners.

____ 5. _____ Squeaky meets a group of girls from the neighborhood while practicing for the race.

____ 6. _____ Squeaky realizes that Raymond could be a good runner and thinks about coaching him.

B. DIRECTIONS: *Look at the sentences you labeled "rising action" and "falling action." On the lines below, write two details that describe the rising action of "Raymond's Run" and two details that describe the falling action. The details might describe events, actions, a conversation, or a character's thoughts.*

Rising action:

1. _____

2. _____

Falling action:

1. _____

2. _____

Name _____ Date _____

"Raymond's Run" by Toni Cade Bambara
Vocabulary Builder

Word List

| prodigy | reputation |

A. DIRECTIONS: *Think about the meaning of the italicized Word List word in each sentence. Then, answer the question.*

1. Because of Cynthia Procter's talent on the piano, Squeaky calls her a *prodigy*. How does Cynthia play the piano?

   _____

2. What kind of *reputation* as a runner would Squeaky have if she never won a race?

   _____

B. DIRECTIONS: *Follow the instructions for writing a sentence using each Word List word. Be sure to make the meaning of the vocabulary word clear.*

   Example: Use *prodigy* in a sentence about a music student.
   Sentence: Soon the prodigy Kayla was playing the violin better than her teacher.

1. Use *prodigy* in a sentence about a child who solves math problems.

   _____

2. Use *reputation* in a sentence about the behavior of an animal.

   _____

C. DIRECTIONS: *On the line, write the letter of the word or phrase that answers the question.*

____ 1. Who is *not* a *prodigy*?
   A. a talented person
   B. a genius
   C. a mean person
   D. a wonder

____ 2. Which word does *not* have anything to do with a *reputation*?
   A. authority
   B. influence
   C. fame
   D. disgust

Name _____ Date _____

Support for Writing a New Ending

Plan a **new ending** to "Raymond's Run" in which Squeaky loses the race to Gretchen. Begin with the announcer saying, "In first place—Miss Gretchen P. Lewis. In second place—Miss Hazel Elizabeth Deborah Parker." Use the following chart to come up with sentences you can use for your ending. In the second column, write your ideas about the thoughts, feelings, or actions you might describe. Base your responses on the personality traits described in the first column. Write in Squeaky's voice and style. As you write your new ending, remember what Squeaky thinks as she sees Raymond climb the fence.

Squeaky's Personality Traits	Thoughts or Feelings Squeaky Might Have, Actions She Might Take
Loves and respects Raymond	
Takes pride in herself, especially as a runner	
Practices and studies hard	
Respects Gretchen's ability as a runner	
Values loyalty	

In your new ending to "Raymond's Run," remember to use the pronouns *I, me,* and *my* in reference to Squeaky and to match the voice and style to Squeaky's personality.

Name _____ Date _____

"**Raymond's Run**" by Toni Cade Bambara
Support for Extend Your Learning

Research and Technology

Use the following chart as you gather information for an **oral report** on the Special Olympics. In your Internet search, try to find out how the Special Olympics got started, who participates in them, what events are scheduled, and why the Special Olympics are important.

History	Participants and Events	Importance

Listening and Speaking

Answer the following questions in preparation for a **radio broadcast** of Squeaky's race in "Raymond's Run." You will be writing and giving the broadcast. Remember to use action verbs so that listeners will feel the rising tension and the excitement of the close race between Squeaky and Gretchen.

1. How does Squeaky look? _____

_____

2. How does Gretchen look? _____

_____

3. How does Squeaky act—what does she do? _____

_____

4. How does Gretchen act—what does she do? _____

_____

5. What happens as Squeaky and Gretchen approach the finish line? How close are they?

_____

_____

Name _____ Date _____

"Raymond's Run" by Toni Cade Bambara
Enrichment: Athletic Coaching

Squeaky is the fastest runner in her neighborhood, and she makes a serious effort to train for her races. She might be even faster, however, if she had a track coach.

Athletic coaches can make the difference between a good athlete and a great one. They teach beginners the fundamentals of the sport, lead athletes through a season, and help world champions sharpen their skills. Coaches and instructors also help amateurs who simply want to increase their enjoyment of a sport or improve their exercise routine. Coaches can be found guiding teams and individuals at the professional and Olympic levels, at schools and colleges, and at local fitness centers, ice rinks, and swimming pools.

All athletic coaches must be good teachers. They must know their sports thoroughly, keep up with the latest techniques, and develop an effective teaching method. Coaches at all levels must also be concerned with safety so that they can be sure their trainees maximize performance without injuring themselves.

Athletic coaches who work in public and private schools are usually required to have a bachelor's degree from an accredited college. Many other sports instructors also hold a college degree. Most coaches and instructors are skilled players of at least one sport.

A. DIRECTIONS: *Use the information in the preceding passage and your knowledge and experience to answer the following questions.*

1. What are some duties of a middle-school athletic coach?

   _____

   _____

2. What are some job opportunities for coaches and sports instructors?

   _____

   _____

3. In your opinion, what personality traits should a coach have to be successful at his or her job?

   _____

   _____

B. DIRECTIONS: *Imagine that you are the principal of a large middle-school and you are looking to hire an athletic coach. Write down four questions that you would ask an applicant during an interview. Then, trade papers with a classmate, and answer each other's questions orally. Do you qualify for the job?*

1. _____

2. _____

3. _____

4. _____

Name _____ Date _____

"A Retrieved Reformation" by O. Henry
"Raymond's Run" by Toni Cade Bambara
Build Language Skills: Vocabulary

The Prefix *pre-*

The prefix *pre-* means "before" or "in advance." Often, you will recognize the word to which it has been attached—for example, *prepay.* When you do not recognize the word, you can use the prefix to try to understand the word and remember its meaning: You will know that the word has something to do with one thing happening before another. For example, you can tell that a *prediction* is something done before something else.

A. DIRECTIONS: *Follow these instructions to write sentences using words formed with the prefix* pre-. *If you need to, look up the definition of the word in a dictionary before you write your sentence.*

1. Use *preview* in a sentence about a movie.

   _____

   _____

2. Use *preface* in a sentence about a book.

   _____

   _____

3. Use *preamble* in a sentence about the Constitution.

   _____

   _____

Academic Vocabulary Practice

B. DIRECTIONS: *Follow these instructions to write sentences using the Academic Vocabulary words.*

1. Use *predict* in a sentence about the weather.

   _____

2. Use *anticipate* in a sentence about a birthday party.

   _____

3. Use *formulate* in a sentence about a plan.

   _____

4. Use *modify* in a sentence about a doghouse.

   _____

5. Use *revise* in a sentence about an essay.

   _____

© Pearson Education, Inc., publishing as Pearson Prentice Hall. All rights reserved.
45

"A Retrieved Reformation" by O. Henry
"Raymond's Run" by Toni Cade Bambara
Build Language Skills: Grammar

Common and Proper Nouns

Nouns may be classified as common or proper. A **common noun** names any person, animal, place, thing, or idea. It is not capitalized unless it is the first word in a sentence.

The girl met another girl on a street and talked about a race they would run the next day.

A **proper noun** names a particular person, animal, place, thing, or idea. A proper noun is always capitalized.

Squeaky met Gretchen on Broadway and talked about the race they would run on May Day.

A. DIRECTIONS: *In the following paragraph, underline the common nouns once and the proper nouns twice.*

It was Sunday morning, the day of the Chicago Marathon. The weather was crisp and

clear, a perfect day for a long race. Sara had trained for six months. She ran long and short

distances every week to build up her endurance and strength. She ran along the lakefront

paths, on the paths in Lincoln Park Zoo, and along the streets of the city neighborhoods.

Sara felt anticipation, sure that she was ready for the race.

B. Writing Application: *Write sentences following the directions in each item. In your sentences, underline the common nouns once and the proper nouns twice.*

1. Use a proper noun in a question you might ask your teacher.

   _____

2. Use a common noun in a sentence about an activity you enjoy.

   _____

3. Use a proper noun in a sentence about your town or city.

   _____

4. Use a common noun in a question you might ask about a marathon race.

   _____

Name _____ Date _____

"Raymond's Run" by Toni Cade Bambara
Selection Test A

Critical Reading *Identify the letter of the choice that best answers the question.*

____ 1. Where does Squeaky get her nickname in "Raymond's Run"?
A. She has a squeaky voice.
B. Her sneakers squeak.
C. The doors on her house squeak.
D. She has a pet hamster that squeaks.

____ 2. How does Squeaky feel about taking care of Raymond?
A. She complains about it.
B. It makes her feel important.
C. She ignores him.
D. She feels protective of him.

____ 3. Why does Squeaky keep Raymond near the sides of the city buildings?
A. He sometimes loses his balance.
B. He sometimes runs into the street.
C. He wears odd clothing.
D. He needs to know who is boss.

____ 4. In "Raymond's Run," why does Squeaky dislike Mary Louise?
A. She is ungrateful.
B. She is too loud.
C. She is a better runner.
D. She is a better student.

____ 5. Why is Squeaky worried when she sees Mary Louise and her friends on the street?
A. They may challenge her to a race.
B. They may make fun of her.
C. They may want to fight.
D. They may laugh at Mr. Pearson.

____ 6. Why does Squeaky get upset when Mary Louise talks to Raymond?
A. Squeaky is jealous of her.
B. Squeaky does not want her to make fun of Raymond.
C. Mary Louise speaks too loudly.
D. Mary Louise is a faster runner than Squeaky.

____ 7. What does Squeaky know about the new girl Gretchen?

    A. She is wealthy.

    B. She likes to fight.

    C. She is loyal to her friends.

    D. She is a good runner.

____ 8. What can you tell about Squeaky from this line in "Raymond's Run"?

    You'd think she'd be glad her daughter ain't out there prancing around the May Pole getting the new clothes all dirty and sweaty and trying to act like a fairy or a flower. . . .

    A. She likes fancy clothes.

    B. She wishes she could dance around the May Pole.

    C. She does not like to get dirty and sweaty.

    D. She thinks the May Pole is a silly waste of time.

____ 9. Squeaky and Gretchen are competing to win the May Day race. What part of the plot does this describe?

    A. the conflict

    B. the falling action

    C. the resolution

    D. the end

____ 10. Why does Squeaky not know at first who has won the race in "Raymond's Run"?

    A. Raymond has climbed the fence.

    B. The May Pole gets in the way.

    C. The finish is very close.

    D. Mr. Pearson speaks too softly.

____ 11. What is the resolution of "Raymond's Run"?

    A. Squeaky and Gretchen meet on the street.

    B. Raymond pretends to drive a stage coach.

    C. Squeaky decides to become Raymond's track coach.

    D. Squeaky watches Raymond run.

____ 12. Based on what you know about Squeaky, what do you predict she will do when Raymond climbs the fence at the race?

    A. She will get angry at him.

    B. She will make sure Raymond does not get hurt.

    C. She will take Raymond home right away.

    D. She will ignore him.

Name _____ Date _____

___ 13. After the race, Squeaky and Gretchen smile at each other. What do you predict about their future?
    A. They will continue not speaking to each other.
    B. They will become friendly with each other.
    C. Squeaky will let Gretchen win the next race.
    D. Gretchen will move to another town.

Vocabulary and Grammar

___ 14. Which word has a meaning similar to *prodigy*?
    A. statue
    B. babysitter
    C. athlete
    D. wonder

___ 15. Which sentence contains a proper noun?
    A. We danced around the May Pole.
    B. We went to a dance last weekend.
    C. They ran in a special race every year.
    D. Her mother came to watch the race.

Essay

16. Do you predict that Raymond will become a runner like Squeaky? In a brief essay, explain why or why not. Use details from "Raymond's Run" to support your answer.

17. Even though they are different in many ways, Squeaky and Raymond are also alike in some ways. Write an essay in which you describe ways Squeaky and Raymond are alike. Include examples from "Raymond's Run."

Name _____ Date _____

"**Raymond's Run**" by Toni Cade Bambara
Selection Test B

Critical Reading *Identify the letter of the choice that best completes the statement or answers the question.*

_____ 1. Squeaky got her nickname because she has a squeaky voice. Why is she also called Mercury?
   A. She is the fastest thing in the neighborhood.
   B. She is a little girl with skinny arms.
   C. She lives on Mercury Street.
   D. She competes in track races.

_____ 2. How does Squeaky feel about the fact that she has to take care of Raymond?
   A. She wishes he would pay more attention.
   B. She is glad to do it because it gives her a sense of importance.
   C. She doesn't mind because he really takes care of himself.
   D. She is very protective of him.

_____ 3. When Squeaky says that Raymond is "not quite right," she means that
   A. he is wrong about an argument they had.
   B. he likes to play practical jokes.
   C. he has a quick temper.
   D. he is mentally challenged.

_____ 4. When Squeaky sees Gretchen and her friends, she is concerned that they will
   A. make fun of George.
   B. make fun of her.
   C. challenge her to a race.
   D. challenge her to a fight.

_____ 5. When Mary Louise asks Raymond what grade he is in, her tone is
   A. friendly.
   B. loving.
   C. puzzled.
   D. mocking.

_____ 6. Which of the following best defines Gretchen's role in "Raymond's Run"?
   A. someone who competes with Squeaky
   B. someone who fights with Squeaky
   C. someone who stands up for Squeaky
   D. someone who teaches Squeaky a lesson

_____ 7. What can you tell about Squeaky's personality from this passage?
   You'd think she'd be glad her daughter ain't out there prancing around the May Pole getting the new clothes all dirty and sweaty and trying to act like a fairy or a flower. . . .

   A. She thinks it's a shame to ruin expensive clothes.
   B. She is envious of girls who dance around the May Pole.
   C. She thinks the May Pole is a silly waste of time.
   D. She thinks it is unladylike to get sweaty.

Unit 1 Resources: Fiction and Nonfiction

____ 8. Which of the following is *not* part of the rising action in "Raymond's Run"?
   A. Squeaky and Raymond confront Mary Louise and her friends on Broadway.
   B. Mr. Pearson hints to Squeaky that she should consider letting the new girl win.
   C. Squeaky is responsible for taking care of Raymond.
   D. Squeaky practices her running to prepare for the race.

____ 9. Squeaky and Gretchen are talented runners who each want to win the May Day race. What part of the plot does this statement describe?
   A. the resolution
   B. the conflict
   C. the exposition
   D. the falling action

____ 10. Which statement is a reasonable prediction of Squeaky's response to Mr. Pearson's hints that Squeaky should let Gretchen win the race?
   A. She will consider letting Gretchen win so that they might become friends.
   B. She will agree to tie with Gretchen because they are both good runners.
   C. She will reject the hint with scorn.
   D. She will agree to let Gretchen win.

____ 11. The resolution of "Raymond's Run" occurs when
   A. Squeaky decides to become Raymond's track coach.
   B. Gretchen wins the race.
   C. Raymond climbs the fence.
   D. Squeaky and Gretchen meet on Broadway.

____ 12. After the race, Squeaky and Gretchen smile at each other with respect. What prediction can you make about their future?
   A. There is a good chance they will become friendly competitors.
   B. Squeaky will let Gretchen win the race next year.
   C. Gretchen will help Squeaky coach Raymond.
   D. Squeaky and Gretchen will probably remain unfriendly toward each other.

Vocabulary and Grammar

____ 13. Which of the following does *not* have a meaning similar to *prodigy*?
   A. mastermind
   B. wonder
   C. ordinary
   D. genius

____ 14. Which sentence contains a proper noun?
   A. We have no school on Memorial Day.
   B. Today is my brother's birthday.
   C. We celebrate every holiday under the sun.
   D. Did you get my mother a gift?

_____ 15. In which sentence is *reputation* used correctly?
    A. She handed him his reputation before they went into the party.
    B. My father has a reputation for winning at checkers.
    C. Has your reputation expired?
    D. He did not know about the new reputation.

Essay

16. Do you predict that Raymond will become a runner like Squeaky? In a brief essay, explain why or why not. Use details from "Raymond's Run" to support your answer.

17. In "Raymond's Run," what readers know about Raymond comes through Squeaky's words and observations about him. In an essay, describe what you know about Raymond. What important lesson does Squeaky learn from her brother? Develop your answer with examples from the story.

Vocabulary Warm-up Word Lists

Study these words from "Gentleman of Río en Medio." Then, complete the activities.

Word List A

additional [uh DISH uh nuhl] *adj.* extra; more
   We were having such a good time at the fair that we bought additional tickets for the rides.

amounted [uh MOWNT id] *v.* added up
   Twelve tickets to the county fair at $5 each amounted to $60.

document [DAHK yuh muhnt] *n.* paper with important information
   A document with proof of age is needed in order to obtain a passport.

insulted [in SUHL tid] *v.* said something rude or upsetting
   She insulted all the party guests by saying that they had no manners.

obediently [oh BEE dee uhnt lee] *adv.* as one has been instructed
   Even though we didn't want to work overtime, we obediently followed the manager's orders.

previous [PREE vee uhs] *adj.* former; earlier
   At my previous school, my lunch break was much earlier than it is here.

quaint [KWAYNT] *adj.* charming in an old-fashioned way
   Some people find the village quaint, but others think it just looks run-down.

rate [RAYT] *n.* standard amount used to figure a total
   Parking garages charge a higher rate to park during their busiest hours.

Word List B

boundaries [BOWN duh rees] *n.* borders; lines that separate one area from another
   After gold was found nearby, the town quickly outgrew its boundaries.

descendants [di SEND uhnts] *n.* one's children, their children, and so on
   We should preserve the parklands for future generations, our descendants.

gnarled [NAHRLD] *adj.* twisted and lumpy with age
   The tiny tree near the timber line was stunted and gnarled.

innumerable [in NOO mur uh buhl] *adj.* uncountable; many
   As we watched, innumerable caribou thundered across the land.

overrun [oh ver RUHN] *v.* spread over in large numbers
   In some years, lemmings overrun the land, creating a population problem.

possession [puh ZESH uhn] *n.* ownership
   After taking possession of the tiny shack, they began to enlarge it.

tilled [TILD] *v.* turned over, or plowed, land for growing crops
   The farmers tilled the soil, then planted seeds in the plowed field.

wretched [RECH id] *adj.* miserable
   During the long, cold winter, the settlers lived a wretched life.

_____ 15. In which sentence is *reputation* used correctly?

　　　A. She handed him his reputation before they went into the party.

　　　B. My father has a reputation for winning at checkers.

　　　C. Has your reputation expired?

　　　D. He did not know about the new reputation.

Essay

16. In "Raymond's Run," what readers know about Raymond comes through Squeaky's words and observations about him. In an essay, describe what you know about Raymond. What important lesson does Squeaky learn from her brother? Develop your answer with examples from the story.

17. Write an essay in which you explain how Squeaky grows and changes in "Raymond's Run." Be specific in your answer by providing details and examples from the story to develop your essay.

"Gentleman of Río en Medio" by Juan A. A. Sedillo
Reading Warm-up A

Read the following passage. Pay special attention to the underlined words. Then, read it again, and complete the activities. Use a separate sheet of paper for your written answers.

Mom and Dad were speechless when Great-aunt Bessie said that she was giving them her house and most of her furniture. It <u>amounted</u> to a gift of half a million dollars.

"Don't say no," Auntie added. "I once <u>insulted</u> a very dear relative by turning down a gift."

Without a fuss, my parents <u>obediently</u> accepted her offer. The <u>previous</u> year, after the twins were born, we had gone house hunting for our growing family. With property valued at a <u>rate</u> of $10,000 an acre, Mom and Dad had always come up short. They told me that we needed an <u>additional</u> $20,000 to make moving out of our crowded apartment possible. Now that Auntie was going to live with her sister, I guess she saw the wisdom in her gift. We saw space and comfort.

Great-aunt Bessie's house was <u>quaint</u> and old-fashioned. Built around the turn of the twentieth century, her grandparents had been the original owners. Her parents had been the second owners. She and her husband had been the third. They'd never had any children of their own, and now Great-uncle Oscar was gone these last three years.

One weekend afternoon, we drove over to Great-aunt Bessie's house to meet with a lawyer. He was going to draw up a deed. Auntie pulled a <u>document</u> out of a crusty old envelope. It was the original bill of sale for the house.

"I want you to have this," she said to my parents. "Keep it safe and pass it along to the next generation." She smiled in my direction. "It's part of our family history."

It felt strange to know that one day I would be part of that history. For now, it felt good to be moving into that big, old house, full of places to explore.

1. Underline the two items that <u>amounted</u> to half a million dollars. Then, write what *amounted* means.

2. Circle the words that caused the relative to be <u>insulted</u>. Rewrite that sentence, using a synonym for *insulted*.

3. Circle the phrase that tells what it means to <u>obediently</u> accept an offer. Then, tell about a time you did something *obediently*.

4. Rewrite the sentence that contains the word <u>previous</u>, using a different phrase for the *previous* year.

5. Circle the phrase that tells the <u>rate</u> at which the narrator says property is valued. Define *rate*.

6. Circle the <u>additional</u> amount of money the family needed in order to move. How does the word *additional* let you know that the family had already saved some money?

7. Circle the synonym for <u>quaint</u>. Give an example of something you know that is *quaint*.

8. Underline the words that tell what the family <u>document</u> was. Name an important *document* belonging to your family or to the country.

Name _____ Date _____

Read the following passage. Pay special attention to the underlined words. Then, read it again, and complete the activities. Use a separate sheet of paper for your written answers.

A popular saying is, "There's no such thing as a free lunch." That may be true. But in 1862, the Homestead Act provided many U.S. citizens with what amounted to free land. The only thing a homesteader needed before taking possession of 160 acres in the Midwest or the West was $12. The only payment for the land after "proving" up, or showing that a home was built and the land was being farmed, was another $6. The real cost of homesteading was a great deal more, however.

To understand the Homestead Act, you have to go back to 1783. Then, our brand-new country was pushing westward and stretching its boundaries mightily. Until the mid-1800s, sale of land by our government helped pay its debts. A struggle began between two groups of people, however. Wealthy people wanted to buy up land to make money. Poor people wanted to live on the land, farm it, and leave it to their descendants, or children.

When President Lincoln signed the Homestead Act, any U.S. head of household over 21 could obtain land. This did not stop the land grab. It did, however, create opportunities for innumerable citizens, including women and ex-slaves, who were willing to brave the frontier.

The cost of starting a farm could be great. Homesteaders in Minnesota, Iowa, and eastern Nebraska and Kansas generally had more success in farming than pioneers who headed farther west. There, they tilled poor, sod-covered soil. Hailstorms and fires could strike. Hordes of grasshoppers could overrun the land and ruin the year's crops. Many farmers wound up with little more than gnarled hands, wretched homes, and little hope for the future.

The whole story of homesteading is too long to tell here. However, there are many records of the process for anyone curious enough to know more about this period in our country's history.

1. Circle three things that the government required of a homesteader to take possession of the land.

2. Write a sentence that tells in what general direction our country stretched its boundaries.

3. Circle a word that gives a clue to the meaning of descendants. Tell who the *descendants* of your parents are.

4. Circle two groups among the innumerable citizens who became homesteaders. Give a synonym for *innumerable*.

5. Underline the words that tell what farmers tilled. Then, write what *tilled* means.

6. According to the passage, what could overrun the land? Use the word *overrun* in a sentence of your own.

7. Why would hands become gnarled from farming poor soil? Use the meaning of *gnarled* to explain your answer.

8. Circle words that give clues to the meaning of the word wretched. Tell what *wretched* means.

"Gentleman of Río en Medio" by Juan A. A. Sedillo
Reading: Make Predictions and Read Ahead
to Confirm or Correct Them

When you **make predictions,** use details in what you read to make logical, informed guesses about what will happen later in a story. **Reading ahead to confirm or correct predictions** helps you remain focused on the connections between events.

As you read, look for details that suggest a certain outcome. Make a prediction about what will happen next. Then, read ahead to see if you were right. Use new details to confirm or correct your original predictions. Finally, make new predictions—and repeat the process. Here are some guidelines for making predictions as you read:

- Consider characters' traits, actions, and relationships to other characters.
- Consider the events that have already occurred.
- Consider the setting and the kinds of events likely to occur in that setting.
- Consider the message that the writer might want to convey.
- Take into account any knowledge you have about similar situations in real life or in books or movies that you are familiar with.

DIRECTIONS: *The following chart lists details from "Gentleman of Río en Medio." Use the questions above to make predictions based on those details as you read the story. Then, read ahead to confirm or correct your prediction. In the third column, note whether your prediction was correct, and write what actually happens.*

Details From Story	Prediction	Confirmation/Correction of Prediction
1. Don Anselmo is offered twice as much money for his land as had been agreed on.		
2. After the sale of the land, the children of the village continue to play in the orchard.		
3. Don Anselmo declares that he did not sell the trees in the orchard when he sold his land.		

"Gentleman of Río en Medio" by Juan A. A. Sedillo
Literary Analysis: Conflict

Conflict is the struggle between two opposing forces.

- In **external conflict,** a character struggles against another character, natural forces, or some aspect of society. In "Gentleman of Río en Medio," the unidentified Americans are in conflict with Don Anselmo as they try to negotiate the purchase of his property.
- **Internal conflict** is a struggle between competing feelings, beliefs, needs, or desires within a single character. For example, if a character faces a loss of some kind, he or she might struggle to maintain a sense of pride or dignity.
- In the **resolution,** problems are worked out to eliminate the conflict.

The following passages from "Gentleman of Río en Medio" tell something about the characters on each side of the story's external conflict. As you reread these passages, think about the internal conflicts with which the characters might be struggling.

> It took months of negotiation to come to an understanding with the old man. He was in no hurry. What he had the most of was time. He lived up in Río en Medio, where his people had been for hundreds of years. He tilled the same land they had tilled.

> "Don Anselmo, about the ranch you sold to these people. They are good people and want to be your friends and neighbors always. When you sold to them you signed a document, a deed, and in that deed you agreed to several things. One thing was that they were to have complete possession of the property. Now, Don Anselmo, it seems that every day the children of the village overrun the orchard and spend most of their time there."

DIRECTIONS: *Use the information in the preceding passages, along with your knowledge of the rest of the story, to answer these questions.*

1. What is the external conflict in "Gentleman of Río en Medio"?

   _____

   _____

   _____

2. With what internal conflict might Don Anselmo be struggling?

   _____

3. With what internal conflict might the Americans be struggling?

   _____

4. How are the conflicts resolved?

   _____

   _____

Name _____ Date _____

Word List

innumerable	preliminary	descendants

A. DIRECTIONS: *Revise each sentence so that the italicized word is used logically. Be sure to include the vocabulary word in your revised sentence.*

Example: When the rain clouds appeared, the baseball fans shouted with *delight*.

Revision: When the rain clouds disappeared, the baseball fans shouted with delight.

1. The Americans could name every one of Don Anselmo's descendants, for to them the children were *innumerable*.

   _____

   _____

2. Don Anselmo's *preliminary* performance followed the meeting.

   _____

3. The children of Río en Medio were proud that Don Anselmo was one of their *descendants*.

   _____

   _____

B. DIRECTIONS: *Answer each question with* yes *or* no. *Then, explain your answer.*

1. Can you count something that is *innumerable*?

   _____

2. Does a *preliminary* event follow the main event?

   _____

3. Are you likely to know any of your *descendants*?

   _____

C. DIRECTIONS: *On the line, write the letter of the best definition of each Word List word.*

____ 1. innumerable
   A. incomparable   B. countless   C. dependable   D. few

____ 2. descendants
   A. ancestors   B. judges   C. advisors   D. offspring

____ 3. preliminary
   A. introductory   B. final   C. explanatory   D. precise

"Gentleman of Río en Medio" by Juan A. A. Sedillo
Support for Writing a Letter

When you write a **letter,** you have a particular audience—a person or group of people—in mind. In addition, you usually have a particular purpose. You might be describing a trip you are taking, telling what you are doing in school or with your friends, requesting a service, or thanking someone for a gift.

As you draft a letter to Don Anselmo, think about these points:

- the person to whom you are writing
- your reason for thanking him or her
- the reasons you appreciate his efforts on behalf of the children

DIRECTIONS: *Answer the following questions. Use your answers in your letter to Don Anselmo.*

1. What does Don Anselmo care about most?

   _____

   _____

2. What gift has Don Anselmo given to the children?

   _____

   _____

3. What did the children probably enjoy about playing in the orchard?

   _____

   _____

4. How have the children benefited from Don Anselmo's solution to the conflict?

   _____

   _____

Now, draft your letter to Don Anselmo. Begin with the salutation "Dear Don Anselmo," and end with the closing "Sincerely yours." Then, sign your name.

"Gentleman of Río en Medio" by Juan A. A. Sedillo
Support for Extend Your Learning

Research and Technology

Use the following chart as you work with the other members of your group to gather information about the Spanish influence in the American Southwest. Working alone or with one or two classmates, research one of the topics in the chart, or choose a related topic. Look not just for written information but also for illustrations you can use in your **oral presentation.** When you have completed your research, meet as a group to make a poster that summarizes your findings. Then, prepare your oral presentation, making sure every member of the group has a part.

Art	Architecture	Music	Food	Other Topic

Listening and Speaking

To prepare to **role-play** the conflict between Don Anselmo and the purchasers of his property, write a script. With your partner, decide who will play the part of Don Anselmo and who will play the part of the narrator, who speaks on behalf of the Americans. Begin by stating your side of the conflict. Remember to use the pronouns *I, me,* and *my* in reference to your character and to write (and speak) in character—that is, as you imagine your character would write (and speak). When you have completed your script, read it over a few times. Then, put it aside, and role-play the conflict without your notes.

Narrator: _____

_____

Don Anselmo: _____

_____

Narrator: _____

_____

Don Anselmo: _____

_____

Narrator: _____

_____

Don Anselmo: _____

_____

"Gentleman of Río en Medio" by Juan A. A. Sedillo
Enrichment: Mathematics

Imagine that you are the **surveyor** who measures Don Anselmo's land. Below is a map showing the land Don Anselmo thinks he owns. You discover that he owns a parcel of land of equal size and shape across the river.

	217.8 Feet	217.8 Feet
200 Feet	One Acre	One Acre
200 Feet	One Acre	One Acre
200 Feet	One Acre	One Acre
200 Feet	One Acre	One Acre

R
I
V
E
R

DIRECTIONS: *Complete the diagram to show the land that Don Anselmo owns across the river. Label its measurements in feet, based on the measurements of the original parcel. Then, answer the following questions.*

1. How many acres of land does Don Anselmo own in all?

   _____

2. What is the total length of the land, in feet?

   _____

3. What is the total width of the land, in feet?

   _____

4. What is the area of one acre, in square feet?

   _____

5. Don Anselmo is selling eight acres of land for $1,200. How many dollars is that per acre?

   _____

6. How much are the Americans willing to pay Don Anselmo for the two parcels of property combined?

   _____

Name _____ Date _____

Selection Test A

Critical Reading *Identify the letter of the choice that best answers the question.*

____ 1. Who tells the story of "Gentleman of Río en Medio"?
A. Don Anselmo
B. a child in the village
C. the American buyers
D. a friend of the Americans

____ 2. Which statement hints that there may be a conflict in "Gentleman of Río en Medio"?
A. It took Don Anselmo months to come to a decision.
B. Don Anselmo had lived in Río en Medio all his life.
C. The orchard is beautiful.
D. Don Anselmo bows to the people at the meeting.

____ 3. Between whom is the conflict in "Gentleman of Río en Medio"?
A. Don Anselmo and the Americans
B. Don Anselmo and the children
C. the Americans and the person helping them with the land
D. Don Anselmo and his relatives

____ 4. Why is Don Anselmo referred to as "Don"?
A. "Don" is a nickname for "Donald."
B. "Don" is another way of saying "dear."
C. "Don" is another way of saying "sir."
D. "Don" means "grandfather."

____ 5. Which sentence best describes Don Anselmo in "Gentleman of Río en Medio"?
A. He is a businessman at heart.
B. He is not a very good negotiator.
C. He is dishonest.
D. He values fairness to all.

____ 6. What is a reasonable prediction about how Don Anselmo will react to the Americans' problem with the children?
A. Don Anselmo will be angry and unreasonable.
B. Don Anselmo will give the problem some thought.
C. Don Anselmo will ask his family's advice.
D. Don Anselmo will tell the children to leave the orchard.

_____ 7. What is Don Anselmo's reason for not selling the trees along with the land?

   A. He doesn't think the Americans want them.

   B. He wants the trees for himself.

   C. The Americans did not ask for them.

   D. The trees belong to his descendants.

_____ 8. Why do you think Don Anselmo brings his young relative to the meetings?

   A. Don Anselmo enjoys having a servant with him at all times.

   B. Don Anselmo is proud of his family and includes them in his life.

   C. Don Anselmo never travels alone.

   D. Don Anselmo wants the company.

_____ 9. How is the conflict resolved in "Gentleman of Río en Medio"?

   A. The person helping the Americans pays for the trees.

   B. The children are allowed to play in the orchard.

   C. The Americans buy the trees from their owners.

   D. Don Anselmo moves back into his house.

_____ 10. To whom does Don Anselmo want to sell his land?

   A. to people he respects

   B. to people who can pay the highest price

   C. to people who will take care of the orchard

   D. to people who will sell the orchard

_____ 11. Based on the behavior of Don Anselmo and the Americans, what prediction can you make about their future together?

   A. Problems will continue to arise.

   B. The Americans will move away.

   C. The children will cause damage to the trees.

   D. They will work out any problems that come up.

Vocabulary and Grammar

_____ 12. Which phrase is closest in meaning to *innumerable*?

   A. not able to be seen

   B. too many to count

   C. not able to be heard

   D. very far away

____ 13. What kind of nouns are the words *women* and *girls*?

  A. proper nouns

  B. pronouns

  C. singular nouns

  D. plural nouns

____ 14. Don Anselmo says that the trees belong to his descendants. Who are his descendants?

  A. his aunts

  B. his grandparents

  C. his offspring

  D. his friends

____ 15. In which sentence is a plural noun used *incorrectly*?

  A. The library had many books on its shelves.

  B. Hundreds of geese flew overhead.

  C. We looked for more berry bushes.

  D. How many childs are in your family?

Essay

16. Don Anselmo is very proud of his large family. He is also very generous to his descendants. Write an essay in which you tell how you know that these are true statements. Give examples from "Gentleman of Río en Medio" to help prove your points.

17. Write an essay in which you predict how Don Anselmo, his relatives, and the Americans will get along as neighbors in the future. Base your answer on events that occur in "Gentleman of Río en Medio."

"Gentleman of Río en Medio" by Juan A. A. Sedillo
Selection Test B

Critical Reading *Identify the letter of the choice that best completes the statement or answers the question.*

_____ 1. Who is the narrator of "Gentleman of Río en Medio"?
   A. Don Anselmo
   B. a child in the village
   C. the Americans who buy the property
   D. the agent handling the sale of the property

_____ 2. Which statement from "Gentleman of Río en Medio" offers the first hint that there may be a conflict between the Americans and Don Anselmo?
   A. "It took months of negotiation to come to an understanding with the old man."
   B. "He lived up in Río en Medio, where his people had been for hundreds of years."
   C. "His orchard was gnarled and beautiful."
   D. "The old man bowed to all of us in the room."

_____ 3. What do you learn about Don Anselmo from the way he dresses?
   A. He tries to appear rich.
   B. He has lived in the same area all his life.
   C. He is proud of his large family.
   D. He is poor, but he has dignity.

_____ 4. In "Gentleman of Río en Medio," why is Don Anselmo referred to as "Don"?
   A. "Don" is a shortened form of his first name, "Donald."
   B. "Don" is a term of affection, similar to "dear" or "darling."
   C. "Don" is a title of respect, such as "sir" in English.
   D. "Don" means "to put on," and shows that he "put on" an act.

_____ 5. Which sentence best describes Don Anselmo?
   A. Don Anselmo is a businessman at heart.
   B. Don Anselmo is not a very good negotiator.
   C. Don Anselmo is stubborn and uncooperative.
   D. Don Anselmo values fairness to all.

_____ 6. Why did Don Anselmo refuse the extra money for his land?
   A. He did not want to cheat the Americans.
   B. He was afraid the Americans were making fun of him.
   C. He felt it was a point of honor to be paid the price they had already agreed upon.
   D. He did not want to lose face in front of the boy who had come with him.

_____ 7. Based on the first meeting described in "Gentleman of Río en Medio," what is a reasonable prediction about what will happen in the second meeting?
   I.   Don Anselmo will be stubborn and unreasonable.
   II. Don Anselmo will put his family first.
   III. Don Anselmo will take his time to reach a decision.
   IV. Don Anselmo will be upset.
   A. I, II   B. I, II, III   C. II, III   D. I, III, IV

____ 8. How do the Americans resolve the conflict over the sale of Don Anselmo's land?
   A. They buy each tree from its owner in the village.
   B. They pay Don Anselmo double the price for his land.
   C. They give up and move away from Río en Medio.
   D. They decide to let the children play in the orchard.

____ 9. The real conflict in "Gentleman of Río en Medio" is between two forces rather than people. Which concepts or traditions are in opposition to other?
   A. the older generation vs. the newcomers
   B. the Americans and their real estate agent
   C. the custom of ownership vs. the law of ownership
   D. the buyers of the land vs. Don Anselmo

____ 10. How might Don Anselmo's internal conflict be described?
   A. his history with the land vs. his family's need for money
   B. his ownership of the land and his descendants' greediness
   C. his need for money and his obligation to the Americans
   D. his attachment to the orchard and his need for new clothes

____ 11. It is important to Don Anselmo to sell his land to
   A. people he respects.
   B. people who can pay the highest price.
   C. people who can care for the orchard.
   D. people who will let the children play in the orchard.

____ 12. Solving the problem by buying the trees from Don Anselmo's descendants is the story's
   A. external conflict.
   B. internal conflict.
   C. resolution.
   D. opposing force.

____ 13. Based on the behavior of Don Anselmo and the Americans, what prediction can you make about their future together?
   A. Problems will continue to arise.
   B. The Americans will move away.
   C. The children will cause damage to the trees.
   D. They will work out any problems that come up.

Vocabulary and Grammar

____ 14. In which sentence is *innumerable* used correctly?
   A. The innumerable guests sat down at the table.
   B. John tried to count the mosquitoes, but they were innumerable.
   C. Without a tape measure, figuring out the table length was innumerable.
   D. The flat tire made the car innumerable.

____ 15. The word *women* is an example of a
      A. plural noun.
      B. singular noun.
      C. phrase.
      D. proper noun.

____ 16. An appropriate word to describe *descendants* is
      A. ancestors.
      B. grandparents.
      C. offspring.
      D. friends.

____ 17. In which sentence are the singular and plural nouns used correctly?
      A. The geese migrated south for the winter.
      B. Three friends shared a tables at the reception.
      C. The library donated many used book to the children in the village.
      D. Daniel took three photography class at schools.

Essay

18. The external conflict in "Gentleman of Río en Medio" involves people of two cultures negotiating a sale of land. Write an essay explaining the point of view of both sides of the conflict, the American buyers and Don Anselmo.

19. Don Anselmo is fair, generous, and proud. Write an essay in which you agree or disagree with this statement. Use examples from "Gentleman of Río en Medio" to support your answer.

Vocabulary Warm-up Word Lists

Study these words from "Cub Pilot on the Mississippi." Then, complete the activities.

Word List A

apprenticeship [uh PREN tis ship] *n.* training for a job
   After high school, Brett started an <u>apprenticeship</u> with a local plumber.

costly [KAWST lee] *adj.* expensive
   Not paying attention while driving can lead to <u>costly</u> errors.

criticized [KRIT uh syzd] *v.* told someone what he or she did wrong
   Ms. Banks <u>criticized</u> Lenny for his selfish attitude.

employment [em PLOY muhnt] *n.* paid work
   Without skills or training, it is hard to find interesting <u>employment</u>.

stingy [STIN jee] *adj.* unwilling to spend or give money
   Mr. Virgil was so <u>stingy</u> that he didn't want to pay me for pet sitting.

tyrant [TY ruhnt] *n.* cruel ruler, or someone who behaves like one
   Whoever disobeyed the <u>tyrant</u> was punished or banished from the land.

varieties [vuh RY uh teez] *n.* different types of the same thing
   How many <u>varieties</u> of melon can you name?

vigorous [VIG uh ruhs] *adj.* lively, strong, or with great energy
   At the age of eighty, Mrs. Dawes was as <u>vigorous</u> as any sixty-year-old.

Word List B

abreast [uh BREST] *adj.* up to date
   Please keep me <u>abreast</u> of the latest news on the election.

aloft [uh LAWFT] *adj.* in the air
   After several tries, the Wright brothers finally got a plane to stay <u>aloft</u>.

blunder [BLUHN der] *n.* mistake
   Calling your sister by the wrong name was an embarrassing <u>blunder</u>.

dialect [DY uh lekt] *n.* type of language that is spoken in a specific place
   It's easy to pick out someone with a southern <u>dialect</u> in a crowd of New Yorkers.

environment [en VY ruhn muhnt] *n.* surroundings; the natural world
   The builder designed the house in harmony with its <u>environment</u>.

homesick [HOHM sik] *adj.* missing one's home and family
   After only two days away at camp, the brothers were already <u>homesick</u>.

impressively [im PRES iv lee] *adv.* in an outstanding way; strikingly
   Both candidates spoke <u>impressively</u> about what they had accomplished.

steamboat [STEEM boht] *n.* boat that uses steam for power
   The <u>steamboat</u> came downriver, its paddle turning and smoke rising into the air.

Name _____ Date _____

Vocabulary Warm-up Exercises

Exercise A *Fill in each blank in the paragraph below with an appropriate word from Word List A. Use each word only once.*

Some jobs require a long [1] _____ period, but I didn't think being a reporter for the middle-school newspaper was one of them. It wasn't as if I had sought [2] _____ at the city desk of a major paper. There were only so many [3] _____ of articles, and I thought I covered them all pretty well: sports, assemblies, elections, contests, and fundraising. Still, that [4] _____ of an editor thought otherwise. He was [5] _____ with his time except when he [6] _____ anything I wrote. He was especially [7] _____ in putting me down when other staff members were around. It wasn't as if I could make some [8] _____ error reporting the news. After all, the paper was given out free to all students!

Exercise B *Revise each sentence so that the underlined vocabulary word is used in a logical way. Be sure to keep the vocabulary word in your revision.*

Example: He played <u>impressively</u>, throwing many incomplete passes and losing much yardage.

He played <u>impressively</u>, throwing many complete passes and gaining much yardage.

1. I always keep <u>abreast</u> of the news, so I know little about current events.

   _____

2. When it rains, the American flag should be hoisted <u>aloft</u>.

   _____

3. A terrible <u>blunder</u> made things better for everyone.

   _____

4. When she recognized the unfamiliar <u>dialect</u>, she realized how <u>homesick</u> she was for a strange town.

   _____

5. If you want to ruin the <u>environment</u>, concern yourself with the loss of habitats.

   _____

6. A flatboat was a great improvement over the slow-moving <u>steamboat</u>.

   _____

Name _____ Date _____

"**Cub Pilot on the Mississippi**" by Mark Twain
Reading Warm-up A

Read the following passage. Pay special attention to the underlined words. Then, read it again, and complete the activities. Use a separate sheet of paper for your written answers.

In colonial America, and in the early days of the republic, <u>apprenticeship</u> was a common way for a boy to learn a trade. He would sign an indenture, or contract, with a master. The master would then train him in all aspects of his livelihood. Usually, no money changed hands until the last year of service. All the same, it was <u>costly</u> to the master. He had to provide the boy with room and board, and he sometimes also taught the boy how to read, write, and keep the business's accounts.

A master could be a <u>tyrant</u> or a gentle teacher, <u>stingy</u> or generous almost to a fault. Some masters <u>criticized</u> their apprentices constantly. Others taught with praise. No matter what, a boy was expected to obey the master's wishes.

The period of service was usually five or seven years. Then, with a small amount of money in his pocket, an apprentice set out into the world. He was known as a *journeyman*. That is because he often had to journey from place to place to find <u>employment</u>. He usually hoped to save up enough money to have his own business.

Modern life offers many opportunities. However, even 200 years ago, there were many <u>varieties</u> of jobs. A boy could train to be a baker or a blacksmith, a cooper (barrel maker) or a chandler (candle maker). These occupations required a boy in <u>vigorous</u> health with a strong desire to learn and the patience to see a job through. Boys with more education and a love of learning might wind up in a printer's shop or a merchant's office.

The Industrial Revolution greatly reduced the apprentice system. In some fields even today, however, it is a necessary route. It is required for learning a craft, such as fine cabinet making, or a service skill, such as plumbing. Also, it is the only way to pass down years of know-how from generation to generation.

1. Underline words that give a clue to the meaning of <u>apprenticeship</u>. Name a trade for which you might like to serve an *apprenticeship*.

2. Circle the words that tell what was <u>costly</u> to the master. Explain why in a sentence.

3. Circle the word that is the opposite of <u>tyrant</u>. Write a sentence that describes someone who is the opposite of a *tyrant*.

4. Circle the word that is the opposite of <u>stingy</u>. Write a sentence that tells at least one way in which a master might have been *stingy*.

5. Rewrite the sentence with the word <u>criticized</u> using a synonym for *criticized*.

6. Circle one form of <u>employment</u> mentioned in the following sentence. Explain in a sentence why a journeyman had to find *employment*.

7. Circle two <u>varieties</u> of trades mentioned in the paragraph. Write a sentence that includes the other *varieties* mentioned.

8. Why did the trades listed require someone with <u>vigorous</u> health?

Name _____ Date _____

"Cub Pilot on the Mississippi" by Mark Twain
Reading Warm-up B

Read the following passage. Pay special attention to the underlined words. Then, read it again, and complete the activities. Use a separate sheet of paper for your written answers.

In 1800, pioneers heading west from the original 13 colonies faced a trek over miles of trails or an equally slow boat trip. Flatboats drifted downstream with the current, and going upstream was impossible.

The invention of the <u>steamboat</u> changed water travel forever. It opened up the Midwest to farming, shipping, and industry. It paved the way for America's great westward expansion. Robert Fulton's *Clermont* began operating on the Hudson River in New York in 1807. Boats that used burning fuel to create steam power reached their height on the Mississippi River shortly before the Civil War.

A steamboat would chug <u>impressively</u> downriver at eight miles an hour, billows of smoke <u>aloft</u>. Docking at ports along the way, it entered the <u>environment</u> of rough, lively river towns. Southern <u>dialect</u> met northern accent in the bustle of St. Louis, Missouri, the steamboat capital. Crews and passengers helped keep folks <u>abreast</u> of the news up and down the river. <u>Homesick</u> river workers would gather around to hear word from their native towns.

Within a few decades, steamboats became "floating palaces." They could be as long as 300 feet, with five decks. Steamboats had a dark side, however. They were dangerous. Sometimes even a minor <u>blunder</u> would cause a boiler explosion, placing people's lives and the boat's cargo in jeopardy.

The Civil War brought a halt to steamboat traffic on the Mississippi. The river turned into a watery battle route. After the war, steamboat traffic resumed. It was soon overshadowed, however, by the growth of another kind of steam transportation: the railroad.

Brought to life in the stage musical *Show Boat*, the steamboat became a form of traveling entertainment. Today, there are still many steamboat lovers. Newly built "floating palaces" operate in some of America's finest river towns, reminding us of days gone by.

1. Underline the words that explain what <u>steamboats</u> are. Write a sentence that tells about the first *steamboat*.

2. Rewrite the sentence with <u>impressively</u> and <u>aloft</u>, substituting different words for them.

3. Circle the words that describe the <u>environment</u> of the river towns. Write a sentence, describing your school *environment*.

4. List the two <u>dialects</u> mentioned in the passage. Then, write a sentence in your own words, telling what a *dialect* is.

5. Rewrite the sentence with the word <u>abreast</u>, using a synonym for the word.

6. Underline the phrase that suggests the river workers might be <u>homesick</u>. Explain in a sentence why they might feel this way.

7. Write a sentence that tells what the results of a <u>blunder</u> might be aboard a steamboat. Define *blunder*.

Name _____ Date _____

Reading: Make Predictions and Read Ahead to Confirm or Correct Them

When you **make predictions,** use details in what you read to make logical, informed guesses about what will happen later in a story. **Reading ahead to confirm or correct predictions** helps you to remain focused on the connections between events.

As you read, look for details that suggest a certain outcome. Make a prediction about what will happen next. Then, read ahead to see if you were right. Use new details to confirm or correct your original predictions. Finally, make new predictions—and repeat the process.

Here are some guidelines to consider for making predictions as you read:

- Consider characters' traits, actions, and relationships with other characters.
- Consider the events that have already occurred.
- Consider the setting and the kinds of events likely to occur in that setting.
- Consider the message that the writer might want to convey.
- Take into account any knowledge you have about similar situations in real life or in books or movies you are familiar with.

DIRECTIONS: *The following chart lists details from "Cub Pilot on the Mississippi." Use the questions above to make predictions based on those details as you read the story. Then, read ahead to confirm or correct your prediction. In the third column, note whether your prediction was correct, and write what actually happens.*

Details From Story	Prediction	Confirmation/Correction of Prediction
1. He was a middle-aged, long, slim, bony, smooth-shaven, horse-faced, ignorant, stingy, malicious, snarling, fault-hunting, mote-magnifying tyrant.		
2. I often wanted to kill Brown, but . . . a cub had to take everything his boss gave, in the way of . . . comment and criticism; and we all believed that there was a . . . law making it a penitentiary offense to strike or threaten a pilot on duty.		
3. The racket had brought everybody to the hurricane deck, and I trembled when I saw the old captain looking up from amid the crowd. I said to myself, "Now I *am* done for!"		

Name _____ Date _____

"Cub Pilot on the Mississippi" by Mark Twain
Literary Analysis: Conflict

Conflict is the struggle between two opposing forces.

- In **external conflict,** a character struggles against another character, natural forces, or some aspect of society.
- **Internal conflict** is a struggle between competing feelings, beliefs, needs, or desires within a single character.

In the **resolution** of a story, problems are worked out in a way that eliminates the conflict.

The following passages from "Cub Pilot on the Mississippi" tell something about the characters' external conflicts and about one character's internal struggle. As you reread these passages, think about the conflicts with which the characters are struggling.

He was a middle-aged, long, slim, bony, smooth-shaven, horse-faced, ignorant, stingy, malicious, snarling, fault-hunting, mote-magnifying tyrant. I early got the habit of coming on watch with dread at my heart. No matter how good a time I might have been having with the off-watch below, and no matter how high my spirits might be when I started aloft, my soul became lead in my body the moment I approached the pilothouse.

I often wanted to kill Brown, but this would not answer. A cub had to take everything his boss gave, in the way of vigorous comment and criticism; and we all believed that there was a United States law making it a penitentiary offense to strike or threaten a pilot on duty.

DIRECTIONS: *Use the information in the preceding passages, along with your knowledge of the rest of the story, to answer these questions.*

1. What is the external conflict in "Cub Pilot on the Mississippi"?

   _____

   _____

2. What is the internal conflict?

   _____

   _____

3. How are the conflicts resolved?

   _____

   _____

   _____

   _____

   _____

   _____

"Cub Pilot on the Mississippi" by Mark Twain
Vocabulary Builder

Word List

pretext	judicious	indulgent

A. DIRECTIONS: *Revise each sentence so that the italicized Word List word is used logically. Be sure to include the vocabulary word in your revised sentence.*

Example: When the rain clouds appeared, the baseball fans shouted with *delight.*

Revision: When the rain clouds disappeared, the baseball fans shouted with delight.

1. Because his motives were sound, Brown needed a *pretext* to find fault with Twain.

   _____

2. By attacking Brown, Twain showed that he was *judicious.*

   _____

3. Brown was *indulgent* in his treatment of the young men who worked with him.

   _____

B. DIRECTIONS: *Answer each question with* yes *or* no. *Then, explain your answer.*

1. Do you need a *pretext* to argue with someone who has irritated you?

   _____

2. Are you being *judicious* when you carefully consider the consequences of your actions?

   _____

   _____

3. Are you being *indulgent* when you point out every mistake that someone has made?

   _____

   _____

C. DIRECTIONS: *On the line, write the letter of the best definition of each Word List word.*

____ 1. indulgent
   A. tolerant   **B.** strict   **C.** demanding   **D.** hungry

____ 2. judicious
   A. thoughtless   **B.** playful   **C.** wise   **D.** unreasonable

____ 3. pretext
   A. preview   **B.** excuse   **C.** novel   **D.** essay

Name _____ Date _____

"Cub Pilot on the Mississippi" by Mark Twain
Support for Writing a Letter

When you write a **letter,** you usually have a particular audience—a person or group of people—in mind. In addition, you usually have a particular purpose for writing. You might be describing a trip you are taking, telling what you are doing in school or with your friends, requesting a service, or thanking someone for a gift.

As you draft a letter to your best friend telling about your first few days as a cub pilot on a steamboat, think about these points:

- the person to whom you are writing
- the purpose of the letter
- the details that best describe your experience on the steamboat

DIRECTIONS: *Answer the following questions. Use your answers in your letter to your friend.*

1. What was your first impression of the steamboat? Did your first impression change? If so, how? What impression do you hold now?

_____

_____

_____

2. What is the pilot like? How does he or she treat you? What are you learning?

_____

_____

_____

3. What are the other crew members like? Do you interact with them?

_____

_____

_____

4. Have you been ashore? What have you seen? What have you done?

_____

_____

_____

Now, draft your letter. Begin with an appropriate salutation (for example, "Dear John") and end with an appropriate closing (such as "Yours truly"). Then, sign your name.

Name _____ Date _____

"Cub Pilot on the Mississippi" by Mark Twain

Support for Extend Your Learning

Research and Technology

Use the following chart as you work with the other members of your group to gather information about the Mississippi River. Working alone or with one or two classmates, research one of the topics in the chart. Look not just for written information but also for visual aids you can use in your **oral presentation.** When you have completed your research, meet as a group to prepare your presentation. Make sure every member of the group has a part.

The River's Role in History	The River's Source, Main Ports, and Mouth	The River's Effect on Transportation in the 1800s
_____	_____	_____

Listening and Speaking

With a partner, write a script to **role-play** the conflict between Twain and Brown. Begin by stating your side of the conflict. Your goal is to find a nonviolent solution.

- What issues divide you?
- What common interests do you have?
- What are your options for resolving the conflict in a way you both find acceptable?

Remember to use the pronouns *I, me,* and *my* in reference to your character and to write (and speak) in character—that is, as you imagine your character would write (and speak). When you have completed your script, read it over a few times. Then, put it aside, and role-play the conflict without your notes.

Brown: _____

_____

Twain: _____

_____

Brown: _____

_____

Twain: _____

_____

Brown: _____

_____

Twain: _____

_____

"Cub Pilot on the Mississippi" by Mark Twain
Enrichment: Conflict Resolution

Mark Twain suffered during his apprenticeship under Mr. Brown. In the end, Twain was so full of anger that he punched a man who was his elder and his boss. How else might the conflict have been resolved?

Conflict at school or work cannot always be avoided. The use of violence, however, is never the answer. Of all the skills you will learn before you enter the workforce, problem solving and **conflict resolution** are among the most essential. Being able to recognize and solve problems early on will help you work well with others and work effectively at your job. If you believe you are being treated unfairly, you might discuss the issue respectfully with the person involved. If that is not an option, ask advice from a responsible individual. Finally, back off, or leave a bad situation before it leads to violence.

DIRECTIONS: *Imagine that Twain and Brown have the chance to resolve their conflict before any violence takes place. Using your imagination and details from "Cub Pilot on the Mississippi," fill in this chart to show how the two men might have used problem-solving skills effectively. The first step has been completed as an example.*

Problem-Solving Steps	Steps Taken by Twain and Brown
1. Recognize that a problem exists: Identify a difference between what is and what could or should be.	Brown continually picks on Twain. Twain says nothing to Brown about how the criticism makes him feel.
2. Identify possible reasons for the problem.	
3. Create a plan to solve the problem.	
4. Evaluate how well the plan is working.	
5. Review the plan, and revise it if necessary.	

"**Gentleman of Río en Medio**" by Juan A. A. Sedillo
"**Cub Pilot on the Mississippi**" by Mark Twain
Build Language Skills: Vocabulary

The Prefix *re-*

The prefix *re-* is retro. That is, it means "back." It can also mean "backward," "again," or "against." In the word *revise*, it means "back" or "backward," and it refers to looking back—making corrections or improvements in something you have planned or written. *Re-* is a handy prefix because it can be attached to many words. For example, if you paint a room and then decide you do not like the color, what you can do next is *repaint* the room.

A. DIRECTIONS: *Follow the instructions to write sentences using the prefix* re-. *If you need to, look up the definition of the word in a dictionary before you write your sentence.*

1. Use *reassemble* in a sentence about an engine. _____

   _____

2. Use *rebate* in a sentence about an appliance. _____

   _____

3. Use *reduce* in a sentence about a diet. _____

   _____

4. Use *reflect* in a sentence about a mirror. _____

   _____

5. Use *repeat* in a sentence about learning something. _____

   _____

Academic Vocabulary Practice

B. DIRECTIONS: *Answer each of the following questions by paying attention to the italicized Academic Vocabulary word. Then, explain your answer.*

1. Can astronomers *predict* a lunar eclipse?

   Yes/No: _____ **Why or why not?** _____

2. If you plan to attend a popular event, do you *anticipate* that few people will be there?

   Yes/No: _____ **Why or why not?** _____

3. If an architect were asked to *formulate* a plan, would he redraw an old plan?

   Yes/No: _____ **Why or why not?** _____

4. If an architect were asked to *modify* a plan, would she make a new plan?

   Yes/No: _____ **Why or why not?** _____

5. If an architect were asked to *revise* a plan, would he look again at the plan he had made?

   Yes/No: _____ **Why or why not?** _____

"Gentleman of Río en Medio" by Juan A. A. Sedillo
"Cub Pilot on the Mississippi" by Mark Twain
Build Language Skills: Grammar

Plural Nouns

A **plural noun** refers to more than one person, place, thing, or idea—for example, *girls, towns, books, beliefs.* The plurals of most nouns are formed by adding an *-s* to the end of the word. The plurals of certain nouns, however, are formed according to different rules. This chart shows some of the rules for forming plural nouns:

Rule	Examples
For words that end in *-x*, *-ch*, or *-sh*, add *-es*.	box, box**es**; church, church**es**; sash, sash**es**
For words that end in a consonant plus *-y*, change the *y* to *i* and add *-es*.	pony, pon**ies**; fly, fl**ies**
For some words that end in *-f* or *-fe*, change the *-f* or *-fe* to *-ves*.	calf, cal**ves**; knife, kni**ves**; *but* roof, roofs.
For some words, the plural form is a different word.	goose, g**ee**se; mouse, m**i**ce; wom**a**n, wom**e**n

A. DIRECTIONS: *Underline each plural noun in the following sentences.*

1. Last year I took a trip west with several friends.
2. We stayed at a ranch where oxen grazed outside our window.
3. We hiked in the desert and found fossils of animal teeth.
4. I found time to read while sitting next to the river, near low bushes of sweet-smelling sage.
5. On our last night, we were lucky enough to see three shooting stars.

B. Writing Application: *Write a paragraph about a trip you have taken or would like to take. Use at least five plural nouns that are not formed by adding -s to the end of the word. Then, underline all the plural nouns in your paragraph.*

_____

_____

_____

_____

_____

_____

"Cub Pilot on the Mississippi" by Mark Twain
Selection Test A

Critical Reading *Identify the letter of the choice that best answers the question.*

____ 1. What does this passage tell you about how young Twain feels about Brown?

> He was a middle-aged, long, slim, bony, smooth-shaven, horse-faced, ignorant, stingy, malicious, snarling, fault-hunting, mote magnifying tyrant.

   A. Twain dislikes Brown intensely.

   B. Twain respects Brown in spite of his flaws.

   C. You can't judge a book by its cover.

   D. Twain finds Brown funny.

____ 2. What do you predict is the possibility of Twain and Brown ever getting along, based on Twain's first experiences with the pilot?

   A. Twain and Brown will find a lot to talk about.

   B. Twain and Brown will never get along well.

   C. Twain and Brown will become friends.

   D. Brown will become a good teacher for Twain.

____ 3. What is Twain feeling in this line from "Cub Pilot"?

> As soon as I could get my voice I said apologetically, "I have had no orders, sir."

   A. eagerness

   B. happiness

   C. discomfort

   D. anger

____ 4. In "Cub Pilot," George Ealer, Ritchie's boss, is the opposite of Brown. Which word describes George Ealer?

   A. lazy

   B. unfair

   C. forgetful

   D. kindhearted

____ 5. What does Twain's friend George Ritchie like to do in "Cub Pilot"?

   A. play tricks on Brown

   B. tease Twain about Brown

   C. eat meals with Brown

   D. tease Twain's brother Henry

Name _____ Date _____

_____ 6. Twain tries to hold his temper when Brown gets angry. What does this describe?
   A. the external conflict
   B. Twain's internal conflict
   C. Brown's internal conflict
   D. the falling action

_____ 7. Why does Brown command Twain to "round the boat to"?
   A. Brown wants to teach Twain a new skill.
   B. Brown knows that Twain will do a good job.
   C. Brown wants Twain to fail so he can yell at him.
   D. Brown has forgotten how to do it himself.

_____ 8. In "Cub Pilot," why does Brown not hear Henry's shouted instruction to stop at the landing?
   A. He dislikes Henry.
   B. He is too busy yelling at Twain.
   C. He has fallen asleep at the wheel.
   D. He is deaf.

_____ 9. Which sentence best describes how the captain treats Twain after Twain's attack on Brown?
   A. The captain supports Twain.
   B. The captain is angry with Twain.
   C. The captain is surprised at Twain's behavior.
   D. The captain is sad about what happened.

_____ 10. What does Twain find out about himself after the conflict with Brown?
   A. He finds out that he has courage.
   B. He finds out that he is reckless.
   C. He finds out that he has steering skill.
   D. He finds out that he has a sense of humor.

_____ 11. How do you predict that Twain would have reacted to Brown's insults if Henry had not been in danger?
   A. Twain would still have attacked Brown.
   B. Twain would have insulted Brown.
   C. Twain would have held in his anger, as usual.
   D. Twain would have leaped off the steamboat.

Vocabulary and Grammar

____ **12.** In which sentence is *ascended* used correctly?

   A. Tom ascended the stairs to the basement.

   B. Sam ascended the stairs to the balcony.

   C. Susan ascended the letter to her father.

   D. The crowded ascended wildly.

____ **13.** What does it mean if parents are *indulgent*?

   A. They are easy-going.

   B. They are strict.

   C. They have many rules.

   D. They are nervous.

____ **14.** What kind of noun is the word *books*?

   A. a proper noun

   B. a plural noun

   C. a singular noun

   D. a phrase

____ **15.** In which sentence are plural nouns used correctly?

   A. There were too many geese in our backyard.

   B. The teacher brought three book to class.

   C. All of the peoples came to the new movie.

   D. Why did you eat all those cookie?

Essay

16. Write an essay in which you agree or disagree with young Twain's decision to fight Brown. If you agree with what he did, give examples and reasons from "Cub Pilot" to support your opinion. If you disagree with what Twain did, give reasons for your opinion and suggest other ways he could have solved the conflict.

17. Write an essay in which you discuss how young Twain and Brown are different. Discuss their physical appearance, use of language, response to anger or frustration, and sense of honesty. Use examples from "Cub Pilot" to support your ideas.

"Cub Pilot on the Mississippi" by Mark Twain
Selection Test B

Critical Reading *Identify the letter of the choice that best completes the statement or answers the question.*

_____ 1. Which sentence best describes how the narrator feels about Brown in this passage from "Cub Pilot"?

> He was a middle-aged, long, slim, bony, smooth-shaven, horse-faced, ignorant, stingy, malicious, snarling, fault-hunting, mote magnifying tyrant.

    A. The narrator despises him.
    B. The narrator respects him.
    C. The narrator envies Brown.
    D. The narrator finds Brown humorous.

_____ 2. What do you predict about how Twain and Brown will get along, based on their first encounter?
    A. Brown and Twain will not get along well.
    B. Brown and Twain will find a lot to talk about.
    C. Brown and Twain will become friends.
    D. Brown will be a valuable teacher for Twain.

_____ 3. Why do you think Brown examines Twain's shoes so carefully?
    A. to make Twain feel uncomfortable and self-conscious
    B. to be sure Twain is using proper hygiene
    C. because he admires the shoes
    D. because he is curious

_____ 4. What do you know about the conflict between Twain and Brown from this passage?

> The moment I was in the presence, even in the darkest night, I could feel those yellow eyes upon me, and knew their owner was watching for a pretext to spit out some venom on me.

    A. Brown imagines that Twain dislikes him.
    B. Brown dislikes Twain because of his poor job performance.
    C. Brown is trying to help Twain.
    D. Brown's dislike for Twain is just part of Brown's disagreeable personality.

_____ 5. In "Cub Pilot," George Ritchie takes great pleasure in
    A. playing pranks on Brown.
    B. teasing Twain about Brown.
    C. showing up Twain in front of Brown.
    D. showing up Twain in front of Ealer.

_____ 6. Brown commands Twain to "round the boat to" because he wants
    A. Twain to fail.
    B. Twain to learn a new skill.
    C. the job done right.
    D. to be a good teacher.

_____ 7. In "Cub Pilot," Brown fails to hear Henry's shouted instruction to stop at a landing because
   A. he dislikes Henry and always ignores him.
   B. he is too busy yelling at Twain.
   C. he has fallen asleep at the wheel.
   D. he is deaf.

_____ 8. Twain struggles to hold his temper during Brown's tirades. This statement describes
   A. the external conflict.
   B. Twain's internal conflict.
   C. Brown's internal conflict.
   D. the falling action.

_____ 9. Which word describes the captain's attitude toward Twain after the attack on Brown?
   A. supportive
   B. sad
   C. angry
   D. surprised

_____ 10. Which personal quality does Twain discover as a result of his conflict with Brown?
   A. courage
   B. recklessness
   C. steering skill
   D. sense of humor

_____ 11. If Henry had not been in danger, how do you predict Twain would have reacted to Brown's insults?
   A. Twain would have attacked Brown.
   B. Twain would have insulted Brown verbally.
   C. Twain would have held in his anger, as usual.
   D. Twain would have leaped off the steamboat.

Vocabulary and Grammar

_____ 12. In which sentence is *ascended* used correctly?
   A. The furnace repairperson ascended the stairs to the basement.
   B. The crowd ascended enthusiastically to the entertainer.
   C. Tom ascended the stairs to the balcony.
   D. Sandy ascended the package to her aunt.

_____ 13. What does it mean if parents are *indulgent*?
   A. They are tolerant.
   B. They are strict.
   C. They are nervous.
   D. They have lots of rules.

Name _____ Date _____

____ 14. The word *hippopotami* is an example of
   A. a proper noun.
   B. a plural noun.
   C. a singular noun.
   D. a phrase.

____ 15. In which sentence are singular and plural nouns used correctly?
   A. The deer grazed on the plains.
   B. The groups enjoyed hiking in the beautiful mountain.
   C. Many peoples attended the convention.
   D. There were too many dog and cat in the room.

Essay

16. Write an essay in which you contrast young Twain and Brown. Discuss similarities and differences in their physical appearance, use of language, response to anger or frustration, and sense of honesty. Use examples from "Cub Pilot" to support your ideas.

17. Given the personalities of Brown and Twain, do you think their conflict was inevitable, or do you think there was some way they could have resolved their differences? Write an essay that addresses this question, using specific examples from "Cub Pilot" to support your answer.

18. In "Cub Pilot on the Mississippi," Twain states that his two and a half years as an apprentice on a steamboat allowed him to become "personally and familiarly acquainted with about all the types of human nature that are to be found in fiction, biography, or history." Write an essay about what you think Twain learns about human nature from the events recounted in the selection. Discuss any characters about whom Twain learns something in the course of the story.

"Old Ben" by Jesse Stuart
"Fox Hunt" by Lensey Namioka
Vocabulary Warm-up Word Lists

Study these words from "Old Ben" and "Fox Hunt." Then, complete the activities.

Word List A

attractive [uh TRAK tiv] *adj.* pretty or pleasant to look at
The plain house looked more <u>attractive</u> after the flowers were planted.

charmer [CHAHR mer] *n.* someone who pleases
The baby is such a <u>charmer</u> that people often stop to look at her.

fascinating [FAS uh nay ting] *adj.* very interesting
I recommend this <u>fascinating</u> book about animals of the rain forest.

mischievous [MIS chuh vus] *adj.* playful; naughty
This <u>mischievous</u> pup kept snatching the children's treats from the picnic blanket.

occurred [uh KERD] *v.* happened
A lunar eclipse <u>occurred</u> last night, and I witnessed the whole event.

tamed [TAYMD] *v.* changed from a wild state
After the wild bird had been <u>tamed</u>, it would perch on her shoulder.

unbelievingly [un buh LEEV ing lee] *adv.* showing doubt
I looked at him <u>unbelievingly</u> when he told me I had won the raffle.

vivid [VIV id] *n.* bright; lively; strong
The painter is known for his <u>vivid</u> hues of red, orange, and yellow.

Word List B

affectionate [uh FEK shun it] *adj.* showing love
The <u>affectionate</u> puppy licked its master's cheek.

ambitious [am BISH uhs] *adj.* having a strong desire to achieve
He is so <u>ambitious</u> that he plans to be a millionaire by age 25!

competitors [kuhm PET i terz] *n.* rivals; opponents
The Yankees and the Red Sox have been bitter <u>competitors</u> for years.

eavesdrop [EEVZ drahp] *v.* listen in secret
He hid outside the window to <u>eavesdrop</u> on the private conversation.

outstanding [owt STAND ing] *adj.* excellent; standing above
There were so many <u>outstanding</u> essays that it was hard to choose the best.

paralyzing [PA ruh lyz ing] *adj.* making unable to move
With a <u>paralyzing</u> bite, the snake made sure its prey was unable to escape.

qualifications [kwahl uh fuh KAY shunz] *n.* conditions that must be met
Few candidates for the job met its tough <u>qualifications</u>.

scholarship [SKAHL er ship] *n.* money award that pays school bills
She was able to attend the expensive college thanks to a full <u>scholarship</u>.

"Old Ben" by Jesse Stuart
"Fox Hunt" by Lensey Namioka
Vocabulary Warm-up Exercises

Exercise A *Fill in each blank in the paragraph below with an appropriate word from Word List A. Use each word only once.*

I still have [1] _____ memories of the time I tried to adopt a homeless, stray cat. He seemed happy enough living the outdoor life, but I couldn't believe that he wouldn't prefer a warm, [2] _____ house to curl up in. He was such a [3] _____, and he seemed fond of me as well. So I placed a bowl of tempting food near the door. Scruffy, as I called him, sniffed at the bowl [4] _____. I found it [5] _____ that he hesitated so long before digging in. Then, something unfortunate [6] _____. My brother made a loud noise, and the cat took off. I never [7] _____ that wild cat, but I still think of his [8] _____ ways.

Exercise B *Answer the questions with complete explanations.*

1. Are <u>competitors</u> likely to be <u>affectionate</u>? Why or why not?
   _____

2. Do people ask permission to <u>eavesdrop</u> on conversations?
   _____

3. Is an <u>outstanding</u> student more likely to win a <u>scholarship</u> than a lazy student?
   _____

4. If you're <u>ambitious</u> to be elected to student council, should you prepare a speech, stating your <u>qualifications</u>?
   _____

5. Why is it a good idea to avoid the kinds of substances that might have a <u>paralyzing</u> effect on your body?
   _____

Name _____   Date _____

Reading Warm-up A

Read the following passage. Pay special attention to the underlined words. Then, read it again, and complete the activities. Use a separate sheet of paper for your written answers.

If your idea of a pet is something warm and fuzzy, then a snake isn't for you. If you want a <u>fascinating</u> creature to marvel at, though, you might enjoy one of these slinky, slithery reptiles.

People may look at you <u>unbelievingly</u> if you suggest the idea of a snake as a pet. They may think you've got to be a snake <u>charmer</u> to know how to manage these reptiles. Through the ages, situations have <u>occurred</u> in which people have kept <u>tamed</u> snakes as pets. You just need to pick your snake carefully. That's true of approaching snakes in general.

For example, the bands of <u>vivid</u> red, yellow, and black on a scarlet king snake may be familiar to you. Be careful, however, if you approach one. The deadly coral snake has similar markings. The two snakes live in overlapping areas in the southeastern part of our country, so you need to be especially cautious if you live within the coral snake's range.

There is one clear difference between the two snakes. Starting from the head, the harmless king snake's first color is red. The coral snake's first color is black. Luckily, there's a trick to remembering the difference. You need to learn two rhymes. Actually the first, about the coral snake, is all you need to know: *If red touches yellow, it can kill a fellow.* The second, true of the scarlet king snake, can keep you from a panic attack: *If red touches black, it's a friend of Jack.*

Even if the idea of keeping a snake at home makes you feel creepy, it is hard to deny that many snakes are <u>attractive</u> in a purely colorful way. Just identify them correctly and don't be <u>mischievous</u>. Keep your distance from the poisonous ones and the ones that can squeeze the life out of you. If you do, there is no reason that you cannot enjoy their beauty from afar.

1. Circle the word that <u>fascinating</u> describes. Then, rewrite the sentence in which it appears, using a synonym for *fascinating*.

2. Underline the words that tell why someone might look <u>unbelievingly</u> at you. Write about a time when you looked *unbelievingly* at someone.

3. Circle the words that tell what a snake <u>charmer</u> can do. What makes someone a *charmer*?

4. Rewrite the sentence with the word <u>occurred</u>, using a synonym for *occurred*.

5. Underline the words in the last paragraph that give a clue to the meaning of the word <u>tamed</u>. Write about an animal you or someone you know has *tamed*.

6. Underline what is described as <u>vivid</u>. Write a short description of something in your house that's a *vivid* color.

7. Circle the word that tells what about snakes is <u>attractive</u>. Do you find snakes *attractive*? Why or why not?

8. In your own words, tell why the narrator warns you not to be <u>mischievous</u> around snakes. Tell what *mischievous* means.

"Old Ben" by Jesse Stuart
"Fox Hunt" by Lensey Namioka
Reading Warm-up B

Read the following passage. Pay special attention to the underlined words. Then, read it again, and complete the activities. Use a separate sheet of paper for your written answers.

I knew from the start that the underlined scholarship contest would not be a piece of cake. In fact, I almost didn't enter it. Still, I wanted the all-expenses-paid tuition, room, and board at the State Science Institute so badly, I could almost taste it.

To tell the truth, I had never even thought about going to a summer school until about a month before the contest was to take place. I will admit that I am ambitious and I enjoy working hard to invent and build gadgets. I just never thought of spending my leisure time on a school project if I didn't have to. I started thinking differently, however, thanks to a habit I have that my mom says will get me in trouble someday: I eavesdrop. I do not hang around at doorways or listen in at keyholes. Still, if someone is talking in a loud voice at the next table in the library, what am I supposed to do, plug up my ears with my fingers?

In any event, that time eavesdropping worked in my favor because I learned about the scholarship that State Science awards to one outstanding student each year. The qualifications include high grades, an interesting and fully-functional project with a written explanation, and a winning personal interview. How could I miss? I would knock out all my competitors. At least, that is what I told myself before I found out that my rivals were not just from my school but from all the schools in the city.

The morning of the big test, I felt a paralyzing fear as if I had to will my feet to move. When Mom went to hug me, I knew she was just trying to be affectionate, but I brushed her aside.

To make a long story short, I choked on the test—but only for a minute. As I recovered my wits, I began to fill in answers. Luckily, this story has a happy ending. Next summer, I'll be inventing and building in a fully equipped modern science lab.

1. Circle the words that tell what a scholarship to State Science consists of. Tell why the narrator might want a *scholarship*.

2. Underline the phrase that gives a clue to the meaning of ambitious. Describe an *ambitious* person.

3. Write a sentence that includes the three ways mentioned in which someone might eavesdrop.

4. In your own words, tell what kind of student is outstanding.

5. Circle the three qualifications for the scholarship. Write a sentence giving three *qualifications* for being good in your favorite sport.

6. Underline the synonym for competitors. Write a sentence telling who have been your *competitors*.

7. Circle the words that tell what caused the paralyzing fear. Write a sentence that explains what a *paralyzing* fear is.

8. Circle the words that tell how Mom tried to be affectionate. Write a sentence in which you list three things that show someone is *affectionate*.

"Old Ben" by Jesse Stuart
"Fox Hunt" by Lensey Namioka
Literary Analysis: Narrative Structure

Narrative structure is the form or pattern a story follows. In some stories, authors may break the straight timeline by using one or both of these two common devices:

- A **flashback** is a scene within a narrative that interrupts the sequence of events to relate events that occurred in the past. A flashback often reveals something important about a character.
- **Foreshadowing** is the use of clues hinting at events that are going to occur later in the plot of a narrative. Foreshadowing creates suspense by keeping readers guessing.

DIRECTIONS: *Read the passages from "Old Ben" and "Fox Hunt." Then, answer the questions.*

One morning in July when I was walking across a clover field to a sweet-apple tree, I almost stepped on him. There he lay coiled like heavy strands of black rope. He was a big bull blacksnake. We looked at each other a minute, and then I stuck the toe of my shoe up to his mouth. He drew his head back in a friendly way. He didn't want trouble. Had he shown the least fight, I would have soon finished him. My father had always told me there was only one good snake—a dead one.

1. Identify one detail that foreshadows the friendship between the narrator and the snake.

_____

2. Identify one detail that hints at what will ultimately happen to Ben.

_____

3. Which of the two details you identified helps the author to create suspense? In what way? _____

One night, while he was struggling to stay awake over his book, [Fujin] heard a soft voice behind him. "A fine, hardworking young man like you deserves to pass the examination."

Fujin whirled around and saw a beautiful girl standing behind him. Somehow she had appeared without making any noise. She had huge, bewitching eyes that slanted sharply. Could he be dreaming?

"Let me help you," continued the girl. "I can act as a tutor and coach you."

"And that was how your ancestor, Liang Fujin, got the coaching he needed to pass the examinations," said Andy's mother.

4. Explain why this passage is a flashback. _____

_____

5. What does this flashback reveal about Andy, his goals, or his motives? _____

_____

6. Explain the element of foreshadowing in this passage. _____

_____

"Old Ben" by Jesse Stuart
"Fox Hunt" by Lensey Namioka
Vocabulary Builder

A. DIRECTIONS: *For each numbered item, write a new sentence so that the underlined vocabulary word makes sense. Be sure not to change the vocabulary word.*

Example: When fresh tomatoes are <u>scarce</u>, we enjoy them at every meal.
Revised sentence: When fresh tomatoes are <u>scarce</u>, we use canned ones.

1. The <u>decadent</u> nobleman was honest and hard working.

   _____

2. The <u>affectionate</u> little girl pinched her cousin.

   _____

3. Carmen was <u>tantalized</u> by the beautiful bracelet she had received.

   _____

4. With the help of a <u>partition</u>, the twins created one large room out of two smaller rooms.

   _____

5. Mom has a hard time persuading my <u>studious</u> brother to do his homework.

   _____

B. DIRECTIONS: *Circle the letter of the word or phrase that is most nearly the same in meaning to the word in CAPITAL LETTERS.*

1. PARTITION:
   A. divider   B. problem   C. conflict   D. request
2. STUDIOUS:
   A. comical   B. strict   C. nervous   D. bookish
3. DECADENT:
   A. everlasting   B. corrupt   C. generous   D. depressed
4. AFFECTIONATE:
   A. mean   B. rebellious   C. loving   D. clinging
5. SCARCE:
   A. abundant   B. fearful   C. not plentiful   D. not sharp
6. TANTALIZED:
   A. tricked   B. lied   C. teased   D. equaled

Name _____ Date _____

"**Old Ben**" by Jesse Stuart
"**Fox Hunt**" by Lensey Namioka

Support for Writing to Compare Narrative Structures

Before you draft your essay comparing and contrasting the narrative structures of these stories, complete the graphic organizers below. For each selection, list examples of foreshadowing and/or flashback that the author uses. Then, for each example, tell how it affects the reader or the story. For example, does the reader feel suspense? Does the example reveal something important about a character? Does it make you think differently about something or someone in the story?

"Old Ben"	
Examples of Foreshadowing	**Effect on Reader or Story**
1.	1.
2.	2.
Examples of Flashback	**Effect on Reader or Story**
1.	1.
2.	2.

"Fox Hunt"	
Examples of Foreshadowing	**Effect on Reader or Story**
1.	1.
2.	2.
Examples of Flashback	**Effect on Reader or Story**
1.	1.
2.	2.

Now, use your notes to write an essay comparing and contrasting the narrative structures of "Old Ben" and "Fox Hunt."

Unit 1 Resources: Fiction and Nonfiction

Name _____ Date _____

"**Old Ben**" by Jesse Stuart
"**Fox Hunt**" by Lensey Namioka
Selection Test A

Critical Reading *Identify the letter of the choice that best answers the question.*

____ 1. At the beginning of "Old Ben," how does the father feel about snakes?
    A. He admires them.
    B. He does not worry about them.
    C. He hates them.
    D. He thinks they are funny.

____ 2. In "Old Ben," why does Old Ben make a good pet?
    A. He drinks milk.
    B. He does tricks for visitors.
    C. He eats the mice in the corncrib.
    D. He gets along with the barn animals.

____ 3. How are Old Ben and the narrator alike?
    A. They are both easily frightened.
    B. They are both trusting.
    C. They both dislike the narrator's father.
    D. They both live in the barn.

____ 4. How does Old Ben die?
    A. He dies of old age.
    B. Fred the horse stomps on him.
    C. He dies of hunger.
    D. He is killed in the hogpen.

____ 5. What purpose does foreshadowing serve in "Old Ben"?
    A. It makes the reader wonder what will happen to Ben.
    B. It tells the reader more about the narrator.
    C. It gives the reader factual information about snakes.
    D. It helps the author describe the setting.

____ 6. Why does Andy feel lonely at the beginning of "Fox Hunt"?
    A. because he does not have a girlfriend
    B. because no other students invite him to study with them
    C. because no one gets off with him at the bus stop
    D. because his parents make him study all the time

___ 7. In "Fox Hunt," how does Andy's father feel about his ancestors?
   A. proud
   B. ashamed
   C. amused
   D. curious

___ 8. Read these sentences from "Fox Hunt."

   Last year, one of the girls in his geometry class had asked him to give her some help after school. . . . But after she passed the geometry test, she didn't look at him again.

   These sentences are an example of what?
   A. narrative structure
   B. foreshadowing
   C. flashback
   D. setting

___ 9. Which of the following is a main idea of both "Fox Hunt" and "Old Ben"?
   A. Good things happen to gentle creatures.
   B. Some creatures are not what they seem.
   C. Snakes make good pets.
   D. It pays to study hard.

___ 10. What happens to both Andy in "Fox Hunt" and the narrator in "Old Ben"?
   A. They fall in love.
   B. They are rewarded for their hard work.
   C. They learn something about their past.
   D. They make an unusual friend.

___ 11. Which of the following is an example of flashback from one of the stories?
   A. Liang Fujin lived with his widowed mother in a small thatched cottage. . . .
   B. I opened the corncrib door and took Old Ben from around my neck. . . .
   C. He, Andy Liang, would have to study for the PSAT the hard way.
   D. Old Ben failed one morning to drink his milk.

___ 12. Which of the following is an example of foreshadowing from one of the stories?
   A. My father had always told me there was only one good snake—a dead one.
   B. But with the change in his pocket, he had to be satisfied with a candy bar.
   C. When I lifted him he was as long as I was tall.
   D. Maybe if he studied less and went in for sports, girls would get interested in him.

Vocabulary

___ **13.** Which sentence uses a vocabulary word *incorrectly*?

   A. In "Fox Hunt," Andy's parents expect him to be studious.

   B. The narrator of "Old Ben" likes the snake because it is affectionate.

   C. One night, Andy has a partition about a fox hunt.

   D. Old Ben would have been tantalized by the mice if they had been out of reach.

___ **14.** In "Fox Hunt," what are *scarce* in Andy's life?

   A. parents

   B. friends

   C. dreams

   D. snacks

Essay

15. The title of a story may give clues about the story's ending. In an essay, tell what you think of the titles of "Old Ben" and of "Fox Hunt." First, tell how each story ends. Then, explain how each title does or does not give clues about its ending. In your opinion, which is the better title?

16. Both "Old Ben" and "Fox Hunt" are told mostly but not entirely in chronological order. The author of each story uses certain story elements to break the flow of time. One of these elements takes the reader back in time, while the other points forward in time. In a short essay, identify these two elements. Then, tell which element(s) each author uses, and give examples from the stories. Finally, explain what purpose the elements serve.

"Old Ben" by Jesse Stuart
"Fox Hunt" by Lensey Namioka
Selection Test B

Critical Reading *Identify the letter of the choice that best answers the question.*

____ 1. Which pair of words best describes the father's attitude toward snakes at the beginning of "Old Ben"?
   A. care, concern
   B. amusement, affection
   C. uncertainty, distrust
   D. fear, dislike

____ 2. "Old Ben" suggests that the narrator's willingness to be friendly toward a snake is
   A. unusual.
   B. dangerous.
   C. perfectly normal.
   D. foolish.

____ 3. In "Old Ben," the narrator's father eventually sees Old Ben as a good pet because he
   A. ignores the cats.
   B. stays away from the dog.
   C. gets rid of all the mice in the corncrib.
   D. gets along with the other barn animals.

____ 4. What story event do these sentences foreshadow?
   > One morning in early October we left milk for Old Ben, and it was there when we went back that afternoon. But Old Ben wasn't there.

   A. Old Ben's return in April
   B. Old Ben's encounter with Fred the horse
   C. the disappearance of Old Ben
   D. the father's first reaction to Old Ben

____ 5. The author of "Old Ben" uses foreshadowing mainly to
   A. give the reader important information about the narrator.
   B. build suspense.
   C. teach the reader about snakes.
   D. describe the setting.

____ 6. In "Fox Hunt," why does Andy plan to study alone for the PSAT examination?
   A. because he does not want the other kids to slow him down
   B. because the only person he wants to study with is Lee
   C. because he wants to avoid studying for as long as possible
   D. because the other kids have not invited him to study with them

____ 7. Read this passage from "Fox Hunt."
   > Last year, one of the girls in his geometry class had asked him to give her some help after school. That went pretty well, and for a while he thought they might have some-thing going. But after she passed the geometry test, she didn't look at him again.

   The author most likely included this information
   A. to give the reader a clue about Lee's feelings for Andy.
   B. to explain why his father wants Andy to study hard.
   C. to cause the reader to feel sorry for Andy.
   D. to help explain why Andy feels unpopular with girls.

____ 8. Near the end of "Fox Hunt," what does Lee mean when she says "I'll get my reward someday"?
A. that she will someday become Andy's wife
B. the she will someday earn a scholarship to college
C. that Andy will someday earn enough money to pay her
D. that Andy will someday realize her true identity

____ 9. Which sentence from "Fox Hunt" does *not* foreshadow Lee's true identity?
A. A girl got off the bus behind him and started walking in the same direction.
B. "My name is Leona Hu."
C. Lee's eyes, on the other hand, definitely slanted upward at the corners.
D. When they passed the corner house on their way home, the German Shepherd went into a frenzy of barking. . . .

____ 10. Which is true of the the snake in "Old Ben" and Lee in "Fox Hunt"?
A. Neither is friendly at first.
B. They are humans posing as animals.
C. They behave in unexpected ways.
D. Neither is treated fairly.

____ 11. What do the fathers in "Old Ben" and "Fox Hunt" have in common?
A. They are unwilling to change their minds about anything.
B. They have strong ideas about some things in life.
C. They allow their sons plenty of free time.
D. They live mainly in the past.

____ 12. Which phrase best describes the narrative structure of both "Old Ben" and "Fox Hunt"?
A. told in strict chronological order
B. told mainly through flashbacks, but with occasional glimpses of the present
C. told only through foreshadowing and flashbacks
D. told in chronological order, but with occasional foreshadowing or flashbacks

____ 13. Which of the following is true of both "Old Ben" and "Fox Hunt"?
A. They have magical elements.
B. They contain mysteries.
C. They are true stories.
D. They have happy endings.

____ 14. Which of the following is an example of flashback from "Old Ben" or "Fox Hunt"?
A. "He crawled from the hayloft down into Fred's feed box, where it was cool. . . . Lucky for Old Ben that he got out in one piece."
B. "There was somebody running with him—another fox, with reddish hair and a bushy tail."
C. "One day early in April I went to the corncrib, and Old Ben lay stretched across the floor. . . . His skin was rough and his long body had a flabby appearance."
D. "Fujin whirled around and saw a beautiful girl standing behind him. Somehow she had appeared without making any noise."

____ 15. Which of the following experiences do Andy in "Fox Hunt" and the narrator in "Old Ben" share?
   A. making an unusual friend
   B. earning a reward for hard work
   C. losing someone or something very dear
   D. discovering something about his family's past

____ 16. How are the narrator in "Old Ben" and Andy in "Fox Hunt" different?
   A. The narrator is trusting, while Andy is cautious.
   B. The narrator is superstitious, while Andy is a realist.
   C. The narrator is scholarly, while Andy enjoys nature.
   D. The narrator is lonely, while Andy is surrounded by friends.

Vocabulary

____ 17. Which sentence uses a vocabulary word *incorrectly*?
   A. Andy's studious nature would help him do well on the PSAT.
   B. Old Ben and the narrator develop an affectionate friendship.
   C. Andy's father constantly praises his decadent ancestors.
   D. Old Ben becomes tantalized by the mice in the hayloft.

____ 18. How might a *partition* be used at an examination like the PSAT?
   A. to keep time
   B. to separate two groups of test-takers
   C. to sort used and unused test booklets
   D. to provide help for students who need it

____ 19. In "Fox Hunt," which of the following are *scarce* in Andy's life?
   A. good grades
   B. daydreams
   C. friends
   D. bus rides

Essay

20. The title of a work of literature may contain a clue about the work's outcome. In an essay, evaluate the titles "Old Ben" and "Fox Hunt." First, summarize the outcome of each story. Then, go on to show how the title does or does not give clues about that outcome. In your opinion, which title is more effective? Why?

21. Write an essay comparing and contrasting the snake in "Old Ben" and Lee in "Fox Hunt." Show similarities and differences between the two characters with regard to their true nature, their behavior, their relationships to the people around them, and their goals and motives.

22. In some ways, the narrative structures of "Old Ben" and "Fox Hunt" are similar, but in other ways the structures are different. In an essay, compare and contrast the pattern each story follows. How does the narrative structure of each story add to or detract from the experience of reading the story? Use examples from the stories to support your ideas.

Name _____ Date _____

Reflection: Description of a Person

Prewriting: Choosing Your Topic

Use the following chart to list people who have influenced you in some important way.
Then, review your list and select one person as a topic for your description.

Family	Friends	Teachers	Coaches

Drafting: Organizing Examples and Details

Use the following chart to organize your examples and details in order of importance.

Least Important	1.
	2.
	3.
	4.
Most Important	5.

Writing Workshop—Unit 1, Part 1
Description of a Person: Integrating Grammar Skills

Concrete, Abstract, and Possessive Nouns

Concrete nouns name people, places, or things that can be perceived by the five senses. Abstract nouns name ideas, beliefs, qualities, or concepts. Possessive nouns show ownership.

Nouns	Examples	How to Use the Nouns
Concrete Noun	child, dog, street, Jeff	Use **specific,** concrete nouns: She cooks *lasagna, fried chicken,* and *blueberry muffins* for me. Avoid **vague,** general nouns: She cooks good *stuff* for me.
Abstract Noun	love, freedom, childhood, kindness	In writing a description, support abstract nouns such as *friendship* with specific, concrete nouns that add vivid details.
Possessive Noun	child's cat, Jeff's computer, boys' team, women's plan	To form the possessive of plural nouns that end in *s,* add an apostrophe. For plural nouns that do not end in *s,* add an apostrophe and an *s.*

Using Vivid, Concrete Nouns

A. DIRECTIONS: *To complete each sentence, circle the letter of the most vivid, specific noun.*

1. César is a great (A) person (B) chef (C) man.
2. He certainly knows how to grill (A) steaks (B) meat (C) food.
3. For the perfect (A) barbecue (B) meal (C) time, invite him to cook.
4. We have our best picnics in that (A) meadow (B) field (C) place.
5. César will need a (A) tool (B) thing (C) spatula to turn the food on the grill.

Fixing Errors in Possessive Nouns

B. DIRECTIONS: *Rewrite each sentence using the correct possessive forms of the nouns.*

1. At the picnic, we will have a girlses' relay race.

   _____

2. Two mens' teams will have a tug-of-war.

   _____

3. This trees' branch is a good place to hang the swing.

   _____

4. Mr. and Mrs. Hodges are coming with their dogs, known as "The Hodge's Three."

   _____

5. Mom is taking her book, <u>Honestys' Reward</u>, to read in the shade.

   _____

Unit 1 Resources: Fiction and Nonfiction

Name _____ Date _____

Unit 1: Fiction and Nonfiction
Part 1 Benchmark Test 1

MULTIPLE CHOICE

Reading Skill: Predicting

1. What are the two main things you should consider to make accurate predictions in a story?
   A. the author and the personalities of the characters
   B. the title and the names of the characters
   C. the plot and the cultural context of the work
   D. story details and your own experience

2. What is the best procedure for making predictions as you read a story?
   A. Make a prediction as you read, and then keep reading to see if it comes true.
   B. Make a prediction as you read, and then peek at the ending to see if you are right.
   C. Never change a prediction you make, no matter what new details the story provides.
   D. Read the story backward so that you know everything that will happen before it happens.

3. What main effect does making predictions have on most readers?
   A. It removes all the suspense from the plot of a story.
   B. It cuts down on the reader's interest in the story.
   C. It makes the story seem more realistic and believable.
   D. It helps keep the reader actively engaged in the story.

4. Read these sentences from a story. Then, choose the best prediction of what will happen next.

   In the early morning, Cara stood at the bus stop on Round Lake Road. She clutched her textbooks to her side and stamped her feet to try to keep warm.

   A. Cara will greet her brother when he comes home from school on the bus.
   B. Cara will get on the bus, when it comes, in order to go to school.
   C. Cara will read her textbooks as she takes the bus to the movies.
   D. Cara and her family will move to a warmer climate.

5. Which of these details most clearly predicts that a bad storm is coming?
   A. A siren sounds as a character looks out the window.
   B. The sky darkens and the winds begin to blow.
   C. A character takes a sailboat to a place called Storm Island.
   D. A character listens to a weather report and shakes her head.

Name _____ Date _____

Read this selection from a short story. Then, answer the questions that follow.

In the ballroom, the orchestra began to play. Jorge listened, tapping a foot to the rhythm. Across the table Anna smiled, tapping a foot as well. Jorge rose from his chair at the table and smiled back at Anna. "Shall we?" he said, motioning toward the dance floor. The tablecloth hung low between them, and as Jorge moved forward, he stepped on it. Then, his legs in a tangle, he fell flat on his face.

6. From the details in the first five sentences of the selection, which of these predictions seems most likely to happen?
   A. Jorge will refuse to ask Anna to dance with him.
   B. Anna will refuse to dance with Jorge when he asks.
   C. Jorge and Anna are going to get up and dance.
   D. Jorge is going to trip and fall on his face.

7. Which detail in the selection should make you reconsider your first prediction and expect a different outcome than before?
   A. Jorge taps his foot to the music.
   B. Anna taps her foot to the music.
   C. Jorge motions toward the dance floor.
   D. Jorge steps on the tablecloth.

Reading Skill: Using Text Aids

8. Which of these are examples of consumer documents?
   A. atlases and almanacs
   B. labels and warranties
   C. textbooks and encyclopedias
   D. newspapers and magazines

9. What does the legend on a map provide?
   A. the meaning of the maps' symbols
   B. the scale to which the map is drawn
   C. directions (north, south, east, west)
   D. an old tale about places on the map

10. What is the term for a document that lists arrival and departure times in rows and columns?
    A. a legend
    B. an orientation
    C. a schedule
    D. an itinerary

Literary Analysis: Plot, Conflict, and Literary Devices

11. What is the term for the part of a story that provides background information about main characters and their situation?
    A. exposition
    B. flashback
    C. falling action
    D. resolution

12. Which of these choices is the best definition of the climax of a story?
    A. the point at which the conflict is introduced
    B. the point where new complications to the conflict are introduced
    C. the point of highest tension or suspense
    D. the point at which all the loose ends of a plot are tied together

13. Which of these is a good example of an internal conflict?
    A. A knight struggles to defeat a fire-breathing dragon.
    B. A lawyer struggles to prove the innocence of her client.
    C. A farmer struggles to bring his crops through a bad drought.
    D. A student struggles to come to the right decision.

14. In what part of the story are problems worked out so that the conflict is eliminated?
    A. exposition
    B. rising action
    C. foreshadowing
    D. resolution

15. What does foreshadowing usually help to create?
    A. suspense
    B. flashbacks
    C. external conflict
    D. internal conflict

16. What does it mean when a story has a chronological narrative structure?
    A. The narrator presents events that happened in a long-ago time.
    B. The narrator presents events in the order in which they happened in time.
    C. The narrator jumps around in time in order to provide his or her memories.
    D. The narrator introduces a character who goes on to tell a story within the story.

Read the selection. Then, answer the questions that follow.

(1) Jean, a high school student, was such a good swimmer that she was able to get a summer job as a lifeguard at the local pool. (2) She had no idea that the experience would test her skill and quick thinking more than anything ever before. (3) One Thursday afternoon, Dean and Frank Rinaldo showed up at the pool. (4) Noisy and reckless, the two teenaged brothers quickly drove the other swimmers away. (5) They paid no attention when Jean told them to behave. (6) Jean was just about to phone her supervisor when she saw the brothers crash into each other and begin to sink. (7) No one was there to help as Jean dove into the pool and struggled to pull them out. (8) They were very heavy, but she finally managed to drag out first Dean and then Frank. (9) Dean was conscious but in pain. (10) Frank was unconscious, and Jean had to give him mouth-to-mouth resuscitation. (11) When he finally began breathing, Jean raced to her cell phone and called an ambulance. (12) After the brothers recovered, they apologized to Jean and never behaved badly at the pool again.

17. Which part of the story is the exposition?
    A. sentence 1
    B. sentence 2
    C. sentence 3
    D. sentence 12

18. Which sentence in the story is an example of foreshadowing?
    A. sentence 1
    B. sentence 2
    C. sentence 5
    D. sentence 6

19. Around what conflict do the events in the story center?
    A. Jean and the doctors' struggle to save the lives of the injured Rinaldo brothers.
    B. Jean's struggle to control the crowds at the swimming pool.
    C. Jean's struggle to get the Rinaldo brothers to behave at the swimming pool.
    D. Jean's struggle to be the best swimmer she can be.

20. Where does the climax of the story take place?
    A. sentence 3
    B. sentences 4–5
    C. sentences 6–11
    D. sentence 12

Vocabulary: Prefixes

21. Which statement is true about the prefixes *pre-* and *re-?*
    A. *Pre-* and *re-* usually have similar meanings.
    B. *Pre-* and *re-* often have opposite meanings.
    C. *Pre-* and *re-* are never used with the same roots.
    D. *Pre-* is much more frequently used than *re-*.

22. Based on your understanding of the prefix *pre-*, where in a textbook chapter would you probably find a *preview*?
    A. before the chapter starts
    B. in the middle of the chapter
    C. at the end of every section
    D. at the end of the entire chapter

23. Based on your understanding of the prefix *re-*, when are you likely to *regain* something?
    A. when you never had it
    B. when you had it at least once before
    C. when you do not want it
    D. when you understand it fully

24. Based on your understanding of the prefix *re-*, what do you conclude the italic word in this sentence must mean?

    As she sang the song, the singer kept having trouble with the high notes of the *refrain*.

    A. the opening notes of a song
    B. an introductory part of a song that has a different tune that the rest
    C. the highest notes in a song
    D. a line or stanza that is sung over and over in a song

Grammar

25. Which statement is true about common and proper nouns?
    A. A proper noun is more specific than a common noun.
    B. A proper noun is more polite than a common noun.
    C. A common noun usually begins with a capital letter.
    D. A proper noun usually does not begin with a capital letter.

26. How many proper nouns are there in this sentence?

    Sally Harding and her brother visited the D-Day Museum in New Orleans.

    A. two
    B. three
    C. four
    D. six

27. Which sentence below uses correct capitalization?
    A. Carmine saw the United Nations and a museum when he visited New York City.
    B. Carmine saw the United Nations and a Museum when he visited New York City.
    C. Carmine saw the united Nations and a museum when he visited New York city.
    D. Carmine saw the United Nations and a museum when he visited new york city.

28. Which of these spelling rules is accurate?
    A. To form the plural of any noun that ends in *y*, change the *y* to an *i* and add *es*.
    B. To form the plural of any noun that ends in *y*, just add *s*.
    C. To form the plural of a noun that ends in a vowel + *y*, change the *y* to an *i* and add *es*.
    D. To form the plural of a noun that ends in a consonant + *y*, change the *y* to an *i* and add *es*.

29. Which of these sentences uses plural nouns correctly?
    A. The wifes used knifes to cut bunchies of berrys from the leafs.
    B. The wives used the knives to cut bunches of berries from the leaves.
    C. The wives used the knives to cut bunchies of berries from the leavs.
    D. The wifes used the knifes to cut bunches of berryes from the leaves.

30. What do you call a noun that names something that can be perceived by one or more of the five sense?
    A. a common noun
    B. a proper noun
    C. a concrete noun
    D. an abstract noun

31. Which word in this sentence is an abstract noun?

    The child showed great kindness to the stray puppy that she found on the street.

    A. child
    B. kindness
    C. puppy
    D. street

32. Which of these sentences uses possessive nouns correctly?
    A. The two brothers' invention was a children's game; each player's marker was an animal.
    B. The two brother's invention was a childrens' game; each player's marker was an animal.
    C. The two brother's invention was a children's game; each players' marker was an animal.
    D. The two brothers' invention was a childrens' game; each players' marker was an animal.

ESSAY

Writing

33. Think of a children's story that you read or heard when you were younger. Then, on a separate piece of paper, write a very short version of the story, but give it a new ending. You can include details that help point to the new ending, or you can make it a complete surprise.

34. Think of a new experience you had that might be of interest to others. It can be something you did recently or something you recall from the past. Then, on a separate piece of paper, write a letter to a close friend in which you describe this experience.

35. Think of a person in your town or neighborhood who has made a strong impression on you. Then, on a separate piece of paper, write a short description of this person. Explain what he or she is like and why he or she has made such a strong impression on you.

Unit 1: Fiction and Nonfiction
Part 2 Concept Map

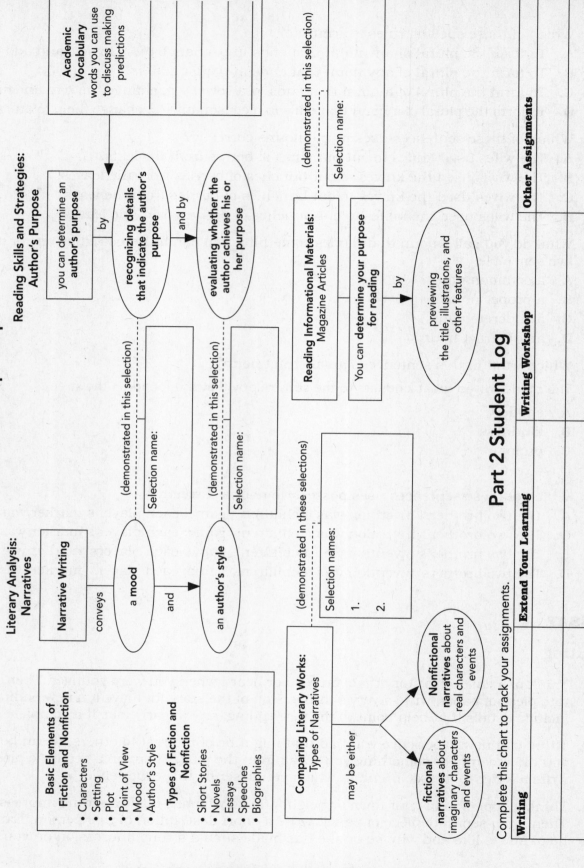

Reading Skills and Strategies:
Author's Purpose

Academic Vocabulary words you can use to discuss making predictions

you can determine an author's purpose

by

recognizing details that indicate the author's purpose

and by

evaluating whether the author achieves his or her purpose

(demonstrated in this selection)

Selection name: _____

(demonstrated in this selection)

Selection name: _____

Literary Analysis:
Narratives

Narrative Writing

conveys

a mood

and

an author's style

Basic Elements of Fiction and Nonfiction
- Characters
- Setting
- Plot
- Point of View
- Mood
- Author's Style

Types of Fiction and Nonfiction
- Short Stories
- Novels
- Essays
- Speeches
- Biographies

Comparing Literary Works:
Types of Narratives

(demonstrated in these selections)

Selection names:
1. _____
2. _____

may be either

Nonfictional narratives about real characters and events

fictional narratives about imaginary characters and events

Reading Informational Materials:
Magazine Articles

(demonstrated in this selection)

Selection name: _____

You can determine your purpose for reading

by

previewing the title, illustrations, and other features

Part 2 Student Log

Complete this chart to track your assignments.

Writing	Extend Your Learning	Writing Workshop	Other Assignments

Unit 1: Fiction and Nonfiction
Part 2 Diagnostic Test 2

Read the selections. Then, answer the questions.

In 1933, when Franklin Delano Roosevelt became president, the United States was in its fourth year of the devastating crisis known as the Great Depression. The crisis began in October 1929 when the stock market crashed. The price of stocks in companies all over America fell dramatically. An estimated $30 billion was lost. Many individuals' savings were wiped out. Companies cut back or closed, and people lost their jobs. The country was stricken with fear of financial catastrophe.

President Herbert Hoover was in office at the time. Unfortunately, he lacked a deep understanding and clear recognition of what had happened. He believed the country's problems were caused primarily by the normal ups and downs of business and would resolve on their own. As a result, President Hoover did little to change things.

Soon, 25 percent of able workers were unemployed. Banks also failed. In December 1931, the Bank of the United States went broke, losing $200 million in depositors' savings.

By 1932, many Americans had lost faith in Hoover's leadership and wanted a take-charge president who could guide the country out of its misery. They got one when they elected Franklin Delano Roosevelt, soon known by all as "FDR." FDR established many new programs that many people believe brought the country out of the Great Depression.

1. What is the main idea of this selection?
   A. During the Great Depression, many people lost their jobs and their entire life's savings.
   B. Herbert Hoover did not understand what had happened.
   C. Because of the misery caused by the Great Depression, people wanted a new president.
   D. Franklin Delano Roosevelt was a strong president.

2. What initially caused many people to lose their jobs during the Great Depression?
   A. Stock prices fell dramatically.
   B. Companies cut back or closed.
   C. Hoover did not understand the crisis.
   D. Banks went broke and lost people's money.

3. Why didn't President Hoover try to change things during the Great Depression?
   A. He believed the bad economy was simply a result of the normal business cycle and would fix itself.
   B. He did not care that so many Americans were poor, hungry, and unemployed.
   C. He was not very intelligent and did not have any good ideas for fixing the problems.
   D. He knew that Roosevelt would do a better job than he could and wanted to step aside.

4. Which of the following details from the selection best supports the idea that Americans were disappointed in Hoover's approach to the crisis?
   A. 25 percent of workers were unemployed.
   B. Hoover did not understand what had happened.
   C. The Bank of the United States went broke.
   D. Voters chose Franklin D. Roosevelt in 1932.

5. What was President Roosevelt's approach to the Great Depression?
   - A. He was stricken with fear of causing further financial catastrophes.
   - B. He did not change things because he believed the problems would fix themselves.
   - C. He forced companies to give workers their jobs back and banks to reopen.
   - D. He started many new programs that were meant to help end people's suffering.

6. What was a result of President Hoover's lack of action?
   - A. The stock market crashed.
   - B. Problems began to fix themselves.
   - C. Many more people lost their jobs.
   - D. People's faith in Hoover grew.

7. What happened to many people's savings during the Great Depression?
   - A. They gave it away to those who were less fortunate.
   - B. They lost it in the stock market crash or in failed banks.
   - C. Their savings grew under Hoover and shrank under Roosevelt.
   - D. Their savings were not directly affected by the Great Depression.

8. Based on the information in the selection, what caused the Great Depression?
   - A. the loss of many people's jobs and savings
   - B. the stock market crash of 1929
   - C. the failure of the Bank of the United States
   - D. the election of Herbert Hoover

Read the selection. Then, answer the questions.

At the dawn of the twentieth century, few people dared to speculate that human beings would ever be able to fly. Yet, two brothers named Orville and Wilbur Wright, were about to make that dream come true.

The adventurous Wright brothers had never been afraid of a challenge. Together, as young men, they opened a bicycle shop in Dayton, Ohio. Their business was a commercial success, but simply making money was not enough to satisfy the Wright brothers. Their curiousity led to an interest in flying and they started building a series of gliders. Fearing that the gliders would be unable to withstand strong winds, they built a sturdier airplane powered by a lightweight gasoline engine. They took their new airplane to Kitty Hawk, North Carolina to test it.

On December 17, 1903, the brothers tossed a coin to see who would go up first. Orville won. He flew for 12 seconds and traveled 120 feet. Although the farthest the plane flew that day was only 825 feet, the airborne brothers were rightfully proud of their extraordinary aerial feat. It didn't take very long for people around the world to realize that the Wright brothers' invention could change the course of history.

9. What did the Wright brothers do for a living?
   - A. They had a bicycle shop in Dayton, Ohio.
   - B. They built lightweight gasoline engines.
   - C. They invented war machines for the United States government.
   - D. They did not work because they were independently wealthy.

10. Why did the Wright brothers decide to build an airplane powered by a gasoline engine?
    A. They liked adventure, and a gasoline-powered airplane was more dangerous than a glider.
    B. They feared that gliders would not be able to withstand strong winds.
    C. They became tired of pedaling their early inventions, which were based on bicycles.
    D. They flipped a coin to decide what kind of airplane they would build.

11. How far did the Wright's airplane fly during its first flight in Kitty Hawk, North Carolina?
    A. 12 feet
    B. 120 feet
    C. 825 feet
    D. 1,000 feet

12. What two details help you conclude that both Orville and Wilbur wanted to pilot the first flight?
    A. They built gliders first, and they went to Kitty Hawk, North Carolina.
    B. They sold bicycles, and they built a gasoline-powered flying machine.
    C. They did not fly very far the first day, but they knew they had made history.
    D. They flipped a coin to decide who would fly first.

13. What is the main idea of this selection?
    A. The Wright brothers were adventurous men who were never afraid of a challenge.
    B. The Wright brothers made history when they invented a gasoline-powered airplane.
    C. Simply making money was not enough for the Wrights, who had a passion for flying.
    D. The brothers were very proud of their first test flights in Kitty Hawk, North Carolina.

14. What quality made the Wright brothers very different from most people in the early twentieth century?
    A. They dared to believe that human beings could fly.
    B. They were extremely intelligent and loved machines.
    C. They owned their own successful bicycle sales business.
    D. They were brothers who were very fond of each other.

15. Based on the information in the selection, which of the following might have prevented the Wrights from inventing a gasoline-powered airplane?
    A. if they had run out of money
    B. if they had been more interested in bicycles
    C. if their gliders had been successful
    D. if they had been satisfied with running their business

Vocabulary Warm-up Word Lists

Study these words from "The Adventure of the Speckled Band." Then, complete the activities.

Word List A

beloved [bi LUHV id] *adj.* dearly loved
 Our <u>beloved</u> cat lived to ten years of age, but I wish he had survived longer.

clad [KLAD] *v.* clothed or dressed
 Remember the story of the emperor who was <u>clad</u> in no clothes at all?

fate [FAYT] *n.* destiny; future; chances
 We wondered about the <u>fate</u> of the dog that had fallen through the ice.

hastening [HAY suhn ing] *v.* moving quickly
 <u>Hastening</u> to complete his chores before game time, Ned forgot to take out the garbage.

objections [uhb JEK shunz] *n.* reasons for disagreeing
 I don't understand your <u>objections</u> to my vacation plans.

satisfying [SAT is fy ing] *n.* doing enough for; having enough
 Curious people often have trouble <u>satisfying</u> their need for exploration.

unfortunate [uhn FAWR chuh nit] *adj.* happening because of bad luck
 The <u>unfortunate</u> car accident left the driver with a broken leg.

withdraw [with DRAW] *v.* go out; leave
 The judge asked the loud man to <u>withdraw</u> from the courtroom.

Word List B

excursion [eks KUR zhuhn] *n.* short trip
 We chose to take the train for our mountain <u>excursion</u>.

ferocious [fuh ROH shuhs] *adj.* fierce
 At the wild animal park, you can safely view <u>ferocious</u> animals roaming around.

massive [MAS iv] *adj.* big, heavy, and solid
 The lawyer seemed tiny behind her <u>massive</u> desk, but her voice was firm.

noiselessly [NOYZ luhs lee] *adv.* without sound
 The thief crept <u>noiselessly</u> through the dark store.

resemblance [ri ZEM bluhns] *n.* likeness in appearance or way of acting
 Many people say that a dog owner often has a <u>resemblance</u> to his or her pet.

residence [REZ uh duhns] *n.* place where a person lives
 The mayor's <u>residence</u> was so big it looked like a palace.

speckled [SPEK uhld] *adj.* covered with spots
 I learned to ride on a <u>speckled</u> pony named Dot.

tragic [TRAJ ik] *adj.* very sad or unfortunate
 The news on TV kept showing the <u>tragic</u> events over and over.

Name _____ Date _____

"The Adventure of the Speckled Band" by Sir Arthur Conan Doyle
Vocabulary Warm-up Exercises

Exercise A *Fill in each blank in the paragraph below with an appropriate word from Word List A. Use each word only once.*

My great-grandfather came from Ireland and talked kindly about his

[1] _____ homeland. He had some [2] _____ times and

as a teen, [3] _____ to find a way out, he came to America. Now, as an

old man, he wondered why he had ever wanted to [4] _____ from such

a beautiful place. We reminded him that it was [5] _____ that brought

him here. [6] _____ in the only clothes he owned, he came despite

the [7] _____ of his family. He came because he knew he was not

[8] _____ his need to see new things. As he spoke, we could still see

that spark of curiosity shining in his deep blue eyes.

Exercise B *Answer each question in a complete sentence. Use a word from Word List B to replace each underlined word or group of words without changing the meaning.*

1. Why would a father ask you to move <u>without sound</u> around the house when his baby is sleeping?

   _____

2. Which two members of your family have the greatest <u>likeness</u> to each other?

   _____

3. What is the best <u>place you have lived</u>?

   _____

4. What story have you read that has an <u>extremely sad</u> ending?

   _____

5. What would you do if you saw a sick person with <u>spotted</u> skin?

   _____

6. Why does a bank safe always have a <u>thick, heavy</u> door?

   _____

7. Why do you suppose people like to see <u>fierce</u> animals?

   _____

8. What was your favorite family <u>trip</u>?

   _____

"The Adventure of the Speckled Band" by Sir Arthur Conan Doyle
Reading Warm-up A

Read the following passage. Pay special attention to the underlined words. Then, read it again, and complete the activities. Use a separate sheet of paper for your written answers.

A life on the move is a <u>beloved</u> life for the roaming people named Gypsies. For centuries, they have been moving from place to place, <u>satisfying</u> their need to travel. Today, Gypsies are scattered all around the globe. However, the largest number of them lives in Europe.

The first Gypsies came from India, not Egypt, as their name might indicate. No one knows why these people decided to <u>withdraw</u> from their country. Only the Gypsy language, called Romany, has carried with it the traditions of India. The Gypsy culture has its own proud heritage.

The Gypsies first left India around A.D. 1000. By the fifteenth century, Gypsies had reached western Europe. People often had <u>objections</u> to Gypsies being in their region. No doubt, they feared the different looks and way of life of the Gypsies. People in many areas seemed hostile toward Gypsies. In Nazi Germany, half a million Gypsies suffered the terrible <u>fate</u> of death in prison camps, alongside Jews and other targets of terrible hatred. Yet, through all the <u>unfortunate</u> events, Gypsies have remained a close group. They also have stayed true to their beliefs and customs.

Because they prefer temporary work, Gypsies have taken many interesting jobs. They have traded everything from horses to crafts to pots and pans. They have worked as farmers and as circus performers. Gypsy women have often made money telling other people's fortunes. Indeed, the picture most people have of a Gypsy is of a woman <u>clad</u> in black, looking into a crystal ball.

Like many other groups in the world today, Gypsies seem to be <u>hastening</u> toward a more modern way of life. Still, their songs and dances as well as their desire to pick up in the spring and be on their way, will surely never leave them completely.

1. Underline the words that describe the Gypsies' <u>beloved</u> life. Then, explain what **beloved** means.

2. Circle the words that describe the need Gypsies have been <u>satisfying</u>. Then, write a sentence using **satisfying**.

3. Underline the name of the country from which Gypsies decided to <u>withdraw</u>. Then, explain what **withdraw** means.

4. Circle the words that name particular things about Gypsies to which Europeans had <u>objections</u>. Then, tell your opinion about these **objections**.

5. Underline the words describing some Gypsies' <u>fate</u> in Germany. Then, explain the saying "a **fate** worse than death."

6. Write a sentence describing an <u>unfortunate</u> event you've read about.

7. Describe your own image of a Gypsy. State clearly how he or she might be <u>clad</u>.

8. Circle the phrase that tells what Gypsies are <u>hastening</u> toward. Define **hastening**.

"The Adventure of the Speckled Band" by Sir Arthur Conan Doyle
Reading Warm-up B

Read the following passage. Pay special attention to the underlined words. Then, read it again, and complete the activities. Use a separate sheet of paper for your written answers.

Have you ever dreamed of seeing rare and <u>ferocious</u> animals in the wild? If so, perhaps one day you can visit India. You might go on an <u>excursion</u>, traveling all around this vast country. Or, you might choose to visit just one wildlife area for a few days.

Corbett National Park was established in 1936 as Hailey National Park. It was India's first attempt to protect the country's wildlife from hunters. Located in a beautiful area of the foothills of the <u>massive</u>, looming Himalayas, the park is the <u>residence</u> of thousands of plant and animal species. You can see crocodiles <u>noiselessly</u> and sneakily moving through the river. You can spot a dole, with its <u>resemblance</u> to a wild dog. You might find a black bear, a mongoose, or a tiger on the prowl for food. You can ride an elephant, go fishing, or simply listen to the monkeys chattering.

For all of these experiences, visitors should thank Jim Corbett. This famous photographer helped set up the park in its modern form. With the aid of the World Wildlife Fund, the park also became the place where Project Tiger was launched in 1973. This effort was aimed at stopping the killing of tigers, which could lead to the <u>tragic</u> and unthinkable wiping out of species. The project has spread, so that many tiger reserves can now be found wherever tigers live in the wild.

Corbett Park, which covers more than 201 square miles, could take years to explore. The time to visit is from November 15 to June 15. The rest of the year, the park is closed because of monsoons. During the season, whether you're in the bright, open grasslands or the huge jungles that are only <u>speckled</u> with sunlight, you will be amazed at all that Corbett National Park has to offer.

1. Explain what <u>ferocious</u> means. Then, list all the *ferocious* animals you can think of.

2. Underline the phrases that describe an <u>excursion</u>. Then, write a sentence describing an *excursion* you'd like to take.

3. Write a sentence describing what the <u>massive</u> Himalayas must look like.

4. Circle the words that tell who makes their <u>residence</u> in the park. Describe your place of *residence*.

5. Explain why crocodiles move <u>noiselessly</u>.

6. Circle the name of the animal with a <u>resemblance</u> to a wild dog. Then, write your own sentence about two animals with a *resemblance* to each other.

7. Circle the words that tell what is <u>tragic</u>. Then, write a sentence using the word.

8. Explain the meaning of <u>speckled</u>, naming something else that could be described this way.

"The Adventure of the Speckled Band" by Sir Arthur Conan Doyle
Reading: Recognize Details That Indicate the Author's Purpose

The **author's purpose** is his or her reason for writing. Learn to **recognize details that indicate the author's purpose.** The author's purpose and the types of details in the work affect the way you read the work. Look for these types of details:

- To *inform*, an author might use facts and technical language. Pause frequently to check your understanding, and take notes from material written to inform you.
- To *persuade*, an author might include reasons that lead readers to agree with an opinion. With this kind of writing, question the author's statements and check facts.
- To *entertain*, an author might provide details that amuse, intrigue, horrify, or fascinate readers. With such material, pay attention to descriptions—especially, to images that appeal to the senses.

Frequently, the author has both a general purpose and a specific purpose in mind. In "The Adventure of the Speckled Band," Doyle's *general* purpose is to entertain you with a mystery. As Doyle tells the story, he provides details that entertain in a *particular* way—for instance, by puzzling you or frightening you, as in the following description of Helen Stoner.

> She raised her veil as she spoke, and we could see that she was indeed in a pitiable state of agitation, her face all drawn and gray, with restless, frightened eyes, like those of some hunted animal.

DIRECTIONS: *Read each passage from "The Adventure of the Speckled Band." From the list, choose the item or items that best identify the author's specific purpose in that passage. Alternatively, you may describe the author's specific purpose in words of your own.*

  to frighten readers   to make readers curious   to give readers a sense of relief

1. A series of disgraceful brawls took place, two of which ended in the police court, until at last he became the terror of the village, and the folks would fly at his approach, for he is a man of immense strength, and absolutely uncontrollable in his anger.

    _____

2. The lady could not move her bed. It must always be in the same relative position to the ventilator and to the rope—or so we may call it, since it was clearly never meant for a bell-pull.

    _____

3. He had ceased to strike and was gazing up at the ventilator when suddenly there broke from the silence of the night the most horrible cry to which I have ever listened. It swelled up louder and louder, a hoarse yell of pain and fear and anger all mingled in the one dreadful shriek.

    _____

4. "It means that it is all over," Holmes answered. "And perhaps, after all, it is for the best. Take your pistol, and we will enter Dr. Roylott's room."

    _____

"The Adventure of the Speckled Band" by Sir Arthur Conan Doyle
Literary Analysis: Mood

Mood, or atmosphere, is the overall feeling that a literary work or passage creates for the reader. The mood of a work might be somber, joyful, sentimental, and so on. A variety of elements contributes to the mood of a work.

- Words, such as *gloomy*, and images, such as "the wind was . . . splashing against the windows"
- Setting, such as "the windows were broken and blocked with wooden boards"
- Events, such as "our door had been suddenly dashed open"

A writer chooses words carefully in order to create a particular mood. As you read the following passage from "The Adventure of the Speckled Band," notice how the underlined words help create a mood of terror.

> There was something else which she would fain have said, and she <u>stabbed</u> with her finger into the air in the direction of the doctor's room, but a fresh <u>convulsion</u> <u>seized</u> her and <u>choked</u> her words.

DIRECTIONS: *Write the words in each story passage that contribute to the mood of terror.*

1. Imagine, then, my thrill of terror when last night, as I lay awake, thinking over her terrible fate, I suddenly heard in the silence of the night the low whistle which had been the herald of her own death. I sprang up and lit the lamp, but nothing was to be seen in the room. I was too shaken to go to bed again. . . .

   _____

   _____

2. A large face, seared with a thousand wrinkles, burned yellow with the sun, and marked with every evil passion, was turned from one to the other of us, while his deep-set, bile-shot eyes, and his high, thin, fleshless nose, gave him somewhat the resemblance to a fierce old bird of prey.

   _____

   _____

3. How shall I ever forget that dreadful vigil? I could not hear a sound, not even the drawing of a breath, and yet I knew that my companion sat open-eyed, within a few feet of me, in the same state of nervous tension in which I was myself. The shutters cut off the least ray of light, and we waited in absolute darkness.

   _____

   _____

"The Adventure of the Speckled Band" by Sir Arthur Conan Doyle
Vocabulary Builder

A. DIRECTIONS: *Answer each question by deciding which italicized word or phrase explains the meaning of the underlined vocabulary word. Write your choice on the line.*

1. If a hissing noise sounds <u>sinister</u> to Jack, does he think it sounds *loud, harmless,* or *threatening?*

   _____

2. If Lisa's large floppy hat were not in <u>compliance</u> with the school dress code, would the principal want Lisa to *continue wearing the hat* or *put the hat in her locker* until the end of the school day?

   _____

3. If an attorney needs to present <u>tangible</u> evidence that her client was out of town during a robbery, should the attorney look for evidence that is *understandable, vague,* or *amusing?*

   _____

B. DIRECTIONS: *Respond to each numbered item by writing a sentence that uses one word from the word list. Underline that word.*

Word List

sinister	compliance	tangible

1. Describe a reason someone catches the flu.

   _____

2. Describe the costume that one student considered wearing to a masquerade party.

   _____

3. Tell why a proposal to build a skyscraper might not be approved by the city.

   _____

C. DIRECTIONS: *For each item, write the letter of the word that is most nearly* opposite *in meaning to the word in CAPITAL LETTERS.*

____ 1. TANGIBLE:
   A. true   B. false   C. unclear   D. understandable

____ 2. SINISTER:
   A. evil   B. kind   C. right   D. unbelievable

____ 3. COMPLIANCE:
   A. complication   B. correctness   C. distrust   D. disobedience

"The Adventure of the Speckled Band" by Sir Arthur Conan Doyle
Support for Writing a Personal Narrative

In a **personal narrative,** a writer tells about an event or experience that has happened in his or her life. The writer usually narrates the event in the order in which it occurred, from first incident to last.

Before you begin writing your own personal narrative, think of an event in your life in which you solved a problem using your reasoning skill. Maybe you have already told others about this event. The event may be funny, scary, sad, or memorable for some other reason.

When you begin to prepare notes for your personal narrative, list what happened first (the first incident), and continue to the end of the event or experience (the last incident). Reexamine the list, and if necessary, move incidents into the proper order, or add incidents you may have left out. Then, jot down thoughts you had along the way for each incident in the overall event. As you write, recall one of Sherlock Holmes's effective narratives in which he explains his thought processes as he solves the mystery. Use the chart to list each incident and the thoughts you had. Add rows if the event involved more than three incidents.

Incidents (First to Last)	What I Was Thinking at This Point
1.	
2.	
3.	

Now, based on your notes, write a personal narrative about a time you used logic, or reasoning, to solve a problem.

"The Adventure of the Speckled Band" by Sir Arthur Conan Doyle
Support for Extend Your Learning

Research and Technology

Most of the time you see wild and exotic animals only on television, in movies, or at a circus or zoo. In some areas, however, pet stores sell animals such as hedgehogs, ferrets, monkeys, and reptiles. Would you be alarmed if your neighbor had a hedgehog for a pet? What about a tiger or wolf?

To start your **report** on local regulations regarding wild or exotic animals in your area, you will have to find out which animals are considered wild or exotic in the first place. A good place to start is with one or all of the following resources. For each general resource, write down at least one specific person or organization you might approach to get information.

<u>General Resources</u>

Individuals _____

_____

Government agencies _____

_____

Other organizations _____

_____

Now, get your research underway.

Listening and Speaking

Which scene in "The Adventure of the Speckled Band" first comes to mind when you think back on the story? As you prepare to **describe the scene** to your partner, think about the effect that the scene had on you. Then, write a sentence explaining why you found the scene so memorable.

_____

_____

Finally, describe the scene to your partner.

Name _____ Date _____

"The Adventure of the Speckled Band" by Sir Arthur Conan Doyle
Enrichment: Consider a Career as a Detective

When Sherlock Holmes solved the case of the speckled band, he showed resourcefulness, intelligence, tenacity, logical thinking, and the desire to help people. These are all characteristics of a good **detective.** Within local and state police departments, the Federal Bureau of Investigation (FBI), and other federal agencies, detectives are the men and women who analyze information to solve crimes.

After a crime has been committed, detectives receive information from the uniformed police officers who respond to the crime and from technicians who collect physical evidence from the scene. Detectives talk to any victims or witnesses, and they interview anyone with possible information about the crime. Detectives must be very organized and able to put together information from many sources. When questioning, interviewing, and observing witnesses and suspects, detectives must also be skilled at judging a person's character. Many colleges and special schools offer degrees in criminal justice.

A. DIRECTIONS: *Use information from the story to answer the following questions.*

1. What was Holmes's first opportunity in the story to use the skill of logical reasoning?

   _____

2. Which other detective skill did Holmes employ during his first meeting with Miss Stoner?

   _____

3. What physical evidence did Holmes first examine at the house of Dr. Roylott?

   _____

   _____

4. What task did Holmes perform when entering Miss Stoner's room?

   _____

B. DIRECTIONS: *Use the information on this page and from your own knowledge and experience to answer these questions.*

1. What do you think is the most important characteristic of a good detective? Give your reasons.

   _____

   _____

2. Which school subjects are important in preparing for a career as a detective? Explain your reasoning.

   _____

   _____

   _____

Name _____ Date _____

"The Adventure of the Speckled Band" by Sir Arthur Conan Doyle
Selection Test A

Critical Reading *Identify the letter of the choice that best answers the question.*

____ 1. In "The Adventure of the Speckled Band," what makes Helen Stoner seek help from Sherlock Holmes?
A. Her father has been murdered, and his money is missing.
B. Her mother is missing, and her stepfather does not seem upset.
C. Her sister was murdered, and Helen fears for her own safety.
D. Her stepfather has threatened to kill her mother.

____ 2. In the mystery by Sir Arthur Conan Doyle, what is the speckled band?
A. a poison necklace
B. a scarf used to strangle Helen's sister
C. a bracelet identifying the murderer
D. a snake

____ 3. In "Speckled Band," Holmes tells Helen Stoner how she got to his office. How does he know how she traveled?
A. He followed Helen after she left her house.
B. He has good powers of deduction.
C. He listened through the door as she told Watson.
D. He made a wild guess.

____ 4. Why does the author or "The Adventure of the Speckled Band" include information about Dr. Roylett's violent past in India?
A. The author wants us to feel sorry for Roylett.
B. The author wants us to believe that Helen's sister died in India.
C. The author wants to set up Roylett as a prime suspect.
D. The author is trying to mislead us.

____ 5. In "Speckled Band," what Indian animals does Helen Stoner say are living on the estate?
A. a monkey and a baboon
B. a baboon and a cheetah
C. a cheetah and a tiger
D. a tiger and a baboon

____ 6. What mood is created in the following sentence from "Speckled Band"? "Imagine, then, my thrill of terror when last night, as I lay awake, thinking over her terrible fate, I suddenly heard in the silence of the night the low whistle which had been the herald of her own death."

    A. fear

    B. curiosity

    C. humor

    D. calm

____ 7. In "Speckled Band," why does Dr. Roylett need Helen to move to her sister's former room?

    A. It is larger and more comfortable.

    B. It has a better view of the estate grounds.

    C. It is more secure.

    D. It is equipped with a bell-rope and ventilator.

____ 8. In "Speckled Band," when Helen Stoner begins sleeping in her sister's former bedroom, what sound does she hear?

    A. a bell tolling

    B. a cheetah howling

    C. a whistling noise

    D. a crying sound

____ 9. In "Speckled Band," what mood does the author create by having Sherlock Holmes and Watson wait in dark silence in the murdered woman's bedroom?

    A. hatred

    B. tension

    C. wonder

    D. sleepiness

____ 10. The author of "Speckled Band" tells readers that Dr. Roylett likes unusual animals from India. Why does this information turn out to be an important clue in the solution to the murder?

    A. because the murderer is an animal trainer from India

    B. because the murder weapon is a rare knife brought from India

    C. because an animal strangled Julia

    D. because a poisonous snake from India killed Julia

Vocabulary and Grammar

____ 11. Which of the following words is a personal pronoun?
A. Mary
C. girl
B. she
D. girls

____ 12. Which sentence does *not* contain a possessive pronoun?
A. David let me borrow his bike.
C. Joanie gave her dog a bone.
B. I drove my car to the beach.
D. Larry ran to the store for a pork chop.

____ 13. Choose the word that is closest in meaning to *sinister*.
A. wicked
C. dramatic
B. bored
D. canister

____ 14. Which of the following words is *not* a possessive pronoun?
A. mine
C. he
B. our
D. his

____ 15. Which word is the opposite of *tangible*?
A. real
C. scary
B. unclear
D. understandable

Essay

16. Do you think "The Adventure of the Speckled Band" is a good mystery story? Write a brief essay evaluating the story. Be sure to include details that show how skillful Holmes is as a detective, how well the author presents the clues, and how successful the author is in keeping you interested in the solution to the mystery.

17. A mystery story usually has suspects. In "The Adventure of the Speckled Band," Sir Arthur Conan Doyle sets up Dr. Roylett to be Holmes's prime suspect in the murder of Julia Stoner. Write an essay in which you explain how the author made Roylett a convincing suspect. Be sure to support your ideas by including specific examples of Roylett's personality and background.

"The Adventure of the Speckled Band" by Sir Arthur Conan Doyle
Selection Test B

Critical Reading *Identify the letter of the choice that best answers the question.*

____ 1. In "The Adventure of the Speckled Band," why does the author show Holmes figuring out how Helen Stoner got to his rooms?
A. to show that the detective has strong powers of deduction
B. to show how silly Helen Stoner is
C. to show what a good memory Watson has
D. to foreshadow how the story will end

____ 2. In "Speckled Band," why does Holmes quickly suspect that Dr. Roylett is the criminal?
A. Dr. Roylett's wife died under mysterious circumstances.
B. Dr. Roylett is violent and has a financial motive.
C. Dr. Roylett has poisoned people in the past.
D. Holmes worked on a previous case involving Dr. Roylett.

____ 3. What might be Doyle's purpose for including the gypsies?
A. The gypsies have gathered poisoned herbs for Dr. Roylett.
B. The gypsies have cast a spell on Dr. Roylett.
C. The gypsies have threatened Dr. Roylett and his two stepdaughters.
D. The gypsies are a false clue and add to the difficulty of solving the mystery.

____ 4. In "Speckled Band," what is Doyle's purpose for mentioning Dr. Roylett's interest in Indian animals?
A. His interest in these animals shows that he is insane.
B. The murder "weapon" turns out to be an animal from India.
C. The cheetah helps track down the murderer.
D. His interest in animals is a false clue and provides no evidence.

____ 5. What reason does Helen Stoner in "Speckled Band" give to explain to Holmes why she and her late sister had locked their bedroom doors at night?
A. They were afraid of the gypsies camping nearby.
B. Locking the door kept out cold drafts.
C. They were afraid of the wild animals roaming the estate.
D. Their stepfather had once killed a man and was dangerous.

____ 6. In Doyle's mystery, what were the final words of Julia Stoner, the murder victim?
A. "Arrest Dr. Roylett!"
B. "It was the band! The speckled band!"
C. "Call Sherlock Holmes. . . . Now!"
D. "He wants our money! Run for your life!"

____ 7. What two sounds are important clues in solving the mystery in "The Adventure of the Speckled Band"?
A. a whistling and a metallic clang
B. a barking dog and a police siren
C. a ticking clock and a ringing bell
D. a tinkling piano and a gypsy's song

____ 8. In "Speckled Band," how is Helen Stoner's situation when she appeals to Holmes similar to that of the murder victim's?
   A. She is poor and running away from home.
   B. She has just returned from India and likes cheetahs.
   C. She is to be married and sleeps in her sister's room.
   D. She is a friend of Holmes and lives in London.

____ 9. What mood does Doyle create in "Speckled Band" by having the detective and the prime suspect meet?
   A. The meeting frightens the detective and slows the action.
   B. The meeting creates tension and motivates the detective.
   C. The meeting explains the mystery.
   D. The meeting creates sympathy for the suspect.

____ 10. Which of the following questions sums up the mystery Holmes must solve in "Speckled Band"?
   A. Why would anyone want to murder an innocent young girl?
   B. Why do the fingerprints on the speckled band not match those of the prime suspect?
   C. How did the murderer get into a locked room and kill someone without a trace?
   D. Why is Helen Stoner lying about where she was on the night of the murder?

____ 11. In "Speckled Band," why does Holmes wait for a signal before returning to the crime scene?
   A. He doesn't want the criminal to know he is there.
   B. He wants to make sure that no one is home.
   C. He wants to make sure that everyone is asleep.
   D. The signal will mean that the mystery is solved.

____ 12. What mood does the author convey in the following sentence from "Speckled Band"? "From outside came the occasional cry of a night bird, and once at our very window a long-drawn catlike whine, which told us that the cheetah was indeed at liberty."
   A. curiosity
   B. peace
   C. horror
   D. anxiety

____ 13. How was Julia Stoner murdered in "The Adventure of the Speckled Band"?
   A. Her stepfather opened the iron bars on the window and poisoned her.
   B. A snake was released into her room through a ventilator slot.
   C. A cheetah came through a trap door in the floor.
   D. A gypsy put some poison in her tea.

____ 14. Why does Holmes say, "Violence does, in truth, recoil upon the violent, and the schemer falls into the pit which he digs for another"?
   A. Holmes himself is injured in the trap he sets for Dr. Roylett.
   B. Helen Stoner is revealed to be the true criminal.
   C. Dr. Roylett is poisoned by the snake he was using to try to kill Helen.
   D. Dr. Roylett turns himself in and goes to prison for life.

___ 15. The author of "Speckled Band" creates a mood of terror and mystery by describing
     A. Holmes's home in London.
     B. Julia Stoner's last night.
     C. Holmes's logical explanation of the solution to the crime.
     D. several of Holmes's past cases.

Vocabulary and Grammar

___ 16. In "Speckled Band," Holmes insists that Julia's death has a *tangible* cause, or a cause that
     A. can be explained logically.   C. can be frightening.
     B. is very suspicious.   D. is difficult to discover.

___ 17. If a person smiles in a *sinister* way, what kind of person might you expect him or her to be?
     A. amusing   C. dishonest
     B. energetic   D. moody

___ 18. Which word in the following sentence is a personal pronoun? "Beth had waited for the bus for an hour before she decided to take the train."
     A. Beth   C. for
     B. she   D. an

___ 19. Which of the following sentences contains a possessive pronoun?
     A. Helen walked her dog around the block.   C. Did they find the lost cat?
     B. He put the ferret back into a cage.   D. Raccoons pick through garbage cans.

___ 20. Which word is the best substitution for *compliance* in the following sentence? "Josh's compliance was necessary before the group could go on the field trip."
     A. contribution   C. cooperation
     B. persistence   D. appliance

Essay

21. How successful were you in solving the mystery along with Holmes in "The Adventure of the Speckled Band"? In a brief essay, explain which relevant clues you were able to identify and which false clues may have led you astray. Did you know how the crime was committed before Holmes explained it in the end? Why or why not?

22. The following sentence is a good example of how the author created a mood of terror and mystery throughout "Speckled Band": "Imagine, then, my thrill of terror when last night, as I lay awake, thinking over her terrible fate, I suddenly heard in the silence of the night the low whistle which had been the herald of her own death." Write an essay in which you explain why this passage is so effective in creating the mood. Refer to specific words and phrases in your explanation.

Study these words from the excerpt of An American Childhood. *Then, complete the activities.*

Word List A

comparison [kuhm PAR uh suhn] *n.* looking at similarities and differences
People always seem to want to make a <u>comparison</u> between twins.

deliberately [duh LIB er uht lee] *adv.* on purpose
I did not <u>deliberately</u> try to hurt the girl's feelings.

depths [DEPTHS] *n.* deep part
Some very strange animals live in the <u>depths</u> of the ocean.

extent [ek STENT] *n.* range; scope; amount
The full <u>extent</u> of the hurricane damage will not be known for weeks.

item [EYE tuhm] *n.* one thing
If you could pack only one <u>item</u> for the trip, what would it be?

precisely [pree SYS lee] *adj.* exactly
I found it hard to define that word <u>precisely</u>.

sensations [sen SAY shuhnz] *n.* physical feelings experienced through the senses
The hot pepper caused burning <u>sensations</u> on my tongue.

transparent [trans PA ruhnt] *adj.* clear; letting light pass through
In cold weather, our usually <u>transparent</u> windows become foggy.

Word List B

basis [BAY sis] *n.* something, such as an idea or reason, on which another thing is based
She had no <u>basis</u> for disliking the new student.

conceivably [kuhn SEE vuh blee] *adv.* possibly
Life on a faraway island <u>conceivably</u> could become boring and lonely.

fiction [FIK shuhn] *n.* made-up stories
My uncle's many travel adventures are as interesting as <u>fiction</u>.

membrane [MEM brayn] *n.* thin layer of skin
The dew was like a <u>membrane</u> covering the lawn.

petals [PET uhlz] *n.* colored outer parts of a flower
The beautiful tulips began dropping their <u>petals</u> one by one.

posing [POHZ ing] *v.* staying in a certain position
The cat, lying quite still on the ledge, seemed to be <u>posing</u> for the camera.

restless [REST lis] *adj.* having trouble concentrating or being still
The crowds grew <u>restless</u> as they continued to wait in long lines.

serene [suh REEN] *adj.* calm and quiet
The small inn was in such a <u>serene</u> setting that we relaxed immediately.

Name _____ Date _____

from An American Childhood by Annie Dillard
Vocabulary Warm-up Exercises

Exercise A *Fill in each blank in the paragraph below with an appropriate word from Word List A. Use each word only once.*

I went to the store looking for one specific [1] _____. Somehow, I left

with many purchases. I am just now figuring out the [2] _____ of my

spending. The first thing that caught my eye was a beautiful red scarf. Next, the CD

playing in the store gave me pleasant [3] _____—as if I were swimming

in the [4] _____ of the cool ocean. I had to buy that, too! Then, my

[5] _____ of this store's prices on the [6] _____ lamp-

shades I wanted with prices I'd seen elsewhere resulted in another purchase. Finally,

having spent [7] _____ one hour and one hundred dollars more than

planned, I left the store. No one would ever believe that I had not

[8] _____ planned on spending so much money.

Exercise B *Decide whether each statement below is true or false. Circle T or F. Then, explain your answer.*

1. Scientists could <u>conceivably</u> find a cure for all diseases in the future.
   T / F _____

2. Race car drivers grow <u>restless</u> during slow laps when they are not allowed to pass
   other cars.
   T / F _____

3. Hours of <u>posing</u> are required when someone is painting a person's portrait.
   T / F _____

4. Mucous <u>membrane</u> is an important part of the respiratory system.
   T / F _____

5. The shelves of <u>fiction</u> in our library include many biographies.
   T / F _____

6. When people are in a <u>serene</u> mood, they want to be in a noisy place.
   T / F _____

7. The <u>basis</u> for most kinds of prejudice is a lack of knowledge about other cultures.
   T / F _____

8. The <u>petals</u> of some flowers are so soft that they feel like velvet.
   T / F _____

from **An American Childhood** by Annie Dillard
Reading Warm-up A

Read the following passage. Pay special attention to the underlined words. Then, read it again, and complete the activities. Use a separate sheet of paper for your written answers.

Most parents of children under five years of age know the <u>extent</u> of childhood fears. Fears of the dark, monsters under the bed, being separated from parents, and loud noises are all common. Some of these fears might seem ridiculous to grown-ups. Nevertheless, a child's <u>sensations</u> of danger, even imagined, are very real. The challenge for a parent is to accept those fears without allowing them to take over a child's life.

The first task is to know what scares a child. Any <u>item</u> can frighten a youngster. Remember, children think differently than adults. They often think an object is alive, and they may feel small and helpless. Just think about how many toddlers fear the loud sound and action of water flushing. They imagine being flushed away to the <u>depths</u> of who knows where. It is this sort of unknown thing that can be most scary and leave a child feeling helpless.

Once you know the sources of a child's fears, you can work <u>deliberately</u> with the child to talk about them. Never treat childhood fears as silly. Instead, figure out <u>precisely</u> what is scaring the child. Then, help the child understand the fear so that everything about it becomes <u>transparent</u> to the child. It's hard to fear things that you understand clearly. Remember, too, that hugs and kind words really do help a scared child.

Try to avoid any <u>comparison</u> of one child's fears to another's. It doesn't matter if a youngster you know is scared of the very things you loved most as a child. What counts is your understanding and careful actions to move the child past the fears that trouble him or her.

1. Underline the sentence that tells the <u>extent</u> of childhood fears. Then, explain what *extent* means.

2. Circle a pair of antonyms that describe a child's <u>sensations</u>. Write a sentence about *sensations* you do not like.

3. Underline a synonym for <u>item</u>. Write a sentence telling about an *item* that scared you as a child.

4. Circle the words that tell where these <u>depths</u> might be. Then, explain what *depths* means.

5. What should parents do <u>deliberately</u>? Write a sentence about how you do something *deliberately*.

6. Write a sentence that identifies <u>precisely</u> something that might scare a child. Give a synonym for *precisely*.

7. Underline the phrases describing how something becomes <u>transparent</u> and less scary. Then, explain what *transparent* means.

8. Circle the words naming the type of <u>comparison</u> you should not make. Then, explain what a *comparison* is.

Name _____ Date _____

from **An American Childhood** by Annie Dillard
Reading Warm-up B

Read the following passage. Pay special attention to the underlined words. Then, read it again, and complete the activities. Use a separate sheet of paper for your written answers.

Almost a teenager and therefore not too closely super-vised, the average twelve-year-old has lots of hours alone during the summer. Many of those hours are spent sleep-ing, and the rest <u>conceivably</u> could be opportunities for getting into trouble.

For me, the long days of my thirteenth summer seemed like a work of <u>fiction</u> that I should fill with interesting events. Unable to do so, I became <u>restless</u>. Eventually, I became downright unhappy. I know now that I should have figured out some decent ways to fill my time, but I didn't.

The difficulty was that I lived in the country, far from any opportunity for intrigue. Just imagine this. My great-est summer adventure as a young child was looking for a plant that had four <u>petals</u>, the lucky "four-leaf clover" that my Irish grandma raved about. Well, maybe the greatest adventure part isn't quite true.

I did have some happy moments, though. I remember the joy of swimming in the smooth, still, <u>serene</u> waters of the local lake in the hot days of summer. My grandma would take me there sometimes. When I was twelve, how-ever, my grandma died and my parents both worked. I had no way to get to the lake, and I had no <u>basis</u> for fig-uring out how to enjoy myself on my own.

I began that summer <u>posing</u> as a happy and lazy pre-teenager who wanted nothing more than to be left to my own devices. Within two weeks, however, the thin <u>membrane</u> dividing that lie from my true state of misery broke. My parents couldn't help but see my boredom and unhappiness. Thinking it would help, they sent me away to summer camp—a great solution, they thought. That is when the worst summer of my life really began. I think it should be in the running to win the prize for the worst waking nightmare of an American childhood.

1. Explain what <u>conceivably</u> can get children into trouble.

2. Underline the words describ-ing what the writer's work of <u>fiction</u> would include. Then, describe what *fiction* means.

3. Underline the phrase describ-ing what might have made the writer feel less <u>restless</u>. Then, describe what you do when you feel *restless*.

4. Circle the words that tell where <u>petals</u> can be found. Then, describe your favorite flower, using the word *petals*.

5. Underline two words that help you picture a <u>serene</u> lake. Write a sentence about *serene* water using these words.

6. Explain why the writer has no <u>basis</u> for knowing how to entertain herself.

7. Write a sentence about a time you were <u>posing</u> as something.

8. Write a sentence explaining why <u>membrane</u> is a good word to use when talking about a lie.

Name _____ Date _____

from **An American Childhood** by Annie Dillard
Reading: Recognize Details That Indicate the Author's Purpose

The **author's purpose** is his or her reason for writing. Learn to **recognize details that indicate the author's purpose.** The author's purpose and the types of details in the work affect the way you read the work. Look for these types of details:

- To *inform*, an author might use facts and technical language. Pause frequently to check your understanding, and take notes from material written to inform you.
- To *persuade*, an author might include reasons that lead readers to agree with an opinion. With this kind of writing, question the author's statements and check facts.
- To *entertain*, an author might provide details that amuse, intrigue, horrify, or fascinate readers. With such material, pay attention to sensory images.

Frequently, the author has both a general purpose and a specific purpose in mind. In the excerpt from *An American Childhood,* Dillard's *general* purpose is to entertain you by telling about an event in her childhood. Dillard provides details that entertain in a *particular* way by arousing curiosity and perhaps frightening you, as in the following sentences.

I lay alone and was almost asleep when the thing entered the room by flattening itself against the open door and sliding in. It was a transparent, luminous oblong.

A. DIRECTIONS: *Read each passage from* An American Childhood. *From the list, choose the item or items that best identify the author's specific purpose in that passage. Alternatively, you may describe the author's specific purpose in words of your own.*

to make readers curious   to frighten readers   to give readers a sense of relief

1. When I was five, growing up in Pittsburgh in 1950, I would not go to bed willingly because something came into my room.

   _____

2. I heard the rising roar it made when it died or left. I still couldn't breathe. I knew— it was the worst fact I knew, a very hard fact—that it could return again alive that same night.

   _____

3. What, precisely, came into the bedroom? A reflection from the car's oblong windshield. Why did it travel in two parts? The window sash split the light and cast a shadow.

   _____

B. DIRECTIONS: *Write one or two sentences in which you entertain readers with details that frighten them. You might tell about something you were afraid of as a young child.*

_____

_____

_____

Name _____ Date _____

from **An American Childhood** by Annie Dillard
Literary Analysis: Mood

Mood, or atmosphere, is the overall feeling that a literary work or passage creates for the reader. The mood of a work might be somber, joyful, sentimental, and so on. A variety of elements contributes to the mood of a work.

- Words, such as *whooping*, and images, such as "two joined parts, a head and a tail, like a Chinese dragon."
- Setting, such as "I could see the door whiten at its touch. . . ."
- Events, such as "When I needed someone most, I was afraid to stir. . . ."

A writer chooses words carefully in order to create a particular mood. As you read the following passage from *An American Childhood*, notice how the underlined words help create a mood of fear.

Most often, <u>restless</u>, it came back. The light stripe <u>slipped</u> in the door, ran <u>searching</u> over Amy's wall, stopped, stretched <u>lunatic</u> at the first corner, raced <u>wailing</u> toward my wall, and <u>vanished</u> into the second corner with a <u>cry</u>.

A. DIRECTIONS: *Write the words in each passage from the selection that contribute to the mood of fear.*

1. Every night before it got to me it gave up. It hit my wall's corner and couldn't get past. It shrank completely into itself and vanished like a cobra down a hole.

   _____

2. Night after night I labored up the same long chain of reasoning, as night after night the thing burst into the room where I lay awake and Amy slept prettily and my loud heart thrashed and I froze.

   _____

3. It raced over the wall, lighting it blue wherever it ran; it bumped over Amy's maple headboard in a rush, paused, slithered elongate over the corner, shrank, flew my way, and vanished into itself with a wail.

   _____

B. DIRECTIONS: *Write one or two sentences using some of the words you underlined in the passages above and any other you think of. Your goal is to create a mood of fear. You might begin by recalling an unusual character or situation in a book or movie. Underline the words you use to help create the mood.*

_____

_____

_____

from **An American Childhood** by Annie Dillard
Vocabulary Builder

A. DIRECTIONS: *Answer the following questions by deciding which one of the italicized words or phrases explains the meaning of the underlined vocabulary word. Write your choice on the line.*

1. If the waters of the lake were <u>serene</u>, were the waters *choppy, flat,* or *shallow?*

   _____

2. If the moon was a <u>luminous</u> guide for Jason as he paddled his kayak over the dark water, was the moon *glowing, dim,* or *romantic?*

   _____

3. If the conductor says, "<u>Conceivably</u>, you will become a great musician," does he mean *it is necessary, it is imaginable,* or *it is unlikely* that you will achieve greatness?

   _____

B. DIRECTIONS: *Respond to each numbered item by writing a sentence that uses one word from the word list. Underline that word.*

Word List

serene	iluminous	conceivably

1. Describe the numbers on a watch that you can read in a dark room.

   _____

   _____

2. Describe the mood you might feel at the end of a day when things went your way.

   _____

   _____

3. How do scientists express the likelihood that temperatures will go up throughout the world in the future?

   _____

   _____

from **An American Childhood** by Annie Dillard
Support for Writing a Personal Narrative

In a **personal narrative,** a writer tells about an event or experience that has happened in his or her life. The writer narrates the event in the order in which it occurred, from first incident to last.

Before you begin writing your own personal narrative, think of an event in your life that bothered, frightened, or puzzled you until you understood what it meant. Maybe you have already told others about this event. The event may be funny, scary, sad, or memorable for some other reason.

When you begin to prepare notes for your personal narrative, list what happened first (the first incident), and continue to the end of the event or experience (the last incident). Reexamine the list, and if necessary, move incidents into the proper order, or add incidents you may have left out. Then, jot down the thoughts you had along the way for each incident in the overall event. Use the graphic organizer to list each incident and the thoughts you had. Add rows if the event involved more than three incidents.

Incidents (First to Last)	What I Was Thinking at This Point
1.	
2.	
3.	

Now, using your notes, tell of a time you learned the truth about something that had previously bothered, frightened, or puzzled you.

from **An American Childhood** by Annie Dillard
Support for Extend Your Learning

Research and Technology

Puzzles have existed in all scientific fields. A biologist puzzled over strange animal behavior. An engineer wondered why certain cars hug the road better than others. A chemist developed a way to make sodas fizzy. As you think about your report on solving a puzzle of the past, list questions you still have about the puzzle and about its solution. After each general category, list at least one specific resource you might approach to ask your questions.

Individuals _____

_____

Government agencies _____

_____

Corporations _____

_____

Other organizations _____

_____

Now, get your research underway.

Listening and Speaking

Which scene in the excerpt from *An American Childhood* first comes to mind when you think back on the selection? As you prepare to **describe the scene** to your partner, think about the effect that the scene had on you. Then, write a sentence explaining why you found the scene so memorable.

_____

_____

Finally, describe the scene to your partner.

from **An American Childhood** by Annie Dillard
Enrichment: Origins of Shadow Puppets

We do not often pay attention to shadows, even though they follow us everywhere. In Annie Dillard's autobiographical story, shadows trigger her imagination. Shadows have played a significant role in storytelling in many cultures, for many purposes.

One of the most intriguing uses of shadows is in a special kind of puppetry. Paper or leather cutouts are held behind a light-colored cloth (called a *screen*) and manipulated with rods. There are usually no more than three rods for a puppet—one for the body and two for the arms. The legs swing freely, but a skilled puppeteer can control their movement. A light shines behind the puppets, creating, on the audience side of the screen, shadows of the puppets. A **shadow puppeteer** can tell epic stories or hilarious comedies.

Most historians consider India to be the birthplace of shadow shows. Since 200 B.C. shadow puppetry has been one method used there to present the *Mahabharata* and the *Ramayana*, two epics of wars, gods, demons, heroes, and kings. Shadow puppetry eventually spread, by way of conquest and trade, to countries such as Malaysia, Indonesia, China, Egypt, and Turkey.

Shadow shows in Indonesia are presented at weddings, births, deaths, and during illness. In Indonesia, all puppetry is called *wayang* (which means "shadow") because Indonesians say that drama is the shadow of life. Shadow puppet performances, called *wayang-kulit*, usually last all night, and the *dalang*, or puppeteer, must have stamina as well as skill. The *dalang* usually adds music and vocals to the performance, often including stories, songs, jokes, and political and philosophical thoughts. The show may be set outside to allow people to come and go throughout the night.

DIRECTIONS: *Write your answers to the following questions.*

1. Why do you think shadow puppetry is so popular in many cultures? Explain.

    _____

    _____

2. Why do you think shadow shows are usually performed at night?

    _____

    _____

3. What is the role of the *dalang* in Indonesian society?

    _____

4. Imagine you have a chance to produce a shadow puppet play. What story would you tell your audience? Why?

    _____

    _____

"Adventure of the Speckled Band" by Sir Arthur Conan Doyle
from **An American Childhood** by Annie Dillard
Build Language Skills: Vocabulary

The Suffixes -*ize* and -*yze*

The suffixes -*ize* and -*yze* mean "to make" or "to become." They are used to form verbs. The suffix -*yze* changes the word *analysis* to *analyze*, meaning "to make an analysis."

You can analyze a character's actions in order to figure out his or her motives.

You will probably recognize the roots of many words ending with the suffix -*ize* or -*yze*. However, even when you don't recognize the root word, you will know that a word ending with one of these suffixes is probably a verb.

A. DIRECTIONS: *Change the words below to verbs by adding the suffix -ize. Then complete each sentence with the appropriate word.*

apology _____

memory _____

emphasis _____

1. It took me a long time to _____ all the states and their capitals.
2. I thought he should _____ for arriving late.
3. My teacher liked to _____ the importance of good study habits.

B. DIRECTIONS: *Follow the instructions to write sentences containing the following Academic Vocabulary words:* analyze; intention; establish; determine; achieve.

1. Use *analyze* in a sentence about the results of a science experiment.

   _____

2. Use *intention* in a sentence about something you plan to do this weekend.

   _____

3. Use *establish* in a sentence about proving your opinion about a topic.

   _____

4. Use *determine* in a sentence about figuring out the answer to a history question.

   _____

5. Use *achieve* in a sentence about hoping to accomplish a goal.

   _____

Name _____ Date _____

"The Adventure of the Speckled Band" by Sir Arthur Conan Doyle
from **An American Childhood** by Annie Dillard
Build Language Skills: Grammar

Personal Pronouns and Case

When you speak and write, you automatically use personal pronouns instead of repeating nouns. Here are the personal pronouns grouped according to their three cases:

Nominative Case: I, we, you, he, she, it, they

Objective Case: me, us, you, him, her, it, them

Possessive Case: my, mine, his, her, hers, its, their, theirs

The personal pronouns are underlined in the following example.

After Carla and I finished lunch, we rode our bikes to the volleyball game. She rode faster and beat me.

In the example

- *I, we,* and *she* are in the nominative case
- *me* is in the objective case
- *our* is in the possessive case

A. PRACTICE: *First, underline the personal pronouns in each sentence. Next, circle each personal pronoun that shows possession.*

1. One day I want to race my sailboat across the lake.
2. Jim and Carol ordered a pizza while they studied for their math test.
3. When the storm hit, it shook the windows in our house.
4. He watched the rain pound on his garage roof.
5. Have you ever lost your way in the fog?

B. Writing Application: *Revise the following sentences by replacing each italicized word or phrase with the appropriate pronoun.*

1. When Paula was younger, *Paula* was afraid of dogs.

   _____

2. Even though dogs usually liked Paul, *Paula* found *dogs* frightening.

   _____

3. Paula's brother Ray had always wanted a dog of *Ray's* own.

   _____

4. Paula and Ray visited a pet store where *Paula and Ray* watched a puppy playing.

   _____

from **An American Childhood** by Annie Dillard
Selection Test A

Critical Reading *Identify the letter of the choice that best answers the question.*

_____ 1. Why does the author of *An American Childhood* resist going to bed when she is five?
   A. She does not want to be in the same bedroom with her sister.
   B. She wants to spend more time with her parents.
   C. She sees something scary in her room at night.
   D. She has nightmares about monsters.

_____ 2. Why does the author of *An American Childhood* not tell anyone about her feelings at bedtime?
   A. She does not think anyone will care.
   B. She is too afraid.
   C. She knows her parents are in the next room.
   D. She does not want anyone else to worry.

_____ 3. In *An American Childhood*, why does the author's sister not feel the same as the author?
   A. She has more courage.
   B. She has a better sense of humor.
   C. She is sleeping.
   D. She is too young to have such feelings.

_____ 4. What does the author of *An American Childhood* see every night in her bedroom?
   A. a mouse
   B. a moving light
   C. her parents
   D. the moon

_____ 5. Which of these sentences from *An American Childhood* does *not* create a mood of fear?
   A. "If I spoke of it, it would kill me."
   B. "It made noise. It had two joined parts, a head and a tail, like a Chinese dragon."
   C. "I lay alone and was almost asleep when the thing entered the room by flattening itself against the open door and sliding in."
   D. "Even at two she composed herself attractively for sleep."

____ 6. The author of *An American Childhood* describes a previous experience in which she heard a loud noise during her naps. How is this similar to her experience at bedtime?

A. Both happen at night.

B. Both happen when her parents are not at home.

C. She figures out that the noise and light are caused by everyday things.

D. She realizes that both experiences occur because of passing cars.

____ 7. What happens after the author of *An American Childhood* figures out the mystery?

A. The occurrence still has the power to frighten her sometimes.

B. She is never afraid again.

C. She explains it to her parents, and they all laugh.

D. She tries to scare her sister with the mystery.

____ 8. When does the mood of *An American Childhood* change to wonder?

A. when the author awakens her sleeping sister

B. when the author realizes that she has been dreaming

C. when the author realizes that what she sees are lights from a passing car

D. when the author moves to another house

____ 9. In *An American Childhood*, what is the author's purpose in describing what she sees as a "spirit" entering her room?

A. to create a feeling of humor

B. to create a feeling of fear

C. to create a feeling of happiness

D. to create a feeling of boredom

____ 10. What facts about the author's life do you learn from *An American Childhood*?

A. The author lived near a road and shared a room with her younger sister.

B. The author spent most of her childhood too frightened to sleep well at night.

C. The author began her career as a writer when she was five.

D. The author spent much of her childhood driving in cars.

Vocabulary and Grammar

____ 11. Which word means the opposite of *serene*?

A. calm

B. quiet

C. peaceful

D. excited

____ 12. Which sentence contains a personal pronoun?
  A. Where did they go for lunch?
  B. Bill read the book over the weekend.
  C. Many people enjoy going to museums.
  D. Is going to the beach fun?

____ 13. What is the possessive pronoun in the following sentence? "Tom walked his dog to the store and back."
  A. Tom
  B. dog
  C. his
  D. and

____ 14. In which sentence is *luminous* used correctly?
  A. The lamp's luminous burned out.
  B. The luminous moon lit the surface of the lake.
  C. We watched a luminous cat climb the tree.
  D. My father read a luminous article aloud at breakfast.

____ 15. Which word is the best definition of *conceivably*?
  A. quickly
  B. correctly
  C. possibly
  D. vividly

Essay

16. In *American Childhood*, the author discovers that she—not the world—can control her feelings. In an essay, tell what she first feels about what she sees at bedtime. Describe what parts of the bedtime experience lead to that feeling. Then, explain how the experience later gives the author pleasure. Use specific details from the piece in your answer.

17. In *An American Childhood*, the author uses many details to entertain the reader. In a brief essay, identify some of the details the author uses to describe what she sees at bedtime and how she feels as a result. Then, tell whether or not these details were successful in entertaining you.

Name _____ Date _____

from **An American Childhood** by Annie Dillard
Selection Test B

Critical Reading *Identify the letter of the choice that best completes the statement or answers the question.*

____ 1. In *An American Childhood,* what does the author call the thing that comes into her childhood bedroom at night?
    A. a swift spirit
    B. a ghost
    C. her friend
    D. a princess

____ 2. Why does the author of *An American Childhood* not wake up her little sister, Amy?
    A. Her parents tell her not to wake up Amy.
    B. Amy is sleeping too soundly.
    C. She is too afraid to move.
    D. She wants to protect Amy.

____ 3. Why does Dillard describe her sleeping sister in *An American Childhood*?
    A. to make fun of her sister
    B. to contrast her sister's calmness and her own fear
    C. to develop sympathy for her sister
    D. to show how frightening the night was for her sister

____ 4. What mood does the author of *An American Childhood* create with the following details? "It made noise. It had two joined parts, a head and a tail, like a Chinese dragon. . . . I dared not blink or breathe."
    A. happiness
    B. fear
    C. peace
    D. jealousy

____ 5. In *An American Childhood,* why does the author tell how she solved the mystery of the lights?
    A. to show that siblings are often envious of one another
    B. to explain how she discovered that inside and outside worlds connect
    C. to explain how passing car lights can cause reflections on indoor walls
    D. to confirm that children are often afraid of the dark

____ 6. What is the author describing in the following passage from *An American Childhood*? "I climbed deliberately from the depths like a diver who releases the monster in his arms and hauls himself hand over hand up an anchor chain till he meets the ocean's sparkling membrane and bursts through it. . . ."
    A. a bad dream that used to make her scream
    B. a trip she took later in life
    C. her struggle to separate fantasy from reality
    D. her father's stories of life at sea

143

_____ 7. In *An American Childhood*, Dillard compares her experience of car lights with what past experience?
   A. carnival lights
   B. noisy children playing outside her window
   C. noise from jackhammers in the street
   D. light streaming in from the moon

_____ 8. Which of the following details does Dillard use to support her main insight in *An American Childhood*?
   A. "All night long she slept smoothly in a series of pleasant and serene, if artificial-looking, positions. . . ."
   B. "There was a world outside my window and contiguous to it."
   C. "When I was five, growing up in Pittsburgh in 1950, I would not go to bed willingly because something came into my room."
   D. "It was a passing car whose windshield reflected the corner streetlight outside."

_____ 9. What is Dillard's purpose in *An American Childhood* for comparing her insight about the car lights with another insight she had had the year before during a nap?
   A. to tell stories of her childhood
   B. to explain why was afraid to take naps
   C. to talk about her sleeping disorder
   D. to express her frustration with herself

_____ 10. How does the mood of *An American Childhood* change during the bedtime experience the author describes?
   A. from wonder to boredom
   B. from terror to control
   C. from boredom to wonder
   D. from control to terror

_____ 11. In *An American Childhood*, how does the experience of solving the mystery change the young girl?
   A. She becomes more fearful.
   B. She learns to confide in her parents.
   C. She learns to share more with her sister.
   D. She learns the difference between reason and imagination.

_____ 12. Which of the following statements is an insight conveyed by *An American Childhood*?
   A. "The things in the world did not necessarily cause my overwhelming feelings. . . ."
   B. "Sometimes it came back, sometimes it didn't."
   C. "I could see the door whiten at its touch . . . ."
   D. "My sister Amy, two years old, was asleep in the other bed."

_____ 13. How can you tell that the little girl in *An American Childhood* continued to value the world of the imagination?
   A. She finally admits that the story is not really true.
   B. She enjoys scaring herself even after she solves the mystery.
   C. She refuses to accept the explanation for the mystery.
   D. She says that parents should not tell children scary stories.

___ 14. Which sentence best describes Dillard's attitude in *An American Childhood* toward imagination?
  A. Imagination can provide a lot of pleasure, but it also can scare people.
  B. Imagination is dangerous for young children because it can keep them from sleeping.
  C. Everyone knows the difference between reality and illusion.
  D. Using the imagination is difficult for adults, who deal mostly with logic.

___ 15. As a child, how did the author of *An American Childhood* come to feel about her place in the world?
  A. She felt she was simply part of a collection of things that made up the world.
  B. She knew that her words and thoughts meant a great deal to the world.
  C. She was fearful because she was not sure if she was real or imaginary.
  D. She felt that her life mattered only in terms of her imagination.

Vocabulary and Grammar

___ 16. Which of the following words is a synonym for *luminous* in "a luminous shape"?
  A. jagged
  B. shining
  C. moving
  D. dark

___ 17. Which of the sentences contains a personal pronoun?
  A. Joe and Carol decided to go to a movie.
  B. They saw a new science-fiction thriller.
  C. Many of the town's teenagers were in the theater.
  D. Everyone was glad to have caught the film.

___ 18. Which sentence does *not* use *conceivably* correctly?
  A. Conceivably, we were the best musicians in the band.
  B. The sun, conceivably, did not rise yesterday.
  C. David's joke was, conceivably, the worst one I had ever heard.
  D. Mr. Oeberst is, conceivably, the most talented teacher I know.

___ 19. Which of the words is a possessive pronoun?
  A. me
  B. they
  C. all
  D. hers

Essay

20. In this excerpt from *An American Childhood*, the author uses vivid details to describe her experience at bedtime. Write an essay in which you give examples of details the author uses. Explain what feelings she conveys through the details.

21. In an essay, tell what you think is the author's purpose in this part of *An American Childhood*. Start by mentioning details Dillard uses to describe her experience. Then explain what these details lead you to determine is Dillard's purpose in reporting the experience.

from **Travels With Charley** by John Steinbeck
Vocabulary Warm-up Word Lists

Study these words from "Travels With Charley." Then, complete the activities.

Word List A

conceal [kuhn SEEL] *v.* hide
When Lisa won first prize, she couldn't <u>conceal</u> her excitement.

creation [kree AY shun] *n.* all things that exist in the world
Rita thinks that a blazing red maple tree in autumn is the most beautiful thing in <u>creation</u>.

genuine [JEN yoo in] *adj.* real or true
Rob thought he was buying a <u>genuine</u> leather belt, but it was vinyl.

landscape [LAND skayp] *n.* land area visible from one spot
Outside the train window, the <u>landscape</u> changed from forest to field.

powerful [POW ur fuhl] *adj.* strong
The horse was so <u>powerful</u> that Winslow could hardly control it.

prefers [pruh FERZ] *v.* likes better
Susan <u>prefers</u> soccer to basketball.

reluctance [ri LUHK tuhns] *n.* unwillingness
Danielle has a great <u>reluctance</u> to get out of bed on Monday morning.

typical [TIP uh kuhl] *adj.* having the qualities of the group
Whiskers was a <u>typical</u> cat, curious and independent.

Word List B

clarity [KLA ruh tee] *n.* clearness
Looking at each step of the problem will help you gain <u>clarity</u> about it.

commotion [kuh MOH shuhn] *n.* noisy activity; fuss
The dog running loose in the cafeteria caused a great <u>commotion</u>.

desolate [DES uh lit] *adj.* deserted
The government chose a <u>desolate</u> area in the Southwest to test the bomb.

foreboding [for BOH ding] *n.* feeling that something bad will happen
When Marco saw the dark storm clouds and lightning, he was filled with <u>foreboding</u>.

omens [OH muhnz] *n.* signs of good or bad luck
Some people think that walking under a ladder and breaking a mirror are bad <u>omens</u>.

publicity [puh BLI suh tee] *n.* attention; advertising
The movie got so much <u>publicity</u> before it opened that crowds lined up to see it.

restrictions [ri STRIK shuhnz] *n.* limits
The reporter agreed to the singer's <u>restrictions</u> on questions he could ask.

suspicion [suh SPI shuhn] *n.* idea, not based on facts, that something is wrong
Jenna had a <u>suspicion</u> that Tyler was dating other girls.

from **Travels With Charley** by John Steinbeck
Vocabulary Warm-up Exercises

Exercise A *Fill in each blank in the paragraph below with an appropriate word from Word List A. Use each word only once.*

In a popular work of fiction, Anastasia, a [1] _____ heroine, lives

with a rich but cold relative who doesn't understand her. She is engaged to a suitable

young man, but she [2] _____ the [3] _____ brute of a

groundskeeper whom she knows is the best man in [4] _____. She

has great [5] _____ to tell anyone of her feelings. She must

[6] _____ her love as he barely acknowledges her existence. In actuality,

for years, he has been planting a magical garden, a colorful [7] _____ in

which he can reveal his own love. Will a [8] _____ opportunity arise for

the two to share their feelings?

Exercise B *Decide whether each statement below is true or false. Circle* T *or* F. *Then, explain your answers.*

1. Dark, whirling funnel clouds, often seen as <u>omens</u>, should fill people with <u>foreboding</u>.
   T / F _____

2. All <u>publicity</u> about movie stars should be believed.
   T / F _____

3. Being grounded because someone thinks you may cause a <u>commotion</u> is fair.
   T / F _____

4. <u>Restrictions</u> must be placed on toddlers so they don't wander.
   T / F _____

5. The North Pole is a <u>desolate</u> place, but the South Pole isn't.
   T / F _____

6. If you have a <u>suspicion</u> that your dog is sick, you should take the dog to the vet.
   T / F _____

7. The more <u>clarity</u> you gain about a problem, the harder it is to solve it.
   T / F _____

Name _____ Date _____

from **Travels With Charley** by John Steinbeck
Reading Warm-up A

Read the following passage. Pay special attention to the underlined words. Then, read it again, and complete the activities. Use a separate sheet of paper for your written answers.

Most of the driving public <u>prefers</u> to travel the interstate highway system. Two-lane roads with traffic lights are too slow for busy lives. I consider my own taste <u>typical</u>. When I have a long distance to go, I show no <u>reluctance</u> to take the modern road. I don't think twice about hopping onto the freeway. Tooling smoothly and forcefully down the highway with the help of a <u>powerful</u> engine makes up for the dull view and boring <u>landscape</u>.

Still, a part of me believes that somehow what came before the interstate was more <u>genuine</u>. The interstate, built by the government, lacks the style of a "real" road such as Route 66.

From the late 1920s to the 1950s, many drivers followed Route 66 west from Chicago to Los Angeles. It is worth your time today to get off at one of the ramps of Interstate 40 in New Mexico or Arizona. You might catch a glimpse of what the slick highway will <u>conceal</u>. Motels with rooms shaped liked tepees, theme diners, and streamlined service stations loom up as if out of nowhere.

One of the best treasures in all of <u>creation</u> is a certain hotel in Winslow, Arizona. It not only sits beside the old route but also backs up onto railroad tracks. These well-used tracks carried many a passenger across the country. In the 1920s and 1930s, many roads were still rough and long-distance air travel was not readily available, so people often took the train. They would stop off at railroad hotels along the way. Tasty meals at fair prices awaited them. So did rooms that were nothing like those in the hotels back home.

Some people have accused the interstate of ruining a whole civilization. The highway has its advantages, however. We can motor along speedily to our heart's content. That gives us the time to take a magical detour into the past.

1. Underline the sentence that gives the reason why the public <u>prefers</u> the interstate. Then, write a sentence about something you *prefer*.

2. Circle the phrase that explains the word <u>typical</u>. Write a sentence telling about a *typical* event in your day.

3. Underline the phrase that describes what the author has no <u>reluctance</u> to take. Write a sentence that tells about something you have no *reluctance* to do.

4. Circle two words that describe riding with a <u>powerful</u> engine. Write a sentence telling why a *powerful* engine is suited to the interstate.

5. Write a sentence that tells what might be part of the <u>landscape</u> you'd see along an interstate.

6. Circle the synonym of <u>genuine</u>. Write a sentence describing what is *genuine* about the older road.

7. Underline the three things that an interstate can <u>conceal</u>. Then, write a sentence telling how the highway can *conceal* them.

8. Circle what the passage says is one of the best treasures in all <u>creation</u>. Explain what you think is a treasure in all *creation*.

from **Travels With Charley** by John Steinbeck
Reading Warm-up B

Read the following passage. Pay special attention to the underlined words. Then, read it again, and complete the activities. Use a separate sheet of paper for your written answers.

Western South Dakota offers two remarkable areas of natural beauty. Just hearing their names—the Badlands and the Black Hills—fills one with the suspicion that these aren't ordinary places.

The name Badlands makes the place sound like a desolate wasteland, deserted and lonely. It's an area of strange, pointy rock formations that some people see as full of foreboding. Some look for signs of bad things to come in omens—a dead bird, a sudden whirlwind—in order to justify making a hasty exit. However, that is only half the story. The other half is acres and acres of grassland, resulting in the largest protected mixed-grass prairie in the United States.

The Badlands were once covered with a shallow sea. Over millions of years, the land rose and the sea disappeared. A warm, humid forest emerged, which later gave way to cooler grasslands. Rocks and soil contain clues to each era. Scientists have dug countless fossils from the land, and many more lie waiting to be found. With each new find, we look into the distant past with greater clarity.

The Black Hills are home to one of the most famous monuments in the United States: Mt. Rushmore, four presidential heads carved in rock. In the Badlands, one goes to look at rock that took millions of years to wear away.

In order to preserve a national park or a monument, the government must enforce restrictions about its use. One rule at Mt. Rushmore is "no climbers." Of course, that does not stop publicity-seeking daredevils from taking their chances. Every so often, the site becomes the scene of commotion. Yet another group has attempted to reach the top of the monument, and officials must get the people down.

If you plan to be in western South Dakota, make sure you visit the Badlands and the Black Hills. They each offer a visual delight unequaled anywhere else on Earth.

1. Underline the phrase that tells why you might have the suspicion that these places aren't ordinary. Then, write a sentence about a *suspicion* you've had.

2. Circle a synonym for desolate. Explain whether you would find many people in a *desolate* place.

3. Circle the words that give a clue to the meaning of foreboding. Write about a time when you were filled with *foreboding*.

4. Circle the words that give examples of omens. Tell why you think some people may look for *omens*.

5. What helps us look into the past with greater clarity? Explain why someone would want to do this.

6. Write a sentence telling what kind of restrictions you have at home.

7. Circle the words that tell what some have done to seek publicity. Tell what it means to seek *publicity*.

8. Would you get much sleep if there were a commotion going on outside your window? Explain.

Name _____ Date _____

from **Travels With Charley** by John Steinbeck
Reading: Evaluate Whether the Author Achieves
His or Her Purpose

The **author's purpose** is the reason he or she has for writing. A purpose might be to persuade readers, to entertain readers, or to provide information to readers. Keep in mind that sometimes an author may try to achieve more than one purpose. One of your jobs as a reader is to **evaluate whether an author achieves his or her purpose(s).** You must ask yourself if the author has included sufficient support to persuade you of an idea or position, to entertain you, or to teach you about something. With that question in mind, read these sentences from the first paragraph of the Steinbeck excerpt, which conveys Steinbeck's purpose: to inform himself and his reader about the landscape and people of America.

> I had not heard the speech of America, smelled the grass and trees and sewage, seen its hills and water, its color and quality of light. I knew the changes only from books and newspapers. But more than this, I had not felt the country for twenty-five years. In short, I was writing of something I did not know about, and it seems to me that in a so-called writer this is criminal.

Think about what Steinbeck has to do in the rest of the piece for you to conclude that, becoming informed about his country, he has in turn informed his readers, and therefore, has achieved his general purpose.

A. DIRECTIONS: *Read each of the following passages, and tell in what way it helps Steinbeck to support the thoughts quoted above and to accomplish his general purpose—informing himself and you about the America through which he travels.*

1. "It is some years since I have been alone, nameless, friendless, without any of the safety one gets from family, friends, and accomplices. There is no reality in the danger. It's just a very lonely, helpless feeling at first—a kind of desolate feeling. For this reason I took one companion on my journey—an old French gentleman poodle known as Charley."

   _____

   _____

2. "She was hungry to talk, frantic to talk, about her relatives, her friends, and how she wasn't used to this. For she was not a native and she didn't rightly belong here. Her native clime was a land of milk and honey and had its share of apes and ivory and peacocks. Her voice rattled on as though she was terrified of the silence that would settle when I was gone. As she talked it came to me that she was afraid of this place and, further, that so was I."

   _____

   _____

Name _____ Date _____

from **Travels With Charley** by John Steinbeck
Literary Analysis: Author's Style

You express yourself through the clothes you wear, the hairstyle you prefer, and the activities in which you participate. All of these things reflect your individual style. **Style** also refers to the way authors express themselves in their writing. It is the stamp that gives their writing its unique character. Among other things, an author's style is characterized by his or her tone, the way in which the writer views a particular subject. Writers also produce their style by their choice or words and sentence structure.

A. DIRECTIONS: *Complete the chart by providing for each numbered item at least three examples from* Travels With Charley *that reflect Steinbeck's style.*

Author's Style	
1. Word Choice: Mostly, the vocabulary of an educated person, but lots of informal, conversational words and phrases, including unusual, homey modifiers	**Examples:**
2. Sentence Length and Rhythm: A lot of mature sentences, but once in a while short, conversational-sounding sentences pop up to give the piece an informal feel	**Examples:**
3. Tone: Personal, modest, open	**Examples:**

B. DIRECTIONS: *In no more than three sentences, state what you think Steinbeck's style is in this excerpt from* Travels With Charley.

_____

_____

Name _____ Date _____

from **Travels With Charley** by John Steinbeck
Vocabulary Builder

A. DIRECTIONS: *From the following alphabetized lists, select one synonym and one antonym for each of the numbered words in the table below. Write your choices in the appropriate boxes.*

<u>Synonyms</u>
difficult
heavenly
unexplainable
weakened

<u>Antonyms</u>
comprehensible
easy
earthbound
strengthened

Vocabulary Word	Synonym	Antonym
1. impaired		
2. rigorous		
3. inexplicable		
4. celestial		

B. DIRECTIONS: *For each of the numbered vocabulary words in the table above, write a sentence that shows you know the meaning of the word.*

1. _____

_____

2. _____

_____

3. _____

_____

4. _____

_____

5. _____

_____

from **Travels With Charley** by John Steinbeck
Support for Writing an Observations Journal Entry

Some people enjoy keeping an **observations journal** in which they record thoughts and ideas about people, places, and things they have seen in person or in print, conversations they have heard, experiences they have had—anything they want to remember. These people may first put their notes into a table such as the one below. When you have identified the place you want to write about, fill in the table with prewriting notes.

Thing I want to remember: _____	
Details about it	
Anecdotes involving it	
Examples of it	
Actions spurred by it	
Changes in attitude toward it over time	

Now, based on your notes, write a two-paragraph entry for your observations journal.

from **Travels With Charley** by John Steinbeck
Support for Extend Your Learning

Research and Technology

Sightseers depend on **brochures** to get information quickly about a place they are visiting. Information in a brochure should be clear, accurate, and concise—to the point. As you locate information about places in the Bad Lands, fill in a chart such as the following. You can work with the three places suggested on the chart or places you come across in your own research.

Information for brochure	Fort Union Trading Post National Historic Site	Knife River Indian Villages National Historic Site	Theodore Roosevelt National Park
Why you should visit			
What you can do there			
Directions for getting there			

Then, use your notes to produce the brochure.

Listening and Speaking

To prepare for the **oral presentation** about Steinbeck, look for information in the categories in the following outline or in categories that you prefer.

    I. Parts of America that Steinbeck mostly wrote about

    II. Steinbeck works most often read in school and beyond school

    III. Steinbeck's best-known characters

    IV. Quotations from Steinbeck's literature

After you have finished your research, used an outline to organize your notes, and practiced your presentation, give it in front of the class.

from **Travels With Charley** by John Steinbeck
Enrichment: Travel Writing Career

A **travel writer** writes books or articles for magazines, special sections of newspapers, and Web sites focused on exploring the world beyond one's own backyard. A travel writer must have a talent not only for writing, but also for interviewing and conducting other research. He or she must develop curiosity, flexibility, and organizational skills. To succeed in this field, a travel writer should want to experience a variety of places, people, and events.

DIRECTIONS: *Imagine that you are a travel writer for a magazine for teenagers and that your editor has asked you to write about teenage life in a city (other than your own) anywhere in the world. Plan your visit and the focus of your article by answering the following questions:*

1. What city do you want to visit? Why? _____
   _____

2. What kind of background research should you do before you get to the city? _____
   _____
   _____

3. Where will you go to locate teenagers to interview in that city? _____
   _____

4. How will you communicate with teenagers in that city if you do not speak their language? _____
   _____

5. What five things do you think your readers want to know about their peers in that city? _____
   _____
   _____
   _____
   _____
   _____

Name _____ Date _____

from **Travels With Charley** by John Steinbeck
Selection Test A

Critical Reading *Identify the letter of the choice that best answers the question.*

____ 1. Why does Steinbeck make the trip he reports on in *Travels With Charley*?
   A. He wants to visit relatives in the West.
   B. He wants to try out his custom camping truck.
   C. He wants to learn about America's landscapes and people firsthand.
   D. He is tired of living in one place and thinks it is time that he explored more.

____ 2. How do Steinbeck's friends respond to the news of the trip he is planning?
   A. They wish him well.
   B. They warn about unpleasantness.
   C. They supply him with equipment.
   D. They ask him if they can go along.

____ 3. Whom or what does Steinbeck take along on the trip that leads to *Travels With Charley*?
   A. his poodle
   B. his brother
   C. his son
   D. his father

____ 4. Which three statements are true about Charley in *Travels With Charley* by Steinbeck?
   I.   He is a good companion.
   II. He is a skillful fighter.
   III. He is protective.
   IV. He makes it easy for Steinbeck to meet strangers.
   A. I, II, and IV
   B. I, II, and III
   C. II, III, and IV
   D. I, III, and IV

____ 5. Which word best describes Steinbeck's style in the following sentence?
   And the night, far from being frightful, was lovely beyond thought, for the stars were close, and although there was no moon the starlight made a silver glow in the sky.

   A. choppy
   B. descriptive
   C. unemotional
   D. humorous

_____ 6. In the Bad Lands, Steinbeck stops to ask about eggs. What is his real reason for stopping?

   A. He has not eaten all day.

   B. He thinks the man looks lonely.

   C. He wants to meet someone from there.

   D. Charley needs a break from driving.

_____ 7. What does Steinbeck mean when he says to Charley, "I have a strong impulse to stay, amounting to a celestial command."

   A. He wants to stay in one place so that he can see shooting stars.

   B. He wants Charley to understand that Steinbeck, not Charley, is in charge of the trip.

   C. He has such a strong feeling about danger ahead that it feels like a message from heaven.

   D. He can tell by reading the stars that it is important that they stay where they are.

_____ 8. How does Steinbeck learn about people on his journey?

   A. He has casual conversations with people he meets at each stop.

   B. He interviews people and takes notes.

   C. He observes people from a distance, so they will not recognize him.

   D. He pays attention to Charley's reactions to the people they met.

_____ 9. Steinbeck names his truck after a horse in a novel, and he records conversations with Charley. What do these acts tell you about Steinbeck's attitude toward his subject?

   A. He is impatient to get home.

   B. He misses his country home and horses.

   C. He can look at things humorously.

   D. He likes company.

_____ 10. What is Steinbeck's purpose in describing the chatty woman in the Bad Lands?

   A. to make fun of her

   B. to explain that she moved there recently

   C. to show how talkative everyone is

   D. to show how landscape affects people

_____ 11. Why does Steinbeck end the excerpt from *Travels With Charley* by saying that each generalization he made about his trip "was canceled by another"?

A. He is thinking about giving up writing.

B. He wants readers to feel sorry for him.

C. He wants sympathy from Charley.

D. He is gently criticizing himself.

Vocabulary and Grammar

_____ 12. Which word means the opposite of *impaired*?

A. weakened

B. strengthened

C. lessened

D. damaged

_____ 13. What does *inexplicable* mean?

A. hard to explain

B. obvious

C. simple

D. unavoidable

_____ 14. In which sentence is a reflexive pronoun used *incorrectly*?

A. Hank gave himself five minutes to finish.

B. We bought ourselves some pencils.

C. Bea wrote a story about herself.

D. I missed yourself when you were gone.

Essay

15. Steinbeck writes, "In the night the Bad Lands had become Good Lands." In an essay, describe Steinbeck's first reaction to the Bad Lands. Then, go on to explain the experience that causes his feelings to change. Support your ideas with details from the selection.

16. Based on the information provided in the selection, what would you expect to find in the Bad Lands? How would you feel traveling through the area? Write a brief essay in which you explain reasons that you would or would not enjoy visiting the Bad Lands.

from **Travels With Charley** by John Steinbeck
Selection Test B

Critical Reading *Identify the letter of the choice that best completes the statement or answers the question.*

_____ 1. In *Travels With Charley*, what does Steinbeck mean by saying that he did not know his own country?
A. He did not know the history of America.
B. He did not understand American art.
C. He had not visited areas for a while.
D. He had never been beyond big cities.

_____ 2. In *Travels With Charley*, what did Steinbeck hope to achieve by living in his truck?
A. He could travel without giving his name.
B. He could avoid paying for hotel rooms.
C. He could travel light.
D. He could take his dog with him.

_____ 3. In *Travels With Charley*, what does Steinbeck mean by saying he ". . . was working from memory, and the memory is at best a faulty, warpy reservoir"?
A. His had no memories left.
B. His memories revolved around Chicago.
C. He did not entirely trust his memories.
D. Memories, like reservoirs, depend on rain.

_____ 4. What view of New York is shared by most people whom Steinbeck meets on the road?
A. They do not want to live there.
B. Most hope to visit it.
C. It is a very exciting place.
D. It is more crowded than the West.

_____ 5. Does Steinbeck achieve his purpose: getting to know America again and writing about it?
A. yes, because he talks to strangers
B. no, because he talks only with Charley
C. no, because he talks only with Charley
D. no, because he cancels the trip

_____ 6. From his actions in *Travels With Charley*, you can conclude that Steinbeck
A. has no sense of humor about himself.
B. does not easily make conversation.
C. tends to be ruled by his emotions.
D. is fearful of new experiences.

_____ 7. Steinbeck's description of the Bad Lands differs from one in a travel guide because it
A. does not describe the landscape.
B. makes observations about human nature.
C. is very lengthy and detailed.
D. concentrates on the climate.

____ 8. Steinbeck makes as many observations about humans as he does about nature because
A. the natural setting is not interesting.
B. he does not like travel guides.
C. he feels close to all the people he meets.
D. one of his main interests is human nature.

____ 9. Which sequence best describes Steinbeck's changing emotions about the Bad Lands?
A. uneasiness, fear, delight
B. boredom, amusement, contentment
C. anxiety, resentment, exhilaration
D. anger, surprise, happiness

____ 10. What does the next sentence from *Travels With Charley* say about Steinbeck's writing style?

Against the descending sun the battlements were dark and clean-lined, while to the east, where the uninhabited light poured slantwise, the strange landscape shouted with color.

A. He uses vague words.
B. He likes long, descriptive sentences.
C. He avoids figures of speech.
D. His sentences are short and choppy.

____ 11. What reaction does Steinbeck have to his conversation with the old woman in the Bad Lands?
A. He is comforted by her friendly manner.
B. He is annoyed by her constant prattle.
C. He realizes that he misses his friends.
D. He realizes that he is afraid of the area.

____ 12. At the end of his day in the Bad Lands, Steinbeck builds a fire in order to enjoy its smell and sound. What might be his purpose in telling readers this anecdote?
A. to show how much he enjoys fires
B. to demonstrate his camping abilities
C. to show his comfort with his surroundings
D. to ward off his fears of the barren land

____ 13. What does the next passage say about Steinbeck's style in *Travels With Charley*?

Someone must have told me about the Missouri River at Bismarck, North Dakota, or I must have read about it. In either case, I hadn't paid attention. I came on it in amazement. Here is where the map should fold.

A. He leans toward short sentences.
B. He leans toward long sentences.
C. He mixes long and short sentences.
D. He hides his emotions.

____ 14. Which of the following sentences illustrates Steinbeck's reflective style?
A. "I was set for some scratch-hen eggs."
B. "I felt I wouldn't like to have the night catch me there."
C. "I stopped where people stopped or gathered."
D. "Before I slept I spread a map on my bed, a Charley-tromped map."

____ 15. Why does Steinbeck carefully describe the man of few words and the chatty woman?
A. The author uses a lot of description regardless of the topic.
B. The contrast helps readers see that the Bad Lands can affect people differently.
C. He remembers meeting them both on past travels.
D. He is about to turn back and wants to record his final experiences with care.

Vocabulary and Grammar

____ 16. In which sentence is *rigorous* used correctly?
A. The story was both exciting and rigorous.
B. The weather was rigorous, so we walked.
C. The hike was rigorous, but rewarding.
D. I was too rigorous to eat dessert.

____ 17. Which word or term is an acceptable reflexive pronoun?
A. themselves
B. him or her
C. everyone's
D. hisself

____ 18. Which sentence contains a reflexive pronoun used *incorrectly*?
A. Sara baked a cake for herself.
B. Sara baked a cake for her.
C. Ray told Mark he would be late.
D. The gift means a lot to myself.

____ 19. Something that is *inexplicable* is
A. understandable.
B. inconclusive.
C. incomprehensible.
D. undebatable.

Essay

20. Steinbeck equipped himself, both physically and emotionally, for the journey that led to *Travels With Charley.* Write an essay in which you tell whether he was adequately prepared, inadequately prepared, or overprepared. Give specific examples.

21. In *Travels With Charley*, Steinbeck states his purpose "to try to rediscover this monster land." Using specific examples from the text, discuss in an essay some of the things Steinbeck discovers about American people and American landscapes.

Vocabulary Warm-up Word Lists

Study these words from "The American Dream." Then, complete the activities.

Word List A

democracy [di MAHK ruh see] *n.* government that is run by the people who live under it
People in a <u>democracy</u> have the privilege of voting for their leaders.

destruction [di STRUHK shun] *n.* end; ruin
Pollution has caused the <u>destruction</u> of many sources of clean water.

emerge [i MERJ] *v.* come into being
Out of a group of four candidates, one will <u>emerge</u> as the winner.

equal [EE kwuhl] *adj.* same in amount, number, size, or value
I will divide the pie into <u>equal</u> slices so we all get our share.

individual [in duh VIJ oo uhl] *n.* person
Every <u>individual</u> has a say in the kind of work he or she will do.

perspective [pur SPEK tiv] *n.* way of looking at things
Paul's <u>perspective</u> on life is different from mine because he grew up in England.

segregation [seg ruh GAY shuhn] *n.* practice of keeping groups apart
<u>Segregation</u> forced African Americans to sit in the back of buses.

slavery [SLAY vuh ree] *n.* the practice of one person owning another
Trying to escape from <u>slavery</u> was dangerous, and runaway slaves were in great peril.

Word List B

development [di VEL uhp muhnt] *n.* growth
The <u>development</u> of the empty lot has provided new housing for many.

dilemma [duh LEM uh] *n.* problem that requires a difficult choice
Learning that Dan cheated on the test has created a <u>dilemma</u> about the right thing to do.

essentially [i SEN shuhl lee] *adv.* basically
A lamp is <u>essentially</u> a fancy object to hold a light bulb.

heir [AIR] *n.* person who receives something from a previous generation
Grandma Rose named me as an <u>heir</u> in her will.

legacy [LEG uh see] *n.* something handed down from one generation to the next
Stories and photos provide a living <u>legacy</u> from our ancestors.

moral [MAWR uhl] *adj.* relating to right and wrong
Many parents expect children to learn <u>moral</u> behavior by their examples.

pursuit [puhr SOOT] *n.* search; finding ways to get something
In <u>pursuit</u> of a goal, don't be afraid to change direction if necessary.

ultimately [UHL tuh mit lee] *adv.* finally; in the end
The roller coaster was worth waiting for, as it was <u>ultimately</u> the best ride.

Name _____   Date _____

"The American Dream" by Martin Luther King, Jr.
Vocabulary Warm-up Exercises

Exercise A *Fill in each blank in the paragraph below with an appropriate word from Word List A. Use each word only once.*

Under the system of [1] _____, one [2] _____ can own another. It is clear to people in our country today that such a system doesn't belong in a [3] _____. In a nation where we are all [4] _____, no one can own someone else. Also, laws have made clear that our country is no place for the [5] _____ of people by skin color. It took too many years for the [6] _____ of such a practice. Why did it take so long for such a different [7] _____ to [8] _____? Attitudes and feelings are often passed down from generation to generation, and changing people's views is a difficult challenge.

Exercise B *Answer each question in a complete sentence. Use a word from Word List B to replace each underlined word or group of words without changing the meaning.*

1. During the <u>search</u> for the <u>right</u> thing to do, have you ever found yourself with a <u>problem that requires a difficult choice</u>?

   _____

2. <u>What might be handed down to you</u> from a grandparent?

   _____

3. Do you believe that people are <u>basically</u> good?

   _____

4. What does the <u>growth</u> of a business require?

   _____

5. Do you believe that <u>in the end</u> how successful you are depends on your own actions?

   _____

6. <u>Who receives</u> parents' possessions after they die?

   _____

"The American Dream" by Martin Luther King, Jr.
Reading Warm-up A

Read the following passage. Pay special attention to the underlined words. Then, read it again, and complete the activities. Use a separate sheet of paper for your written answers.

In 1954, Oliver Brown—an African American railroad worker—sued the Topeka, Kansas, Board of Education. The board wouldn't allow his daughter to attend an all-white school in his neighborhood. At the time, <u>segregation</u> was widespread in public schools.

From the <u>perspective</u> of the board, and according to many other people's way of looking at the situation, it was only business as usual. The rule of "separate but <u>equal</u>" was law in the land. That meant it was acceptable for black people to be required to have different schools, neighborhoods, lunch counters, bathrooms, and many other things. These places were supposed to be of the same quality as the ones white people had. Mostly, however, that wasn't the case.

The matter went all the way to the Supreme Court. A young African American lawyer named Thurgood Marshall took the case. From a lawsuit brought by just one <u>individual</u>, the movement to allow black children into white schools grew. The justices decided other similar cases at the same time.

Brown and his side won. Their victory helped achieve the <u>destruction</u> of these unfair practices, thus opening doors which had long been closed to blacks. It was a long but clear fight. Soon, civil rights bills were passed. One hundred years had passed since black people had been freed from <u>slavery</u>. Finally, they could start to <u>emerge</u> as full citizens and enjoy the same rights as other Americans, such as voting.

In a <u>democracy</u>, people vote for representatives who make the laws of the land. But after civil rights laws pass, people's hearts and minds still have to change. African Americans have many more opportunities today than they did fifty years ago. Still, more change must occur to make sure that all citizens of the United States have the same rights and opportunities.

1. Underline the sentence that explains <u>segregation</u>. Then, write a sentence describing another form of *segregation*.

2. Circle the phrase that tells what <u>perspective</u> is. Then, write a sentence explaining your *perspective* on an issue at your school.

3. Underline the phrase in the paragraph that explains <u>equal</u>. Then, write a sentence using *equal*.

4. Rewrite the sentence with <u>individual</u>, using a synonym for the word. Then, write a sentence about an *individual* whom you admire.

5. Underline words that describe the <u>destruction</u> of unfair practices. What helped with the *destruction* of these practices? Explain.

6. Underline the sentence that tells what happens when someone is freed from <u>slavery</u>. Use *slavery* in a sentence.

7. Explain what it means in this passage to <u>emerge</u> as a citizen.

8. Underline the words that explain what a <u>democracy</u> is. Then, write a sentence about living in a *democracy*.

Name _____   Date _____

"The American Dream" by Martin Luther King, Jr.
Reading Warm-up B

Read the following passage. Pay special attention to the underlined words. Then, read it again, and complete the activities. Use a separate sheet of paper for your written answers.

I sat at my desk rereading the letter, wondering what was the best way around this unexpected <u>development</u>. I had not anticipated this precise turn of events. I was indeed faced with a <u>moral dilemma</u> and would have to wrestle with it. What was right and what was wrong?

I had been working diligently in <u>pursuit</u> of my goal to be elected to City Council. A life in politics had been my dream since my days as class president. I had always been convinced that with positive intentions and concern for all people, one person really could make a difference. Many thought that I was overly optimistic and would soon see things differently. As time went on, though, the more I looked for the good in people, the more I seemed to find it. My belief was confirmed: A <u>legacy</u> of mistrust and prejudice is not a proud inheritance, but a shameful one.

The letter that arrived today came from a group whose ideas troubled me. I knew these people dealt unfairly with others and were <u>essentially</u> dishonest at heart. Yet, they were offering a large contribution in support of my campaign. A check for $3,000 was attached to the letter. Did they consider me an <u>heir</u> to their way of thinking, someone who would follow in their footsteps? If I accepted the money, they would expect me to support their side of issues. However, I would not be required to do this, I thought, and my campaign was in serious need of funding. Perhaps some compromise was possible.

As I pondered, the answer finally revealed itself: <u>Ultimately</u>, accepting this support would mean selling part of my good character. It might be foolish to reject such a large contribution. I might lose the election as a result. Nevertheless, my reply would be, "No, thank you."

As I ripped the check into pieces, I felt at peace. My moral dilemma was solved.

1. Underline the phrase that means the same thing as <u>development</u>. Write a sentence describing something that would be an unexpected *development*.

2. Circle the sentence that describes the problem when facing a <u>moral dilemma</u>. Then, tell about a *moral dilemma* you have wrestled with.

3. Underline the words that tell what the author is in <u>pursuit</u> of. Then, write a sentence about a *pursuit* of yours.

4. Circle the word that means the same as <u>legacy</u>. Is there more than one kind of *legacy*? Explain your answer in a complete sentence.

5. Circle the phrase that gives a clue to the meaning of <u>essentially</u>. Write a sentence about yourself that begins, "I feel that *essentially* . . ."

6. Underline the phrase that gives clues to the meaning of <u>heir</u>. Then, write a sentence what you might be *heir* to.

7. Underline the word that is a synonym for <u>ultimately</u>. Think of one more word or phrase that means the same as *ultimately*, and use it in a sentence.

Name _____ Date _____

"The American Dream" by Martin Luther King, Jr.
Reading: Evaluate Whether the Author Achieves His or Her Purpose

The **author's purpose** is the reason he or she has for writing. A purpose might be to persuade readers, to entertain readers, or to provide information to readers. Keep in mind that sometimes an author may try to achieve more than one purpose. One of your jobs as a reader is to **evaluate whether an author achieves his or her purpose(s).** You must ask yourself if the author has included sufficient support to persuade you of an idea or position, to entertain you, or to teach you about something. With that question in mind, read the opening of "The American Dream," which conveys King's purpose: to persuade you to accept his argument.

America is essentially a dream, a dream as yet unfulfilled. It is a dream of a land where men of all races, of all nationalities and of all creeds can live together as brothers.

Think about what King has to do in the rest of the piece for you to conclude that he has persuaded you of his opening remark, and therefore, has achieved his general purpose.

A. DIRECTIONS: *Read each passage, and tell in what way it helps support King's opening statement and accomplish his purpose—persuading you to agree with him.*

1. On the one hand we have proudly professed the principles of democracy, and on the other hand we have sadly practiced the very antithesis of those principles. Indeed slavery and segregation have been strange paradoxes in a nation founded on the principle that all men are created equal.

   _____

   _____

2. The hour is late; the clock of destiny is ticking out. It is trite, but urgently true, that if America is to remain a first-class nation she can no longer have second-class citizens. Now, more than ever before, America is challenged to bring her noble dream into reality, and those who are working to implement the American dream are the true saviors of democracy.

   _____

   _____

3. Through our scientific genius we have made of this world a neighborhood; now through our moral and spiritual development we must make of it a brotherhood. In a real sense, we must all learn to live together as brothers, or we will all perish as fools.

   _____

   _____

Name _____   Date _____

"The American Dream" by Martin Luther King, Jr.
Literary Analysis: Author's Style

You express yourself through the clothes you wear, the hairstyle you prefer, and the activities in which you participate. All of these things reflect your individual style. **Style** also refers to the way authors express themselves in their writing. It is the stamp that gives their writing its unique character. Among other things, an author's style is characterized by his or her tone, the way in which the writer views a particular subject. Writers also produce their style by their choice of words and sentence structure.

A. DIRECTIONS: *Complete the chart by providing for each numbered item at least three examples from "The American Dream" that reflect King's style.*

King's Style	
1. Word Choice: Many formal, sophisticated words and phrases	**Examples:**
2. Sentence Length and Rhythm: Repetition in short sentences; some long, complicated but smooth, even sentences	**Examples:**
3. Tone: Mostly serious, urgent, authoritative, preaching	**Examples:**

B. DIRECTIONS: *In no more than three sentences, state what you think King's style is in "American Dream."*

_____

_____

_____

_____

"The American Dream" by Martin Luther King, Jr.
Vocabulary Builder

A. DIRECTIONS: *From the following alphabetized lists, select one synonym and one antonym for each of the numbered words in the table below. Write your choices in the appropriate boxes.*

Synonyms

abuse

contradictions

opposite

sure

Antonyms

agreement

doubtful

respect

same

Vocabulary Word	Synonym	Antonym
1. antithesis		
2. paradoxes		
3. unequivocal		
4. exploitation		

B. DIRECTIONS: *For each of the numbered vocabulary words in the table above, write a sentence that shows you know the meaning of the word.*

1. _____

2. _____

3. _____

4. _____

Name _____   Date _____

"The American Dream" by Martin Luther King, Jr.

Support for Writing an Observations Journal Entry

Some people enjoy keeping an **observations journal** in which they record thoughts and ideas about people, places, and things they have seen in person or in print, conversations they have heard, experiences they have had—anything they want to remember. These people may first put their notes into a table such as the one below.

For your journal entry about an aspect of today's society that needs improvement, think about something you believe is unfair, unhealthy, or inefficient. It can be something you have noticed at your school, in your community, or in the country or the world at large. When you have identified a topic, fill in the table with prewriting notes.

Problem: _____	
Details about it	
Anecdotes involving it	
Examples of it	
Solution: _____	
Actions spurred by it	
Changes in attitude toward it over time	

Now, based on your notes, write a two-paragraph entry for your observations journal.

"**The American Dream**" by Martin Luther King, Jr.
Support for Extend Your Learning

Research and Technology

Sightseers depend on **brochures** to get information quickly about a place they are visiting. Information in a brochure should be clear, accurate, and concise, or to the point. As you locate information about the places associated with Martin Luther King, Jr., fill in a chart such as the following:

Information for Brochure	Site 1: _____ _____	Site 2: _____ _____	Site 3: _____ _____
Reason for King's visit			
Message delivered			
Form of message (speech? act of civil disobedience)			

Then, use your notes to produce the brochure.

Listening and Speaking

To prepare for the **oral presentation** about King, look for information in the categories in the following outline or in categories that you prefer.

   I. Preparations for the march
   II. Coverage by the media
   III. Most notable moments of the day
   IV. Popularity of the "I Have a Dream Speech" since 1963

After you have finished your research, used an outline to organize your notes, and practiced your presentation, give it in front of the class.

"The American Dream" by Martin Luther King, Jr.
Enrichment: Delivering a Speech Effectively

Some **public speakers** speak totally without notes. Some use notes to remind themselves of the major points they want to make. Some write out a speech word for word, but in delivering a speech make an effort not to sound like they are reading. Here is an opportunity for you to practice the third approach.

DIRECTIONS: *Read the following excerpt from "The American Dream" to yourself several times. When you are convinced that you understand every word and every sentence, move on to thinking about how you want to present the speech orally. With a writing instrument (a marker or a pencil), mark up the speech to indicate where you want to (a) put emphasis; (b) speed up; (c) slow down; (d) pause; (e) speak loudly and authoritatively, (f) speak more quietly and casually; and so on. You can mark the text with words (for example, "speed up") or symbols (for example, a wavy line to show which words you want to emphasize, a vertical line to show where you want to stop and pause for a few seconds, two vertical lines to indicate where you want a longer pause). Finally, present the excerpt to your class. Afterward, ask for comments on the strengths and weaknesses of your presentation.*

Man's specific genius and technological ingenuity has dwarfed distance and placed time in chains. Jet planes have compressed into minutes distances that once took days and months to cover. It is not common for a preacher to be quoting Bob Hope, but I think he has aptly described this jet age in which we live. If, on taking off on a nonstop flight from Los Angeles to New York City, you develop hiccups, he said, you will hic in Los Angeles and cup in New York City. That is really *moving.* If you take a flight from Tokyo, Japan, on Sunday morning, you will arrive in Seattle, Washington, on the preceding Saturday night. When your friends meet you at the airport and ask you when you left Tokyo, you will have to say, "I left tomorrow." This is the kind of world in which we live. Now this is a bit humorous, but I am trying to laugh a basic fact into all of us: the world in which we live has become a single neighborhood.

Name _____ Date _____

Build Language Skills: Vocabulary

The Suffixes *-tion* and *-sion*

The suffixes *-tion* and *-sion* mean the act or process of doing something or the result of doing something. For example, the word *prediction* is formed when the suffix *-tion* is added to the verb *predict*. A prediction is the thing you predict. If you predict that there will be a full moon, then the moon is your *prediction*.

A. DIRECTIONS: *Complete each sentence by changing the underlined word to a word with the suffix -tion or -sion. The first one is done for you.*

1. I like to <u>create</u> collages using leaves and sticks.

   <u>My creation is a collage made of leaves and sticks.</u>

2. Bob will <u>decide</u> whether to go to Wisconsin or Michigan this weekend.

   Bob made a _____ to go to Wisconsin this weekend.

3. Luke knew he could <u>solve</u> the geometry problem.

   Luke figured out the _____ to the geometry problem.

4. I think Sarah will <u>conclude</u> that the chocolate cake is better than the pie.

   Sarah's _____ is that the chocolate cake is better than the pie.

Academic Vocabulary Practice

analyze	intention	establish	determine	achieve

B. DIRECTIONS: *Use an Academic Vocabulary word to complete each of the following sentence pairs.*

1. Dylan's plan was to finish his project on the weekend. It was Dylan's _____ to finish his project on the weekend.

2. Jill began to figure out the reasons for the misunderstanding. She started to _____ the reasons.

3. After Don started a regular practice schedule, his piano pieces improved. When Don practiced more piano he began to _____ better results.

4. Betsy told the twins to stand next to each other so she could decide who was taller. She wanted to _____ which twin was taller.

5. Jack decided to set up a new plan for distributing food. He worked to _____ a new plan.

Name _____ Date _____

from **Travels With Charley** by John Steinbeck
"The American Dream" by Martin Luther King, Jr.
Build Language Skills: Grammar

Reflexive Pronouns

A reflexive pronoun ends in *-self* or *-selves* and indicates that someone or something performs an action to, for, or upon itself. A reflexive pronoun points back to a noun or pronoun stated or implied earlier in the sentence.

He told *himself* to remember his algebra book. [points back to *He*]

Jacob wrote a poem about *himself*. [points back to *Jacob*]

My father said, "You should be generous to *yourself*." [points back to *You*]

My father said, "Be generous to *yourself*." [points back to an unstated *you*]

A reflexive pronoun is formed by adding the suffix *-self* or *-selves* to a personal pronoun.

my + self = myself	her + self = herself
our + selves = ourselves	him + self = himself
your + self = yourself	it + self = itself
your + selves = yourselves	them + selves = themselves

A. PRACTICE: *Write a reflexive pronoun on the line in each sentence below. Be sure that the pronoun is appropriate for the noun or pronoun to which it refers.*

1. Joanna forced _____ to eat the dried beets.

2. Jack and his friends wrote a play about _____.

3. My uncle put a note to _____ next to the phone to remember to call the doctor.

4. The dog barked _____ hoarse.

5. My teacher said, "Have confidence in _____."

6. Herbert hurt _____ climbing the barbed wire fence.

7. We wanted to try solving the problem by _____.

8. Janet repeated the lines to _____.

B. Writing Application: *Use each of the following reflexive pronouns in a complete sentence.*

1. myself _____

2. herself _____

3. ourselves _____

4. itself _____

5. yourself _____

"The American Dream" by Martin Luther King, Jr.
Selection Test A

Critical Reading *Identify the letter of the choice that best answers the question.*

____ 1. What historic document does King quote to express "the American dream"?
A. the Constitution of the United States
B. the Declaration of Independence
C. the Emancipation Proclamation
D. the Mayflower Compact

____ 2. How does King define the American dream?
A. Every person has a right to a job.
B. Each person should live in America.
C. All people have equal rights.
D. All people should have the right to vote.

____ 3. King wants readers to act morally for the good of all. What is King's goal called?
A. inspiration
B. a statement
C. author's purpose
D. author's opinion

____ 4. King repeats a story about traveling fast by airplane. What tone does King convey to readers through the story?
A. an angry tone
B. a logical tone
C. a serious tone
D. a humorous tone

____ 5. What is King's tone in the following sentence?
The American dream reminds us that every man is heir to the legacy of worthiness.

A. hope
B. irony
C. peace
D. despair

____ 6. Why does King describe how planes have made distances between countries seem smaller?
A. He is encouraging inventors to design even faster modes of travel.
B. He would like to see more people have the opportunity to travel.
C. He wants to make the point that the world has become like a neighborhood.
D. He wants to show his pride in American creativity.

Unit 1 Resources: Fiction and Nonfiction

____ 7. According to King, what must America eliminate to remain a "first-class nation"?

    A. politicians

    B. inventors

    C. second-class citizens

    D. third-class travel

____ 8. King says that Americans talk about personal freedom, but that they practiced slavery and segregation. What has a sociologist called this paradox, according to King?

    A. the American dilemma

    B. America's tragic past

    C. a blight on the nation

    D. universalism

____ 9. What does King say will make the American dream come true?

    A. making speeches

    B. learning about other cultures

    C. inventing more high-tech solutions

    D. thinking of everyone as brothers

____ 10. What does King fear will happen if Americans do not respond to his pleas to live in peace?

    A. We will be forced to go to war.

    B. We will perish as fools.

    C. Many people will leave the country.

    D. Neighborhoods will disappear.

____ 11. Which word does *not* describe King's style in "The American Dream"?

    A. direct

    B. serious

    C. educated

    D. uneducated

Vocabulary and Grammar

____ 12. Which of the following words is closest in meaning to *antithesis*?

    A. same

    B. opaque

    C. opposite

    D. separate

____ **13.** In which sentence is *devoid* used correctly?

   A. She filled devoid with ice cream.

   B. A desert is devoid of water.

   C. The movie was suspenseful and devoid.

   D. He asked the customer to devoid the sale.

____ **14.** In which sentence is a reflexive pronoun used *incorrectly*?

   A. You and myself are best friends.

   B. You wrote a note to yourself.

   C. I can get to the office myself.

   D. We baked the cake ourselves.

____ **15.** In which sentence is a reflexive pronoun used *incorrectly*?

   A. They gave themselves no time for lunch.

   B. I'm going to miss yourself when you go.

   C. Patrick taught himself to play the clarinet.

   D. Penny saw herself in the mirror.

Essay

16. Write a brief essay in which you explain what view, or opinion, King wants you to accept in "The American Dream." Then, tell whether you think King accomplished what he set out to do in this speech, and give examples to support your evaluation of the speech.

17. Write an essay in which you discuss King's explanation of how the world has become smaller. Then, decide whether or not you agree with King that a smaller world means we have more opportunities to treat other countries as "neighbors." Defend your opinion with specific reasons.

Name _____ Date _____

"**The American Dream**" by Martin Luther King, Jr.
Selection Test B

Critical Reading *Identify the letter of the choice that best answers the question.*

_____ 1. According to King, the American dream is that
   A. every person has equal rights, dignity, and worth.
   B. every person is exactly the same.
   C. some people are better than others and deserve more.
   D. human rights are granted by the state.

_____ 2. Why does King call America "a schizophrenic personality, tragically divided against herself"?
   A. Blacks and whites, Gentiles and Jews, and Protestants and Catholics are in conflict.
   B. Americans refuse to develop a world perspective.
   C. Americans have professed democracy yet have practiced the direct opposite.
   D. Many support technological advances, but many others oppose them.

_____ 3. What price does King say America will pay for treating people as "second-class citizens"?
   A. unemployment
   B. lower self-esteem
   C. higher taxes
   D. destruction

_____ 4. Which of the following is the view King wants Americans to accept?
   A. Distances are shorter.
   B. We are brothers.
   C. We are beyond the American dilemma.
   D. Quote Bob Hope when appropriate.

_____ 5. What does King mean when he refers to the "American dilemma"?
   A. helping industry but saving environments
   B. defining "American"
   C. claiming equality, but segregating races
   D. promising citizens too much

_____ 6. Why does King say that the world has become "a single neighborhood"?
   A. People respect one another.
   B. All people watch the same television shows.
   C. People can travel so quickly.
   D. People all over want to come to America.

_____ 7. Why does King refer to the Declaration and to the Founding Fathers?
   A. to ground himself in American history
   B. to quote a rhythmic passage
   C. to make his speech longer
   D. to move people to rewrite the document

_____ 8. King quotes this line from the Declaration of Independence:

We hold these truths to be self-evident, that all men are created equal, that they are endowed by their Creator with certain unalienable rights, that among these are life, liberty, and the pursuit of happiness.

Why does he choose this particular line?
A. The line promotes nonviolence.
B. The line is very recognizable.
C. The line is easy to remember.
D. The line stresses the equality of people.

_____ 9. The following sentence is a good example of King's style of writing and speaking.

The American dream will not become a reality devoid of the larger dream of a world of brotherhood and peace and good will.

Which word best describes up this style?
A. passionate
B. vague
C. illogical
D. clipped

_____ 10. Given his strong language about America's potential for change, what is King's purpose?
A. to persuade his audience to vote for him
B. to persuade people to act morally
C. to persuade immigrants to vote
D. to change the Constitution

_____ 11. What does King mention to introduce a lighter tone?
A. an original joke
B. a story told by Bob Hope
C. a story told by President Kennedy
D. a quotation from the Constitution

_____ 12. Which word best describes King's tone in the following sentence?

But the shape of the world today does not permit us the luxury of an anemic democracy.

A. ironic
B. hopeful
C. critical
D. despairing

_____ 13. What does King say Americans must do to make the American dream a reality?
A. see the world as a brotherhood
B. produce more ingenious inventions
C. travel to learn about other cultures
D. stop moving so quickly and work harder

____ 14. According to King, what principle separates totalitarian regimes from democratic governments?
   A. the right to vote in elections
   B. a belief in individual rights
   C. peace and brotherhood
   D. technology and ingenuity

____ 15. Whom does King credit as the "true saviors of democracy"?
   A. sightseers
   B. the writers of the Constitution
   C. those who bring justice to all citizens
   D. those who fight in America's wars

Vocabulary and Grammar

____ 16. What is the *antithesis* of freedom?
   A. liberty
   B. free
   C. slavery
   D. America

____ 17. Which sentence contains a reflexive pronoun?
   A. We gave the gift to her.
   B. She gave herself only five minutes to eat.
   C. Everyone enjoyed the speech.
   D. Will he make a contribution?

____ 18. What situation is *not* an example of exploitation?
   A. paying workers less than the job is worth
   B. taking advantage of one's good nature
   C. making false claims about a product
   D. paying an employee a fair salary

____ 19. Which of the words is a reflexive pronoun?
   A. himself
   B. him
   C. his
   D. self

Essay

20. Write a short essay summarizing King's opinion in "The American Dream." Explain how that opinion logically leads to his conclusion that "we must all learn to live together as brothers, or we will all perish together as fools."

21. Write an essay in which you agree or disagree with the views King expresses in "The American Dream." Begin by clearly stating your opinion about equality in America. Then, support your view with three or more pieces of evidence.

Vocabulary Warm-up Word Lists

Study these words from "Up the Slide" and "A Glow in the Dark." Then, complete the activities.

Word List A

ascent [uh SENT] *n.* act of climbing or rising
Our <u>ascent</u> up the mountain wasn't scary—if we didn't look down.

barren [BA ruhn] *adj.* bare; having no plant life
The desert was <u>barren</u> as far as we could see.

ebbed [EBD] *v.* faded little by little
The light, once so strong, had <u>ebbed</u> to just a faint glow.

firewood [FYR wood] *n.* wood to be burned on a fire
Because the cabin did not have central heating, we gathered <u>firewood</u>.

gully [GUHL ee] *n.* small, narrow valley
Between the two hills was a <u>gully</u> through which a stream flowed.

pose [POHZ] *v.* present; put forth
The roughness of the road did not <u>pose</u> a problem for our all-terrain vehicle.

pulse [PUHLS] *v.* move in a rhythmic way
The light was not steady; it seemed to <u>pulse</u> with a regular rhythm.

rig [RIG] *n.* a cart pulled by animals
The dogs did not seem to mind pulling the <u>rig</u> through the snow.

Word List B

consumed [kuhn SOOMD] *v.* used up completely
Getting ready for the ski slope <u>consumed</u> nearly half an hour.

convulsively [kuhn VUL siv lee] *adv.* with jerking and uncontrollable movements
As Tim started to fall, he <u>convulsively</u> grabbed for the railing.

eerie [EER ee] *adj.* strange or weird and frightening
The soundtrack set an <u>eerie</u> tone for the horror film.

favorable [FAY ver uh buhl] *adj.* helpful; likely to bring success
Because the winds were <u>favorable</u>, our boat reached land quickly.

nausea [NAW zee uh] *n.* sick feeling in the stomach
After eating ten hot dogs, Martin was overcome with <u>nausea</u>.

outcropping [OWT krahp ing] *n.* portion of a substance that sticks out from the surface
The <u>outcropping</u> of rock gave us something solid to hold on to as we climbed.

treacherous [TRECH er uhs] *adj.* extremely dangerous
The river's white water can become <u>treacherous</u>.

upright [UHP ryt] *adj.* standing or sitting straight up; vertical
Even in the darkness, we could make out the snowman's <u>upright</u> form.

Name _____ Date _____

Vocabulary Warm-up Exercises

Exercise A *Fill in each blank in the paragraph below with an appropriate word from Word List A. Use each word only once.*

The dogs pulling the [1] _____ were eager to race across the frozen,

[2] _____ land. Here, there were no forests to get lost in or even

any small trees to use as [3] _____ for a warm fire. This did not

[4] _____ a problem to Martin because he planned to reach the village

before dark. There were small rises in the land, but the [5] _____ caused

the team no difficulty. There were low areas, too, but nothing you could call even a

ditch, let alone a [6] _____. Martin must have figured the distance

wrong because now the sunlight [7] _____ and darkness closed in. As he

watched the stars appear and begin to [8] _____ in the sky, he felt confi-

dent that the dogs would get him to the village before long.

Exercise B *Decide whether each statement below is true or false. Circle T or F. Then, explain your answer.*

1. If your homework <u>consumed</u> ten minutes, then you did not spend enough time on it.
   T / F _____

2. An <u>outcropping</u> can be a <u>favorable</u> place for a mountain climber to get a grip.
   T / F _____

3. A nightlight with an <u>eerie</u> glow would comfort a young child.
   T / F _____

4. Extreme <u>nausea</u> can cause a person to throw up <u>convulsively</u>.
   T / F _____

5. A winter snowstorm can be <u>treacherous</u> to drive in.
   T / F _____

6. An <u>upright</u> sign is one that fell over because of high winds.
   T / F _____

Name _____ Date _____

"Up the Slide" by Jack London
"A Glow in the Dark" *from* Woodsong by Gary Paulsen
Reading Warm-up A

Read the following passage. Pay special attention to the underlined words. Then, read it again, and complete the activities. Use a separate sheet of paper for your written answers.

In 1896, three men found gold in a stream that emptied into the Klondike River in Canada's Yukon Territory. Newspapers ran stories about the fortune to be made.

In the summer of 1897, thousands of people seeking gold boarded ships in ports along the Pacific Coast and headed north. Little did they know that something had occurred that would <u>pose</u> a problem to their dreams of becoming rich. People before them had already staked their claim to most of the gold fields.

Do you have a picture in your mind of these gold seekers? Are they driving a team of dogs, hooked up to a <u>rig</u>? Are they on a frozen, <u>barren</u> landscape? That was not the reality. Many started out in summer. Their trip included the difficult <u>ascent</u> and descent of mountains. Treasure hunters had to carry a year's worth of gear on their backs, up and down the steep trails. Often, they had to prevent it, their pack animals, and themselves from falling down into a <u>gully</u>.

Those who made it to Dawson, the town near the gold fields, were not pleased to find they had come for nothing. People who sold supplies to would-be gold seekers, however, did well. They provided food, clothing, and medical care. Sawmills could barely keep up with the demand for lumber to build houses and for logs that would be used as <u>firewood</u>. Prices for everything rose steeply.

Within a year, nearly twenty thousand people had crowded into Dawson. Lights seemed to <u>pulse</u> like bright stars in the night from buildings where those who had struck gold spent it so fast it was like water trickling through their fingers. Those who had nothing to show for their efforts watched with envy. Soon, most of the disappointed adventurers packed up and went home. In time, the brilliance of the lights <u>ebbed</u>, and Dawson lost most of its residents. A chapter in gold rush history came to a close.

1. Circle the sentence that tells what would <u>pose</u> a problem to the gold seekers. Write about something that might *pose* a problem in your life.

2. Underline the words that help you picture a <u>rig</u>. Tell whether you would like to drive a dog *rig*.

3. Circle the word that gives you a clue to the meaning of <u>barren</u>. Write about an area of the world that is *barren*.

4. Underline the antonym for <u>ascent</u>. Tell what would be a difficult *ascent* for you.

5. Underline the words that help you figure out what a <u>gully</u> is. Describe a *gully* you know or that you can imagine.

6. Circle the two smaller, words in <u>firewood</u>. Describe a time when you might use *firewood*.

7. Circle the words that tell to what the lights that <u>pulse</u> are compared. Write about something else that would *pulse*.

8. Underline what <u>ebbed</u>. Explain what *ebbed* means.

Name _____   Date _____

"Up the Slide" by Jack London
"A Glow in the Dark" *from* Woodsong by Gary Paulsen
Reading Warm-up B

Read the following passage. Pay special attention to the underlined words. Then, read it again, and complete the activities. Use a separate sheet of paper for your written answers.

If you are ever hiking with a group in the dark woods, you might see an <u>eerie</u> light coming from a tree or a log. Neither of them is haunted; it is only foxfire—wild mushrooms that are glowing with their own natural light.

As you draw closer, you will be able to see an <u>outcropping</u> of mushrooms on an <u>upright</u> tree. On a fallen log, you may see the mushrooms growing on both the outside and the inside of the dying wood.

Unlike plants, mushrooms—which belong to a group of living things called *fungi*—do not make their own food. They get it from other living things. Sometimes mushrooms can grow on a tree without destroying it; sometimes they eat away at it until it dies. Other times, the tree is already dying, and the mushroom helps it break down, or decay.

Why do mushrooms glow? They probably shine at night to attract insects. Then, the insects brush up against the mushrooms or eat them, picking up spores, which are the part of the mushroom that makes new mushrooms. It is <u>favorable</u> to the mushroom to spread its spores, and flying insects can help out.

Some mushrooms that glow in the dark are edible, including the honey mushroom. Just because you can eat it, however, does not mean it tastes good. Another mushroom, the jack-o'-lantern, is poisonous. Its bright color and attractive appearance mask the fact that it is <u>treacherous</u> to pick and eat. You should never pick any wild mushroom without an expert's OK.

People who eat a jack-o'-lantern mushroom do not die but become very sick. They will feel great <u>nausea</u> in their stomachs and throw up <u>convulsively</u>.

So, if you ever "see the light" of a mushroom, walk up to it and snap a picture, but do not take it home for dinner. Still, don't feel that the hike has <u>consumed</u> your time for nothing. You can always buy mushrooms at the store and know that they are safe to eat.

1. Circle the word in the next sentence that suggests the meaning of <u>eerie</u>. Describe something *eerie* that you have seen.

2. Rewrite the sentence beginning, "As you draw closer," using different words for <u>outcropping</u> and <u>upright</u>. Do not change the meaning of the sentence.

3. Circle the words that hint at what <u>favorable</u> means. Write about something that is *favorable* to you.

4. Underline the word in the paragraph that suggests the meaning of <u>treacherous</u>. Tell about something *treacherous* that you know of.

5. Underline the words in the paragraph that help explain <u>nausea</u> and <u>convulsively</u>. Tell what else might make someone feel *nausea* and throw up *convulsively*.

6. Circle the word that tells what was <u>consumed</u>. Tell about a situation in your life that *consumed* this thing.

Unit 1 Resources: Fiction and Nonfiction

"Up the Slide" by Jack London
"A Glow in the Dark" *from* **Woodsong** by Gary Paulsen

Literary Analysis: Fictional and Nonfictional Narratives

A **narrative** is any type of writing that tells a story. In a **fictional narrative,** the author tells a story about imaginary characters and events. "Up the Slide" is a fictional narrative. Because it does not describe real events, the author had complete control over the basic story elements of *character, setting,* and *plot.*

In a **nonfictional narrative,** such as "A Glow in the Dark," the author tells a story about real characters and events. The author of this work describes an event that actually happened to him. Although he cannot alter any of the details, he does emphasize some of them to give the story a kind of excitement.

DIRECTIONS: *Read each passage, and answer the questions that follow.*

from "Up the Slide" by Jack London

> For, coming up from the Siwash village the previous day, he [Clay] had noticed a small dead pine in an out-of-the-way place, which had defied discovery by eyes less sharp than his. And his eyes were both young and sharp, for his seventeenth birthday was just cleared.
>
> A swift ten minutes over the ice brought him to the place, and figuring ten minutes to get the tree and ten minutes to return made him certain that Swanson's dinner would not wait.
>
> Just below Dawson, and rising out of the Yukon itself, towered the great Moosehide Mountain, so named by Lieutenant Schwatka long ere the Yukon became famous.

1. Which elements of this fictional narrative did the author make up? Identify two.

   _____

2. Which details did the author borrow from real life? Identify two. _____

   _____

from "A Glow in the Dark" by Gary Paulsen

> They were caught in the green light, curved around my legs staring at the standing form, ears cocked and heads turned sideways while they studied it. I took another short step forward and they all followed me, then another, and they stayed with me until we were right next to the form.
>
> It was a stump.
>
> A six-foot-tall, old rotten stump with the bark knocked off, glowing in the dark with a bright green glow. Impossible. . . . I found out later that it glowed because it had sucked phosphorus from the ground up into the wood and held the light from day all night.

3. What detail provides a clue that this is a nonfictional narrative? _____

   _____

   What kind of detail is this? _____

4. What details give the narrative a fictional feel? Why? _____

   _____

Name _____   Date _____

Vocabulary Builder

A. DIRECTIONS: *Complete each sentence in a way that proves you know the meaning of the italicized word.*

1. When we completed our *ascent,* _____
   _____

2. _____ requires great *exertion.*

3. It is difficult to *sustain* _____
   _____

4. The upward-facing lampshade *diffused* _____
   _____

5. Before our *descent,* _____
   _____

6. Using a careful *maneuver,* _____
   _____

B. DIRECTIONS: *Circle the letter of the word or phrase that is most nearly* opposite *in meaning to the word in CAPITAL LETTERS.*

1. ASCENT
   A. flight
   B. leap
   C. descent
   D. tumble

2. SUSTAIN
   A. let go
   B. strengthen
   C. reject
   D. maintain

3. DIFFUSED
   A. confused
   B. weakened
   C. diluted
   D. condensed

4. MANEUVER
   A. manipulate
   B. bumble
   C. trick
   D. stunt

Name _____ Date _____

"Up the Slide" by Jack London
"A Glow in the Dark" *from* **Woodsong** by Gary Paulsen
Support for Writing to Compare Use of Details in Narratives

Before you draft your essay comparing and contrasting the use of details in these narratives, complete the graphic organizers below. First, list details that reveal aspects of each character. Then, tell specifically what each detail reveals about the character. Finally, discuss how the details affect your view of the character and his challenges.

Clay Dilham in "Up the Slide"	
Invented Details	**What They Reveal About the Character**
How do these details affect your view of the character's challenge?	

Gary Paulsen in "A Glow in the Dark"	
True Details	**What They Reveal About the Character**
How do these details affect your view of the character's challenges?	

Now, use your notes to write an essay comparing and contrasting the use of details in the two narratives.

Name _____ Date _____

"Up the Slide" by Jack London
"A Glow in the Dark" *from* **Woodsong** by Gary Paulsen
Selection Test A

Critical Reading *Identify the letter of the choice that best answers the question.*

____ 1. Which word best describes Clay at the beginning of "Up the Slide"?
    A. playful
    B. confident
    C. fearful
    D. wise

____ 2. Based on the events of "Up the Slide," how long did Clay's trip take?
    A. about thirty minutes
    B. two days
    C. more than two hours
    D. ten minutes

____ 3. Which detail in "Up the Slide" comes from real life?
    A. the Yukon River
    B. Clay's climb
    C. Clay's slide down the slope
    D. Swanson

____ 4. In "Up the Slide," what does Swanson believe?
    A. Firewood is plentiful and easily found.
    B. Clay is a stronger, braver man than he.
    C. Traveling to the Yukon was a huge mistake.
    D. Clay will not return as quickly as he predicts.

____ 5. In "Up the Slide," what does Clay do with the tree after he cuts it down?
    A. He uses it to build a fire.
    B. He sells it for firewood.
    C. He leaves it on the mountain.
    D. He uses it to build a shelter.

____ 6. In "A Glow in the Dark," why does Paulsen run his dogs at night without a light?
    A. to improve the dogs' eyesight
    B. because he has an emergency
    C. because his headlight goes out
    D. to get away from the glow

____ 7. In "A Glow in the Dark," what do Paulsen's actions *after* he sees the glow tell the reader?

    A. He is curious.

    B. He is foolish.

    C. He is confident.

    D. He is cowardly.

____ 8. In "A Glow in the Dark," what does the strange shape turn out to be?

    A. a dog

    B. moonlight

    C. a lantern

    D. a tree stump

____ 9. What phrase best describes "A Glow in the Dark"?

    A. a fictional story about phosphorus

    B. a fictional story about a frightening event

    C. a nonfiction piece about the danger of traveling at night

    D. a nonfiction piece about an event in the author's life

____ 10. Which word best describes both Clay of "Up the Slide" and the narrator of "A Glow in the Dark" at the end of the stories?

    A. afraid

    B. relieved

    C. puzzled

    D. regretful

____ 11. What is true of Clay Dilham in "Up the Slide" and Gary Paulsen in "A Glow in the Dark"?

    A. They both exist in real life.

    B. They are both writers.

    C. They both travel by sled.

    D. They are both loggers.

____ 12. What is true of a fictional narrative such as "Up the Slide"?

    A. It can borrow details from real life.

    B. It must contain only facts.

    C. It cannot tell a story.

    D. It must contain only made-up details.

___ **13.** Despite differences between "Up the Slide" and "A Glow in the Dark," what is true of both works?

   A. They are both speeches.

   B. The both deal with mysteries.

   C. They are both adventure tales.

   D. They are both written in the third person.

Vocabulary

___ **14.** In "Up the Slide," where does Clay Dilham go on his *descent*?

   A. up the slide   C. into a river

   B. around rocks   D. down a mountain

___ **15.** To approach the strange glow, what does Gary Paulsen have to *sustain*?

   A. his dogs   C. his fear

   B. his courage   D. his sled

Essay

16. A character's actions and decisions tell a great deal about his or her personality. In an essay, identify two actions or decisions made by the main character of "Up the Slide" and two actions or decisions by the narrator of "A Glow in the Dark." What does each action or decision tell you about the character? Which character do you find more likable? Why?

17. In a short essay, explain the difference between a fictional narrative and a nonfictional one. How can one type of narrative resemble the other? Give examples from both "Up the Slide" and "A Glow in the Dark" to illustrate your ideas.

Name _____ Date _____

"Up the Slide" by Jack London
"A Glow in the Dark" *from* Woodsong by Gary Paulsen
Selection Test B

Critical Reading *Identify the letter of the choice that best completes the statement or answers the question.*

____ 1. Which word best describes Clay's attitude toward his mission in "Up the Slide"?
A. confident
B. vengeful
C. negative
D. insecure

____ 2. In "Up the Slide," why has the tree Clay discovers escaped the eyes of others?
A. It is covered by a thick blanket of snow.
B. It is hidden by thick cloud cover.
C. It is in an area patrolled around the clock by soldiers.
D. Its gray color blends with the surrounding rock.

____ 3. Based on the information in "Up the Slide," a reader can conclude that Clay's venture took
A. less than thirty minutes.
B. less than an hour.
C. more than two hours.
D. just under two hours.

____ 4. Which aspect of Clay's character is revealed in this passage from "Up the Slide"?
Fully ten minutes passed ere he could master these sensations and summon sufficient strength for the weary climb. His legs hurt him and he was limping, and he was conscious of a sore place in his back, where he had fallen on the ax.

A. pride
B. cowardice
C. eagerness
D. determination

____ 5. In "Up the Slide," the act of felling the tree turns out to be
A. very time consuming.
B. easy.
C. impossible.
D. difficult.

____ 6. The author of "Up the Slide" borrowed which story element from real life?
A. the setting
B. the main character
C. the plot
D. the conclusion

_____ 7. In "A Glow in the Dark," why is Paulsen running his dogs?
A. to keep them warm
B. to get to the nearest town
C. to train them
D. to get away from the glow

_____ 8. In "A Glow in the Dark," Paulsen's actions *after* he sees the glowing form show that he is
A. less brave than readers are first led to believe.
B. more curious than afraid.
C. less adventuresome than readers are first led to believe.
D. more afraid than curious.

_____ 9. The mysterious green form in "A Glow in the Dark" turns out to be
A. a rock.
B. the Northern Lights.
C. a lantern.
D. a tree stump.

_____ 10. Read this passage from "A Glow in the Dark."

> Two more steps, then one more, leaning to see around the corner and at last I saw it and when I did it was worse.
>
> It was a form. Not human. A large, standing form glowing in the dark. . . .
>
> I felt my heart slam up into my throat.

Which of the following descriptions of the passage is most accurate?
A. a nonfictional passage with details that make it seem fictional
B. a fictional passage about something strange that occurs in nature
C. a fictional passage with details make it seem nonfictional
D. a nonfictional passage about a fictional event

_____ 11. Which is *not* true of a fictional narrative?
A. The author may invent characters, settings, and plots.
B. Some of its details can be borrowed from real life.
C. The author may only tell about real people and events.
D. It is usually told in chronological order.

_____ 12. Which word best describes both Clay Dilham of "Up the Slide" and Gary Paulsen of "A Glow in the Dark" at the end of the narratives?
A. desperate
B. self-critical
C. remorseful
D. relieved

_____ 13. How are both "Up the Slide" and "A Glow in the Dark" organized?
A. They present the most important idea first.
B. They move back and forth in time.
C. They do not follow a set pattern.
D. They are told in time order.

____ **14.** Which phrase best describes "Up the Slide" and "A Glow in the Dark"?
   A. narrative essays
   B. first-person narratives
   C. adventure stories
   D. science fiction

____ **15.** In what way are fictional and nonfictional narratives alike?
   A. They can both have conflict.
   B. They both use made-up characters.
   C. They are both factual.
   D. They always have flashbacks.

Vocabulary

____ **16.** In "Up the Slide," during his *ascent*, Clay Dilham must go
   A. up the slide.
   B. down the mountain.
   C. into the gully.
   D. around the rock outcropping.

____ **17.** To accomplish his goal, Clay Dilham in "Up the Slide" has to use a complicated
   A. exertion.
   B. maneuver.
   C. descent.
   D. sustain.

____ **18.** Smoke might be *diffused* by
   A. batteries.
   B. the sun's rays.
   C. the wind.
   D. water.

____ **19.** To win the Iditarod or any other sled race, the dogs must put forth great
   A. exertion.
   B. sustain.
   C. descent.
   D. maneuver.

Essay

20. Facing danger can reveal a great deal about someone's personality. What is revealed about Clay Dilham in "Up the Slide" and Gary Paulsen in "A Glow in the Dark" by the danger each faces? Do you think the two men are admirable or foolish? Write your answer in a brief essay, and support your opinions with examples from the text.

21. In an essay, define *narrative*. Then, tell whether "Up the Slide" is a fictional or a nonfictional narrative and whether "A Glow in the Dark" is fictional or nonfictional. What elements make each story fictional or nonfictional? What elements does each story borrow from the other type of narrative?

Name _____ Date _____

Narration: Autobiographical Essay

Prewriting: Gathering Details

Once you have chosen your topic—the event from your life that you would like to narrate—list details that will help in your writing. Use the following chart. Spend about three minutes listing words and phrases that apply to each heading.

People	Time	Place	Events	Emotions

Drafting: Ordering Events

Use the graphic organizer below to organize the events of your narrative around the conflict.

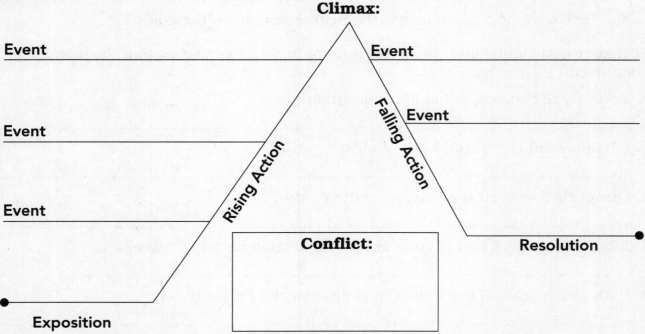

Climax: _____

Event _____   Event _____

Event _____   Event _____

Rising Action   Falling Action

Event _____

Conflict: _____

Resolution

Exposition

Writing Workshop—Unit 1, Part 2

Autobiographical Essay: Integrating Grammar Skills

Revising for Pronoun-Antecedent Agreement

A **pronoun** is a word that stands for a noun or another pronoun. An **antecedent** is the word or group of words for which the pronoun stands. Pronouns should agree with their antecedents in person and number.

Person	Singular in Number	Plural in Number
First person	I paid for *my* ticket, so please send it to *me*.	We ate *our* dinner when the waitress served it to us.
Second person	Simon, who gave that to *you*?	Girls, would *you* like some dessert?
Third person	Sara said *she* might be late because *her* watch was lost.	The boys brought *their* swimsuits so *they* could play in the pool.

An antecedent can be an **indefinite pronoun.** Indefinite pronouns vary in their number: some are always singular, some are always plural, and some can be either.

Indefinite Pronouns		
Singular: another, anyone, anything, either, everybody, everything, little, much, one, nothing, other, somebody	**Plural:** both, few, many, others, several	**Either:** all, any, more, most, none, some

A. DIRECTIONS: *Underline each pronoun, and draw an arrow to its antecedent.*

1. Raul runs daily because he wants to compete next year in ninth grade.
2. Daniel lifts weights for his workout.
3. Bethany and I do 15 push-ups as part of our exercise routine.
4. Ms. Deavers said that some did their exercises, but others didn't.

B. DIRECTIONS: *On the lines provided, rewrite these sentences so that the pronouns agree with their antecedents.*

1. Several are running in his first marathon.

_____

2. Lilianna said she would bring their own water.

_____

3. One of the boys left their towel on the ground.

_____

4. All of the runners had to turn in his registration forms last week.

_____

5. Both girls sprained her ankles sprinting for the finish line.

_____

Name _____ Date _____

Spelling Workshop—Unit 1
Commonly Misspelled Words

Research has shown that **words commonly misspelled by students** are not necessarily hard words. They are everyday words that students have just never learned to spell correctly. Make sure you know how to spell all the words on this list.

Word List

beginning	especially	friends	really	we're
caught	favorite	happened	they're	weird

A. DIRECTIONS: *Write the word from the Word List that matches each clue.*

1. actually and truly   _____

2. took place   _____

3. the one you like best   _____

4. captured   _____

5. contraction for "we are"   _____

6. the start of something   _____

7. strange and unusual   _____

8. people you like a lot   _____

9. contraction for "they are"   _____

10. particularly   _____

B. DIRECTIONS: *Write three sentences about each topic below. Use every list word at least once.*

1. a movie you particularly like

   _____

   _____

   _____

2. a strange event

   _____

   _____

   _____

3. why you get along well with certain people

   _____

   _____

   _____

Communications Workshop—Unit 1
Effective Listening and Note-Taking

After choosing two television interviews to watch, fill out the following chart to complete the note-taking activity.

Topics of interviews: 1. _____

2. _____

What are some of the main points and suporting details of the interview? 1. 2.
What is the purpose of the interview? 1. 2.
What perspective does the subject of the interview have on the topic? 1. 2.
Does the subject of the interview offer enough facts to support the main point? Why or why not? 1. 2.
Do you agree with these ideas? Why or why not? 1. 2.

For Further Reading—Unit 1

DIRECTIONS: *Think about the books you have read. Then, on a separate sheet of paper, answer the discussion questions and take notes for your Literature Circle.*

Why We Can't Wait by Martin Luther King, Jr.

Discussion Give three reasons to explain why 1963 was a "breaking point" for African Americans.

Connections—Literature Circle Why do you think the civil rights movement was so effective? How might it have been different if it had not adopted the philosophy of nonviolent resistance?

Rules of the Road by Joan Bauer

Discussion What is the main **external conflict** in this story? What **internal conflict** does Jenna face in this story? How has Jenna's father affected her life?

Connections—Literature Circle Jenna says, "It's funny the things we hold onto from our parents and the things we leave behind. What do you think Jenna will take from her father? What things do you think she will leave behind?

Woodsong by Gary Paulsen

Discussion Paulsen describes the personalities of the different dogs. Why do you think he mentions the dogs' personalities? What does Paulsen see as the differences between dogs and humans? What might be his feelings about these differences?

Connections—Literature Circle Paulsen sees a change that he went through about finishing the race. What is the change he goes through? What has he learned about himself that causes this change?

Adventures of Huckleberry Finn by Mark Twain

Discussion One of the **themes** of this story is that slavery is brutal and inhumane. What event supports this theme?

Connections—Literature Circle Use examples from this work, other literature, history, science, and your own experience to support your ideas during discussion. Why do you think Huck feels he is doing wrong in helping Jim escape? Why does he decide to do it?

Unit 1: Fiction and Nonfiction
Part 2 Benchmark Test 2

MULTIPLE CHOICE

Reading Skill: Author's Purpose

1. In a detective story or mystery, what is usually the author's main purpose?
   A. to entertain readers with an interesting puzzle
   B. to inform readers about police procedures
   C. to describe the appearance of a crime scene
   D. to persuade readers that crime does not pay

2. For which type of writing is the author's main purpose usually to persuade readers to think or act in a certain way?
   A. biography and autobiography
   B. nonfiction travel writing
   C. newspaper editorial
   D. magazine articles

3. Which of these most often signals writing that is written to inform the reader?
   A. highly emotional language
   B. images and figurative language
   C. interesting characters and situations
   D. facts and technical language

4. For which type of writing is it most important to question the author's statements?
   A. persuasion
   B. description
   C. explanation
   D. narration

Read this selection. Then, answer the questions that follow.

When I was a young man, I worked as an extra in Hollywood. Once, I worked on a film called *Spartacus* about a slave revolt in ancient Rome. I had to arrive at the Hollywood sound stage wearing my toga at five A.M. each morning. It was so early, I wore my watch to make sure I got there on time. During shooting one day, I forgot to take off my watch. No one on the set noticed, and no one noticed it later when they were making the final cut of the film. So if you ever see *Spartacus*, look for the Roman slave wearing a modern wrist watch. That fellow would be me.

5. What is the main purpose of this selection?
   A. to inform
   B. to entertain
   C. to explain
   D. to persuade

6. What is the specific purpose of this selection?
   A. to inform the reader about the difficulties in making a film that is set in the past
   B. to convince the reader to see the film *Spartacus*
   C. to share the writer's interesting and amusing experiences as an extra in films
   D. to explain the process by which a person can become an extra in films

7. What type of detail most clearly points to the main purpose of the selection?
   A. the technical language
   B. the factual information
   C. the reasons for the author's behavior
   D. the surprising event at the end

Read the selection from a magazine article. Then, answer the questions that follow.

Snoring: Comical Ailment or Serious Symptom?

Snoring is often the subject of comedy, but it can be more serious than most people realize. Sometimes it is a sign of obstructive sleep apnea, a medical condition in which the upper air passages narrow during sleep because of the combined effect of a blockage, relaxing muscles, and gravity. As the air passages narrow, breathing lessens, the oxygen level in the blood drops, and the patient snores to try to get more air. When the throat tissues collapse further, the patient stops breathing altogether, at which point he or she awakens, regains control of the throat muscles, and begins breathing normally. The patient then falls back asleep, but the cycle repeats throughout the night. In fact, a patient suffering from severe sleep apnea may awaken more than a hundred times a night. In most cases, since the patient awakens only partially, he or she is unaware of what is happening.

8. What seems to be the main purpose of this magazine article?
   A. to entertain
   B. to inform
   C. to narrate
   D. to persuade

9. Which phrase best describes the attitude of the magazine article's author?
   A. humorous and witty
   B. technical and informative
   C. serious and sad
   D. tense and frightening

10. Imagine that you are doing a science report on snoring. What is the first thing you should do when you come across this magazine article?
    A. Preview it to see if it will be a useful source of information.
    B. Take detailed notes on the information that it supplies.
    C. Compare it to another article on the subject to see which is longer.
    D. Summarize the article in language that you can understand.

Literary Analysis: Mood, Tone, and Author's Style

11. In a discussion of literature, to what does the term *mood* refer?
    A. the author's attitude toward his or her subject or audience
    B. the attitude or feelings that each character expresses
    C. the time and place in which the work happens
    D. the feeling or atmosphere that the work creates for the reader

12. In a discussion of literature, to what does the term *tone* refer?
    A. the author's attitude toward his or her subject and audience
    B. the loudness or softness of the dialogue that characters speak
    C. the polished literary style that some authors display
    D. the feeling or atmosphere that the work creates for the readers

13. Which of these details are most likely to contribute to the mood of a story?
    A. the title and the events
    B. the characters and the ending
    C. the images and the setting
    D. the characters and the dialogue

Read this selection from a short story. Then, answer the questions that follow.

A cold wind raked across the barren moor and night was beginning to set in when we reached our final destination. The horses' hooves beat a steady drum as the carriage proceeded up the sweeping length of the driveway. At last we came to a stop in front of a crumbling mansion. One light shined brightly near an upper window, but the rest of the house was in inky darkness.

14. Which phrase best describes the mood of the selection?
    A. sad and mournful
    B. bleak and eerie
    C. angry and resentful
    D. charming and whimsical

15. Which of these images from the selection most clearly contributes to the mood?
    A. the cold wind raking across the moor
    B. the steady drum of the horses' hooves
    C. the sweeping length of the driveway
    D. the light shining in an upper window

16. Which of these words from the selection most clearly contribute to the mood?
    A. *cold, final,* and *steady*
    B. *sweeping, brightly,* and *inky*
    C. *final, crumbling,* and *brightly*
    D. *barren, crumbling,* and *inky*

17. Based on the selection, which of these qualities seems characteristic of the author's style?
   A. a highly emotional tone
   B. fairly long sentences
   C. lack of imagery
   D. frequent use of slang

Literary analysis: Fictional and Nonfictional Narratives

18. Which of these elements must a narrative contain?
   A. plot
   B. dialogue
   C. figurative language
   D. fictional characters

19. Which type of writing is a nonfiction narrative?
   A. a novel
   B. a biography
   C. a stage drama
   D. a poem that tells a story

Read this selection from a nonfiction narrative. Then, answer the questions that follow.

Aaron and I had hiked quite a distance and were tired when we made camp. By the time dinner was over, we were more than ready for bed. Because of our exhaustion, we did not clean up properly. I should have known better than to leave food around in Yellowstone Park at night. At any rate, some time during the night, I was awakened by a noise. Glancing over, I saw a big, dark shape in the dim light. Blinking my eyes, I realized it was a grizzly bear. The leftovers we had foolishly left near camp had attracted the menacing beast! Deeply afraid, I remained very still and hoped that Aaron would do the same. I breathed a sigh of relief when the bear went lumbering off into the night.

20. How would you describe the mood of this nonfiction narrative?
   A. lighthearted and humorous
   B. sad and sentimental
   C. tense and exciting
   D. serious and unemotional

21. In what way does this nonfiction narrative borrow from the elements of fictional narratives?
   A. It includes invented characters and events.
   B. It resets the events in an imaginary setting.
   C. It emphasizes certain details to add excitement.
   D. It uses chronological order to recount events.

Vocabulary

22. How does the suffix *-ize* or *-yze* affect the word or root to which it is attached?
    A. It changes the word or root into a verb.
    B. It changes the word or root into an adjective.
    C. It changes the word or root into a noun.
    D. It makes the word or root have an opposite meaning.

23. Which of these words is generally used as a noun?
    A. invent
    B. inventive
    C. reinvent
    D. invention

24. In this sentence, what does the word in italics mean?

    The potters will *individualize* each mug by putting a different design on the handle.

    A. people who show unique qualities
    B. to make special or appropriate to each person
    C. to turn something into something else
    D. special; unique

Grammar

25. What is the case of the personal pronoun in this sentence?

    The tune is borrowed, but the words are mine.

    A. nominative
    B. objective
    C. possessive
    D. reflexive

26. What is the complete antecedent of the pronoun *ourselves* in this sentence?

    Since the train was nearly empty, Yvonne and I had a whole car to ourselves.

    A. Yvonne
    B. I
    C. Yvonne and I
    D. train and car

27. Which sentences uses pronouns correctly?
    A. The boys tried to take care of the problem themselves.
    B. Alyson and myself went to the computer store.
    C. You students should do yourself a favor and study more.
    D. No one but myself understood the situation.

28. Which of these sentences uses pronouns correctly?
    A. Each of the girls had their own bicycle.
    B. All of the girls had her own bicycle.
    C. Both of the girls had their own bicycle.
    D. Few of the girls had her own bicycle.

Spelling

29. Which word is spelled correctly?
    A. allways
    B. agravate
    C. bussiness
    D. career

30. In which sentence is the italicized word spelled correctly?
    A. Mom's birthday is an important *occassion* at our house.
    B. *Parallell* lines run side-by-side and never meet.
    C. They took *possession* of the house last Tuesday.
    D. I am waiting *untill* six o'clock before I turn the soup on.

31. What should you do to spell the italic word in this sentence correctly?

    I hope that you will *reccommend* me for this job.

    A. Drop one of the *c*'s only.
    B. Drop one of the *m*'s only.
    C. Drop one *c* and one *m*.
    D. Leave the word alone; it is correct as is.

ESSAY

Writing

32. Think of something that happened to you that changed your view of someone or something. Then, on a separate piece of paper, write a brief personal narrative about the incident.

33. Think about a situation in your school that you think could be improved. Then, on a separate piece of paper, write an observations-journal entry about the situation. Indicate the problem and your ideas about the solution.

34. Recall an incident in your life that you think others would find entertaining or interesting to read about. Then, on a separate piece of paper, write a brief autobiographical essay about the incident. Tell what happened, how you felt at the time, and why the experience has made an impression on you.

ANSWERS

from *The Baker Heater League*
by Patricia C. and Fredrick McKissack
"The 11:59" by Patricia C. McKissack

Vocabulary Warm-up Exercises, p. 2

A. 1. communication
2. courtesy
3. powerful
4. performance
5. loyalty
6. shattering
7. individual
8. customary

B. Sample Answers

1. False. A <u>hostile</u> environment is unfriendly, which would not make visitors feel comfortable.
2. True. Folk tales are known for their exaggerated versions of heroic <u>exploits</u>, but they are still passed down, creating <u>legacies</u>.
3. True. In the 1950s, space travel seemed like a wild idea.
4. False. A <u>storyteller</u> is named that because he or she tells stories rather than reading them.
5. True. The <u>predictions</u> of Y2K occurred before the turn of the millennium.
6. False. Swimmers are <u>competing</u> against the clock and would never waste time.
7. False. Something <u>erupts</u> only when it bursts; a pimple that erupts would be visible.

Reading Warm-up A, p. 3

Words that students are to circle appear in parentheses.

Sample Answers

1. <u>seemed to shrink</u>; *Powerful* means "strong or mighty."
2. (5:00 A.M.); *Customary* means "usual."
3. <u>too lonely to live</u>; My favorite *communication* channels are writing and talking face-to-face.
4. (Thoughts like these); *Shattering* means "breaking apart."
5. <u>even when the rudest people would holler at him about ticket prices or schedules</u>; *Courtesy* includes using kind words and helping others in need.
6. When Rosa Parks refused to give up her bus seat, her *individual* action made a lot of difference in the world.
7. <u>taking pride in yourself and in your own efforts</u>; Job *loyalty* means doing your best on the job to help a company reach its goals.
8. (daily excellence); *Performance* means "an action that has been completed."

Reading Warm-up B, p. 4

Words that students are to circle appear in parentheses.

Sample Answers

1. <u>back-breaking work in the face of great hardships</u>; *Legacy* means "something handed down from previous generations."
2. The natural obstacles were more *hostile* because they could not be reasoned with like people.
3. (anyone who said the idea of a Transcontinental Railroad was nothing but a crazy dream); I *scoffed* when my little brother said that I couldn't learn a difficult skateboarding trick.
4. <u>to lay the most track the most quickly</u>; Track stars are always *competing* against the clock as well as against other runners.
5. (produced 10 miles of track in 12 hours); Since *erupted* is used to describe something that bursts, the word *spurt* matches the meaning.
6. Many people viewed the building of a Transcontinental Railroad as an impossible idea, and so they *predicted* it would never happen.
7. <u>heroic deeds and efforts</u>; A good *storyteller* likes to hold people's attention, so he or she will often choose to exaggerate details in describing the exploits of story heroes.

Patricia C. McKissack

Listening and Viewing, p. 5

Sample Answers and Guidelines for Evaluation

Segment 1. Patricia and Fredrick McKissack discuss ideas together, get feedback from each other, and often take trips while on vacation in order to get ideas and information for stories. Students may suggest that writing with a coauthor encourages greater productivity: two people can work together to gather information, brainstorm ideas, and edit each other's work.

Segment 2. Patricia C. McKissack includes real details in her fiction to convince the reader that the story is really happening. Students may suggest that the "tick-tock" is a device that intensifies the tension in the story and draws in the reader.

Segment 3. Patricia and Fredrick first discuss ideas. Fredrick gathers information by researching. Patricia then types up an outline for the chapters and adds the information to the story; Fredrick revises her writing and digs up interesting facts to add detail to a draft. Students may suggest that brainstorming, outlining, researching, drafting, or revising are important stages because they all contribute to the complete book.

Segment 4. Patricia C. McKissack believes that writing allows writers to interpret an idea in many different ways, show their personalities, and discuss their interests. Students may agree that writing is a good form of self-expression because it allows them to express their opinions and interests to others.

Learning About Fiction and Nonfiction, p. 6

1. fiction; 2. nonfiction; 3. nonfiction; 4. nonfiction;
5. fiction

"The 11:59" by Patricia C. McKissack

Model Selection: Fiction, p. 7

Sample Answers

1. Lester hears the whistle of the 11:59, but does not want to die.
2. stubbornness, creativity
3. Lester's stubbornness makes him want to avoid death. His creativity helps him to devise a plan to try to avoid death.
4. Resolution—Lester dies of a heart attack at 11:59 P.M.

from *The Baker Heater League*
by Patricia and Fredrick McKissack

Model Selection: Nonfiction, p. 8

Sample Answers

1. John Henry. He was a steel-driver.
2. Fact 1. In about 1870, he joined the West Virginia steel-driving team hired to dig out the Big Bend Tunnel for the C. & O. Railroad. Fact 2. He was six feet tall and weighed 200 pounds.
3. The authors include both facts and legends because they want to inform readers about early railroad heroes, and because they want to entertain readers with tall tales.

"The 11:59" by Patricia C. McKissack
from *The Baker Heater League*
by Patricia and Fredrick McKissack

Selection Test A, p. 9

Learning About Fiction and Nonfiction

1. ANS: A	DIF: Easy	OBJ: Literary Analysis
2. ANS: D	DIF: Easy	OBJ: Literary Analysis
3. ANS: C	DIF: Easy	OBJ: Literary Analysis
4. ANS: D	DIF: Easy	OBJ: Literary Analysis
5. ANS: B	DIF: Easy	OBJ: Literary Analysis

Critical Reading

6. ANS: B	DIF: Easy	OBJ: Interpretation
7. ANS: C	DIF: Easy	OBJ: Comprehension
8. ANS: D	DIF: Easy	OBJ: Interpretation
9. ANS: D	DIF: Easy	OBJ: Literary Analysis
10. ANS: A	DIF: Easy	OBJ: Comprehension
11. ANS: A	DIF: Easy	OBJ: Literary Analysis
12. ANS: C	DIF: Easy	OBJ: Comprehension
13. ANS: D	DIF: Easy	OBJ: Literary Analysis
14. ANS: B	DIF: Easy	OBJ: Interpretation
15. ANS: C	DIF: Easy	OBJ: Literary Analysis

Essay

16. Students should note that in "The 11:59," Lester entertains the porters by telling the story of the Death Train. According to this story, any porter who hears the whistle of the 11:59 has only twenty-four hours to live. When Lester himself hears the whistle, he attempts to avoid death, but the 11:59 comes for him anyway—and he ends up "living" the story he loved to tell.

Difficulty: *Easy*

Objective: *Essay*

17. Students should tell about either Casey Jones, John Henry, or Daddy Jones. They should describe particular feats attributed to the hero, and should identify special qualities such as strength, loyalty, bravery, or resourcefulness. Students should observe that, like modern-day superheroes, the railroad hero possesses admirable qualities and often works for the good of others; but that unlike modern-day superheroes, the railroad hero was a real-life person whose heroic qualities became exaggerated over time.

Difficulty: *Easy*

Objective: *Essay*

Selection Test B, p. 12

Learning About Fiction and Nonfiction

1. ANS: D	DIF: Average	OBJ: Literary Analysis
2. ANS: B	DIF: Average	OBJ: Literary Analysis
3. ANS: B	DIF: Average	OBJ: Literary Analysis
4. ANS: C	DIF: Average	OBJ: Literary Analysis
5. ANS: A	DIF: Average	OBJ: Literary Analysis
6. ANS: B	DIF: Average	OBJ: Literary Analysis

Critical Reading

7. ANS: B	DIF: Challenging	OBJ: Literary Analysis
8. ANS: A	DIF: Challenging	OBJ: Literary Analysis

9. ANS: C	DIF: Average	OBJ: Comprehension
10. ANS: D	DIF: Challenging	OBJ: Literary Analysis
11. ANS: B	DIF: Average	OBJ: Comprehension
12. ANS: A	DIF: Average	OBJ: Interpretation
13. ANS: A	DIF: Average	OBJ: Literary Analysis
14. ANS: A	DIF: Average	OBJ: Comprehension
15. ANS: D	DIF: Average	OBJ: Comprehension
16. ANS: B	DIF: Challenging	OBJ: Interpretation
17. ANS: D	DIF: Challenging	OBJ: Interpretation
18. ANS: C	DIF: Challenging	OBJ: Interpretation
19. ANS: C	DIF: Average	OBJ: Literary Analysis
20. ANS: A	DIF: Challenging	OBJ: Literary Analysis

Essay

21. Students should note that while the stories and legends are fictional, it is a fact that early railroad workers told these stories for their own entertainment. The authors probably chose to include some of the legends in their article in order to bring this period of history to life. Students should support their ideas with references to specific legends or heroes.

   Difficulty: *Average*

   Objective: *Essay*

22. Students should explain that in the first half of the story, the author depicts Lester Simmons as a talented storyteller by having him tell (among others) the story of the "Death Train." Students should then identify the major plot events of the story's second half, including Lester's chest pain, the sounding of the whistle, Lester's attempts to evade death, the arrival of the 11:59, and Lester's death. Finally, students should observe that the legend Lester tells in the first half of the story is the legend he actually experiences in the second.

   Difficulty: *Challenging*

   Objective: *Essay*

Unit 1, Part 1 Answers

Diagnostic Test 1, p. 16

MULTIPLE CHOICE

1. ANS: B
2. ANS: D
3. ANS: C
4. ANS: B
5. ANS: D
6. ANS: B
7. ANS: A
8. ANS: D
9. ANS: A
10. ANS: B

11. ANS: A
12. ANS: C
13. ANS: D
14. ANS: B
15. ANS: D

"A Retrieved Reformation" by O. Henry

Vocabulary Warm-up Exercises, p. 20

A. 1. active
2. extremely
3. inspection
4. successful
5. drugstore
6. flourishing
7. café
8. typical

B. Sample Answers

1. How you act <u>socially</u> lets people see how well you can get along with others.
2. A good punishment for <u>burglary</u> might be the thief giving back twice as much as was stolen.
3. A <u>warden</u> should have a strong personality that is centered on fairness.
4. I always enjoy the <u>commotion</u> that occurs at our Fourth of July parade.
5. I felt <u>anguish</u> when we had to put our dog to sleep.
6. I find it easy to do my homework and listen to music <u>simultaneously</u>.
7. Schoolwork is most <u>worthwhile</u> when it prepares me for life in the real world.
8. Everyone says there is a strong <u>similarity</u> between my aunt and me.

Reading Warm-up A, p. 21

Words that students are to circle appear in parentheses.

Sample Answers

1. (Morrilton, Arkansas); It's *extremely* interesting to find something unexpected when I look for facts.
2. <u>main street, row of red brick businesses</u>; *Typical* means "showing common traits."
3. Since a *drugstore* sells many things that people need, it makes sense it would be found in a town's main shopping and business area.
4. <u>Tourists, shoppers, and farmers</u>; *Flourishing* means "succeeding."
5. (food); Since people always need to eat out when they're away from home, a *café* would get a lot of business during tourist season.
6. (reveals); Since an *inspection* means that you are taking a close look at something, *closer* would be a good word to use.

7. (No Limits); If there are no limits to what you can achieve, then the chances of being *successful* are great.

8. (walk the trails or explore caves); When you are *active*, you are involved in what is going on.

Reading Warm-up B, p. 22

Words that students are to circle appear in parentheses.

Sample Answers

1. <u>if each person left prison knowing that he or she would never commit a crime again</u>; *Worthwhile* means "important or useful."

2. (feelings of progress toward a better life); *Anguish* means "strong feelings of suffering."

3. (society); Reformed prisoners needed to make new friends and do work that was *socially* acceptable.

4. <u>honest work</u>; An act of *burglary* occurs when someone breaks into a place and steals things.

5. (nasty fights, bad feelings, and poor behavior); If my life were filled with *commotion*, I would feel nervous, upset, and angry.

6. (the new prisons were designed so that each person had some space of his or her own), (the jobs of people in charge at prisons changed); When I was in fourth grade, I got a new baby brother and moved to a new town *simultaneously*.

7. The prison *warden* must set an example for all the other workers.

8. One *similarity* among all prisoners is that they are in prison for commiting crimes. Another similarity, I believe, is that all prisoners can be reformed.

"A Retrieved Reformation" by O. Henry

Reading: Make Predictions and Support Them, p. 23

Sample Answers

1. Jimmy will go back to cracking safes. / Jimmy cracks several safes.

2. Ben Price will try to build a strong case against Jimmy. / Ben Price finds Jimmy.

3. Jimmy will reform so that he can marry the woman. / Jimmy works honestly and becomes engaged to the woman.

4. Ben Price will arrest Jimmy before he marries Annabel. / Ben watches as Jimmy cracks a safe to save the life of Annabel's niece. Ben lets Jimmy go.

Literary Analysis: Plot, p. 24

A. 1. 6; resolution
2. 2; conflict
3. 1; exposition
4. 4; climax
5. 3; rising action
6. 5; falling action

B. Sample Answers

Rising action:

1. Jimmy opens a shoe business in Elmore.

2. Jimmy makes friends in Elmore and gains respect in the community.

Falling action:

1. After Jimmy frees the child from the safe, he hears a familiar voice calling him by his new name.

2. Jimmy greets Ben and surrenders to him.

Vocabulary Builder, p. 25

A. 1. unobtrusively
2. virtuous
3. anguish
4. retribution

B. 1. B; 2. A; 3. C; 4. D

Enrichment: Nineteenth-Century Science, p. 28

Sample Answers

1. Ben Price would have been helped by knowledge of fingerprinting and use of the FBI fingerprint file.

2. He probably would not have worn gloves because he would not have been concerned with leaving fingerprints, and gloves would have made working with his tools more difficult.

3. Ben Price might have benefited from a telephone, a fax machine, and Internet access.

4. Safecracking is not a likely criminal activity today because of stronger bank vaults, electronic security, and modern forensic laboratories.

Selection Test A, p. 29

Critical Reading

1. ANS: B	DIF: Easy	OBJ: Interpretation
2. ANS: B	DIF: Easy	OBJ: Interpretation
3. ANS: B	DIF: Easy	OBJ: Comprehension
4. ANS: A	DIF: Easy	OBJ: Reading
5. ANS: B	DIF: Easy	OBJ: Comprehension
6. ANS: D	DIF: Easy	OBJ: Literary Analysis
7. ANS: C	DIF: Easy	OBJ: Interpretation
8. ANS: A	DIF: Easy	OBJ: Literary Analysis
9. ANS: D	DIF: Easy	OBJ: Reading
10. ANS: D	DIF: Easy	OBJ: Interpretation

Vocabulary and Grammar

11. ANS: B	DIF: Easy	OBJ: Vocabulary
12. ANS: A	DIF: Easy	OBJ: Grammar
13. ANS: D	DIF: Easy	OBJ: Vocabulary
14. ANS: C	DIF: Easy	OBJ: Grammar

Essay

15. Some students will say Jimmy tells the whole truth to Annabel and her father, because now he is free from the fear of being caught by Ben Price for his past robberies. He will build his shoe business and remain a part of the community. Others might say that Jimmy will be too ashamed to tell Annabel the truth, and he will leave town. If he does that, he may decide to make a clean start in another town, or he may return to his life of crime.

    Difficulty: *Easy*

    Objective: *Essay*

16. Students may say that both Jimmy and Ralph dress well, get along well with people, are good at their work, and keep secrets. Both men are smart, energetic, and successful, but they put these qualities to very different uses. Jimmy is a bank robber, and he pretends to be a businessman. Ralph is a businessman, but he hides his criminal past.

    Difficulty: *Easy*

    Objective: *Essay*

Selection Test B, p. 32

Critical Reading

1. ANS: B	DIF: Average	OBJ: Interpretation
2. ANS: B	DIF: Challenging	OBJ: Reading
3. ANS: D	DIF: Challenging	OBJ: Reading
4. ANS: B	DIF: Average	OBJ: Interpretation
5. ANS: A	DIF: Average	OBJ: Comprehension
6. ANS: D	DIF: Average	OBJ: Comprehension
7. ANS: A	DIF: Challenging	OBJ: Reading
8. ANS: A	DIF: Average	OBJ: Comprehension
9. ANS: C	DIF: Average	OBJ: Interpretation
10. ANS: B	DIF: Average	OBJ: Literary Analysis
11. ANS: C	DIF: Average	OBJ: Literary Analysis
12. ANS: C	DIF: Challenging	OBJ: Reading
13. ANS: D	DIF: Average	OBJ: Literary Analysis

Vocabulary and Grammar

14. ANS: D	DIF: Average	OBJ: Vocabulary
15. ANS: C	DIF: Average	OBJ: Vocabulary
16. ANS: A	DIF: Average	OBJ: Grammar
17. ANS: B	DIF: Average	OBJ: Grammar

Essay

18. Some students may say that the Adamses are so grateful that they forgive his past criminal life, and he will go on to marry Annabel. Others may say that he will go out West, as he mentioned in his letter. Students may say

that he does not go back to cracking safes, whether or not he marries Annabel, because he sees new value in "going straight."

Difficulty: *Average*

Objective: *Essay*

19. Students may respond that Jimmy is smart, easy-going, a risk-taker, and not one to conform to the expectations of others. He is one who is interested in getting ahead in life, and he is not concerned with issues of legality along the way. He chooses to rob banks, despite the possibility of a prison term, because he is good at it and he seems to enjoy the risk. However, when he meets Annabel, Jimmy changes his priorities. He chooses to "go straight" because Annabel is more important to him than the excitement of safecracking.

Difficulty: *Average*

Objective: *Essay*

"Raymond's Run" by Toni Cade Bambara

Vocabulary Warm-up Exercises, p. 36

A.
1. pageant
2. Fantasy
3. energy
4. prefer
5. satin
6. zoom
7. recipe
8. strawberries

B. Sample Answers
1. No, something only becomes a <u>tradition</u> over time.
2. No, a <u>periscope</u> is typically used by a submarine to see above the water.
3. The water in a <u>hydrant</u> should be saved for use in emergencies such as fires.
4. A <u>gorilla</u> must live in its natural habitat, so a residential neighborhood would not be suitable.
5. <u>Shoelaces</u> are too hard for small hands to tie.
6. A <u>loudspeaker</u> is annoying when it is too loud and when it squeaks.
7. When you <u>congratulate</u> someone you let them know you are happy for their success, yet it's hard to be happy for someone who won what you hoped to win.
8. No, a brand-new car would glide smoothly along and not make a <u>chugging</u>, puffing sound.

Reading Warm-up A, p. 37

Words that students are to circle appear in parentheses.

Sample Answers
1. <u>work and play</u>; I need *energy* to get through softball practice after a long day at school.

2. (fire, singing, dancing); A *pageant* is "a well-planned public presentation of a play or performance."

3. I *prefer* to spend time with people who are kind, funny, open-minded, and generous.

4. (seasonal treats), (fresh), (juicy); *Strawberries* are small, red fruits with a sweet taste.

5. Someone who loves flowers would find May Day celebrations, with all of the flowers around, as a fantasy come true.

6. leftover oatmeal; My mother's recipe for cornmeal tamale pie includes ground beef, green peppers, and fresh tomatoes.

7. (prom decorations); Lots of girls have *satin* trim on their prom gowns, or would wear *satin* shoes to match their dress.

8. gently winding their way; Tony Hawk can really *zoom* on his skateboard.

Reading Warm-up B, p. 38

Words that students are to circle appear in parentheses.

Sample Answers

1. A runner avoiding a fire *hydrant* would probably be running along a city sidewalk.

2. your own breathing; *Chugging* means "making puffing sounds while moving."

3. (the annual Halloween cross-country track meet); My favorite sports tradition is the Super Bowl, which I watch every year with my whole family.

4. Running shoes that fit snugly are important for runners, so they care about having the right *shoelaces*.

5. hairy ape; A *gorilla* suit would cover your whole body from head to toe and would be black and hairy.

6. The writer was impressed that the runner could finish the race at all and felt that this deserved to be *congratulated*. *Congratulate* means "to let others know you are happy about their success."

7. (the other side); I'd like to have a *periscope* to look at the top bunk and find out if my brother is really sleeping or not.

8. my name; A *loudspeaker* makes sounds louder so that many people can hear them in a large area.

"Raymond's Run" by Toni Cade Bambara

Reading: Make Predictions and Support Them, p. 39

Sample Answers

1. The race will be close. / The race is close, but Squeaky wins.

2. Squeaky will object. / Squeaky makes a face to show that she would not even think of letting Gretchen win.

3. Squeaky will feel proud of Raymond. / Squeaky thinks that if she loses the race, she can coach Raymond.

4. Squeaky and Gretchen will become friends. / The outcome is not stated in the story.

Literary Analysis: Plot, p. 40

A. 1. 6; resolution
   2. 1; exposition
   3. 3; conflict
   4. 4; climax
   5. 2; rising action
   6. 5; falling action

B. Sample Answers

Rising action:

1. Squeaky remembers that Mary Louise used to be a friend of hers.
2. Rosie speaks disrespectfully to Squeaky. She asks her if she is Raymond's mother.

Falling action:

1. Squeaky remembers how Raymond always keeps up with her when she runs.
2. Squeaky thinks that Raymond has nothing that he can call his own.

Vocabulary Builder, p. 41

Sample Answers

A. 1. Cynthia plays the piano unusually well.
   2. She would have a terrible reputation.

B. 1. Everyone called the girl a prodigy because she did long division when she was three years old.
   2. Dogs have the reputation of being man's best friend.

C. 1. C; 2. D

Enrichment: Athletic Coaching, p. 44

A. 1. Students should explain that a middle-school coach must demonstrate and explain skills, teach the fundamental procedures and rules of a sport, teach safety, organize and run the school's sports program, and encourage all students to do their best.

   2. Students should recognize that there are careers for athletic coaches in professional sports; in college, high-school, and middle-school sports programs; in gyms; and with individuals.

   3. Students might mention attention to detail, patience, fairness, an easy-going nature, compassion, and a sense of humor.

B. Students may ask about an applicant's educational background and teaching experience, how he or she would manage and motivate students, and the ways in which he or she might handle specific hypothetical situations.

"A Retrieved Reformation" by O. Henry
"Raymond's Run" by Toni Cade Bambara

Build Language Skills: Vocabulary, p. 45

Sample Answers

A. 1. The *preview* made me think that I would love the movie, but I did not like it at all.

2. The *preface* of a book tells you what the book is about.

3. The *preamble* to the Constitution describes the purpose of the document.

B. 1. The weather forecasters *predict* an ice storm.

2. My brothers and sisters and cousins *anticipate* the party in celebration of our great-grandfather's ninetieth birthday.

3. Everyone in the community worked to *formulate* a plan to preserve the wetlands.

4. After we adopted a second dog, my sister had *to modify* her plans for the one-room doghouse she was building.

5. It was foolish of me to think that my essay would be perfect and I would not need to *revise* it.

Build Language Skills: Grammar, p. 46

A. It was Sunday morning, the day of the Chicago Marathon. The weather was crisp and clear, a perfect day for a long race. Sara had trained for six months. She ran long and short distances every week to build up her endurance and strength. She ran along the lakefront paths, on the paths in Lincoln Park Zoo, and along the streets of the city neighborhoods. Sara felt anticipation, sure that she was ready for the race.

B. 1. Where is Dodge City?

2. I like to listen to music.

3. Duluth is on Lake Superior.

4. Does your city hold a marathon?

"Raymond's Run" by Toni Cade Bambara

Selection Test A, p. 47

Critical Reading

1. ANS: A	DIF: Easy	OBJ: Comprehension
2. ANS: D	DIF: Easy	OBJ: Interpretation
3. ANS: B	DIF: Easy	OBJ: Comprehension
4. ANS: A	DIF: Easy	OBJ: Comprehension
5. ANS: C	DIF: Easy	OBJ: Comprehension
6. ANS: B	DIF: Easy	OBJ: Interpretation
7. ANS: D	DIF: Easy	OBJ: Comprehension
8. ANS: D	DIF: Easy	OBJ: Comprehension
9. ANS: A	DIF: Easy	OBJ: Literary Analysis
10. ANS: C	DIF: Easy	OBJ: Comprehension
11. ANS: C	DIF: Easy	OBJ: Literary Analysis
12. ANS: B	DIF: Easy	OBJ: Reading
13. ANS: B	DIF: Easy	OBJ: Reading

Vocabulary and Grammar

14. ANS: D	DIF: Easy	OBJ: Vocabulary
15. ANS: A	DIF: Easy	OBJ: Grammar

Essay

16. Students may predict that Raymond will become a runner like Squeaky because, at the end of the story, Squeaky says she should give up running and devote herself to coaching her brother. She sees a lot of potential in his ability, and she is a determined person. Students might also point out that despite Raymond's physical stamina and agility, he is physically challenged in other ways. Because of this, he probably could not compete at the same level as Squeaky, but he could easily become an excellent runner.

Difficulty: *Easy*

Objective: *Essay*

17. Both Squeaky and Raymond enjoy walking around the city, and they seem to enjoy each other's company. The two siblings care about each other. They are physically agile and enjoy running. In addition, both have a sense of fun and imagination. Raymond pretends he is on a circus tightrope or driving a stagecoach. Squeaky likes to pretend she is flying before a race.

Difficulty: *Easy*

Objective: *Essay*

Selection Test B, p. 50

Critical Reading

1. ANS: A	DIF: Average	OBJ: Comprehension
2. ANS: D	DIF: Average	OBJ: Interpretation
3. ANS: D	DIF: Average	OBJ: Interpretation
4. ANS: D	DIF: Average	OBJ: Comprehension
5. ANS: D	DIF: Challenging	OBJ: Interpretation
6. ANS: A	DIF: Average	OBJ: Comprehension
7. ANS: C	DIF: Average	OBJ: Interpretation
8. ANS: C	DIF: Challenging	OBJ: Literary Analysis
9. ANS: B	DIF: Average	OBJ: Literary Analysis
10. ANS: C	DIF: Challenging	OBJ: Reading
11. ANS: A	DIF: Average	OBJ: Literary Analysis
12. ANS: A	DIF: Average	OBJ: Reading

Vocabulary and Grammar

13. ANS: C   DIF: Average   OBJ: Vocabulary
14. ANS: A   DIF: Average   OBJ: Grammar
15. ANS: B   DIF: Challenging   OBJ: Vocabulary

Essay

16. Students may mention that Raymond is mentally challenged and looks different from other people. He needs someone to watch over him. For example, Squeaky makes clear that on their walks through the city, he stays on the inside of the curb so he doesn't run into others. Although it is a difficult and sometimes painful job to take care of her brother, Squeaky has learned important lessons about what is truly important in life from Raymond. She realizes that it is more important to help Raymond train to run and have something of his own than for her to win races. Raymond, too, gets the benefit of learning how to tackle challenges head-on by watching his sister.
    Difficulty: *Average*
    Objective: *Essay*

17. Students should note some of the characteristics of Squeaky: her love and protectiveness toward her disadvantaged brother Raymond; her distaste for snobbery, phoniness, and cruelty shown in various ways by some of her classmates; her pride in running and her competitive spirit. Students might note that Squeaky changes and grows in several ways: after meeting Gretchen and Mary Louise on the street, she realizes that too much competitiveness can lead to personal hurt and conflict; after the May Day race, she realizes that helping Raymond to reach his potential is more important than yet another victory for herself; she realizes that her rivalry with Gretchen might be keeping them from being good friends. Students might note that the virtues we see in Squeaky at the story's outset—her compassion and honesty—are strengthened by the end of the story. We see her more concerned with love and friendship than with competition and winning.
    Difficulty: *Challenging*
    Objective: *Essay*

"Gentleman of Río Medio" by Juan A. A. Sedillo

Vocabulary Warm-up Exercises, p. 54

A. 1. document
2. obediently
3. previous
4. insulted
5. quaint
6. rate
7. amounted
8. additional

B. Sample Answers
1. Weak defenses allowed armies to <u>overrun</u> the country's <u>boundaries</u>.
2. Pioneers in the dusty valley <u>tilled</u> their <u>wretched</u> fields.
3. <u>Innumerable</u> trees in the orchard grew straight and tall, but a few were <u>gnarled</u>.
4. After two generations, <u>descendants</u> of the original owners took <u>possession</u> of the land.

Reading Warm-up A, p. 55

Words that students are to circle appear in parentheses.

Sample Answers
1. <u>house</u>, <u>most of her furniture</u>; *Amounted* means "added up."
2. (turning down a gift); I once *offended* a very dear relative by turning down a gift.
3. (Without a fuss); I cleaned up my room *obediently*.
4. The year *before*, after the twins were born, we had gone house hunting for our growing family.
5. ($10,000 an acre); *Rate* is "the amount used to calculate a total."
6. ($20,000); *Additional* means "more," so the family must have already saved some money.
7. (old-fashioned); An old fishing town near where I live is *quaint*.
8. <u>the original bill of sale for the house</u>; *Examples of a family document:* a birth certificate, a marriage license; *examples of a national document:* the Declaration of Independence, the Constitution

Reading Warm-up B, p. 56

Words that students are to circle appear in parentheses.

Sample Answers
1. ($12), (showing that a home was being built and the land was being farmed), (another $6)
2. Our country stretched its *boundaries* to the west.
3. (children); *Descendants* of my parents include my brothers, my sisters, and myself.
4. (women), (ex-slaves); *Many* is a synonym for *innumerable* in this passage.
5. <u>poor, sod-covered soil</u>; *Tilled* means "turning over land for growing crops."
6. Hordes of grasshoppers could *overrun* the land; At the start of a sale, customers *overrun* the store, looking for bargains.
7. Hands that become *gnarled* from farming show that a farmer has had to do much hard work. If his or her hands were smooth instead of twisted and lumpy, it would show that the work was easy.
8. <u>little more than, little hope for the future</u>; *Wretched* means "miserable, terrible."

"Gentleman of Río en Medio"
by Juan A. A. Sedillo

Reading: Make Predictions and Read Ahead to Confirm or Correct Them, p. 57

Sample Answers

1. Don Anselmo will accept the money. / Don Anselmo does not accept the money. He is angered by the offer and insists on taking only the agreed-upon amount.
2. Don Anselmo will say that he cannot control where the children play. / Don Anselmo claims that he never sold the trees to the Americans.
3. The Americans will pay Don Anselmo the money he had originally turned down so that he will stop the children from playing in the orchard. / Don Anselmo explains that the trees were planted in honor of the children in the village. The Americans spend the winter paying off the children who had trees in the orchard planted in their honor.

Literary Analysis: Conflict, p. 58

Sample Answers

1. The Americans have bought their land from Don Anselmo, but children from the village are spending all their time in the trees in their orchard. The Americans want the children to leave the property. They learn that Don Anselmo believes that the trees were not his to sell. He believes the trees belong to the children because he planted them in their honor when they were born.
2. Don Anselmo has agreed to sell his land, probably because he needs the money. He probably has taken a great deal of pride in ownership of the land, so he may be struggling to keep his pride.
3. The Americans may be struggling to get along in a community where they are seen as foreigners, but also to take possession of the trees on their land.
4. The conflict is resolved when the Americans pay each of Don Anselmo's descendants for the tree planted in his or her honor. In this way, Don Anselmo provides for his family's future, and the Americans gain possession of their orchard.

Vocabulary Builder, p. 59

Sample Answers

A. 1. The Americans could not name Don Anselmo's descendants, for to them the children were *innumerable.*
   2. Don Anselmo's *preliminary* performance came before the meeting.
   3. Don Anselmo was proud that the children of Río en Medio were his *descendants.*
B. 1. No, *innumerable* means "too many to be counted," so something that is innumerable cannot be counted.

2. No, *preliminary* means "introductory," so a preliminary event would come before the main event.
3. Yes, *descendants* are offspring, so if I have children and grandchildren, I will know my descendants.
C. 1. B; 2. D; 3. A

Enrichment: Mathematics, p. 62

1. 16 acres
2. 871 feet ($217.8 \times 4 = 871.2$)
3. 800 feet ($200 \times 4 = 800$)
4. 43,560 square feet ($217.8 \times 200 = 43,560$)
5. $150 per acre ($1,200 \div 8 = 150$)
6. $2,400 ($1,200 \times 2 = 2,400$)

Selection Test A, p. 63

Critical Reading

1. ANS: D	DIF: Easy	OBJ: Comprehension
2. ANS: A	DIF: Easy	OBJ: Literary Analysis
3. ANS: A	DIF: Easy	OBJ: Literary Analysis
4. ANS: C	DIF: Easy	OBJ: Comprehension
5. ANS: D	DIF: Easy	OBJ: Interpretation
6. ANS: B	DIF: Easy	OBJ: Reading
7. ANS: D	DIF: Easy	OBJ: Comprehension
8. ANS: B	DIF: Easy	OBJ: Interpretation
9. ANS: C	DIF: Easy	OBJ: Literary Analysis
10. ANS: A	DIF: Easy	OBJ: Interpretation
11. ANS: D	DIF: Easy	OBJ: Reading

Vocabulary and Grammar

12. ANS: B	DIF: Easy	OBJ: Vocabulary
13. ANS: D	DIF: Easy	OBJ: Grammar
14. ANS: C	DIF: Easy	OBJ: Vocabulary
15. ANS: D	DIF: Easy	OBJ: Grammar

Essay

16. Students may point out that Don Anselmo talks at length about his family to the real estate agent, and he brings along a young relative when he does business. He has bought each new child a tree for the orchard, and he refuses to include the trees in the sale of his land to the Americans. In the same spirit of generosity, though, he does not take more money from the Americans than he had originally agreed on, even though it was discovered he owned more than all had thought.

Difficulty: *Easy*
Objective: *Essay*

17. It appears that any possible conflicts or misunderstandings will be handled in a friendly way in the future, since all people involved show flexibility and a willingness to discuss issues. Students might describe the fair negotiations for the land sale, which progressed over several months but ended fairly. When a problem arose about the ownership of the orchard, each side dealt calmly and fairly with the other to reach a solution. The Americans noted that the village children were always friendly and respectful when they played in the orchard. Don Anselmo says at the second meeting that the village people enjoy their new neighbors.

Difficulty: *Easy*

Objective: *Essay*

Selection Test B, p. 66

Critical Reading

1. ANS: D	DIF: Average	OBJ: Comprehension
2. ANS: A	DIF: Average	OBJ: Literary Analysis
3. ANS: D	DIF: Challenging	OBJ: Interpretation
4. ANS: C	DIF: Average	OBJ: Comprehension
5. ANS: D	DIF: Average	OBJ: Interpretation
6. ANS: C	DIF: Challenging	OBJ: Interpretation
7. ANS: C	DIF: Challenging	OBJ: Reading
8. ANS: A	DIF: Average	OBJ: Literary Analysis
9. ANS: C	DIF: Challenging	OBJ: Literary Analysis
10. ANS: A	DIF: Challenging	OBJ: Literary Analysis
11. ANS: A	DIF: Average	OBJ: Comprehension
12. ANS: C	DIF: Average	OBJ: Literary Analysis
13. ANS: D	DIF: Average	OBJ: Reading

Vocabulary and Grammar

14. ANS: B	DIF: Average	OBJ: Vocabulary
15. ANS: A	DIF: Average	OBJ: Grammar
16. ANS: C	DIF: Average	OBJ: Vocabulary
17. ANS: A	DIF: Average	OBJ: Grammar

Essay

18. Students may say that the Americans had the legal point of view. They wanted to pay Don Anselmo a certain amount for each acre and, in return, own all the property within the agreed-upon boundaries. Don Anselmo has a traditional and honorable point of view. Since he had agreed upon a price, the amount of land did not affect the money he would take for his property. Also, since he had planted the trees for the children born in the village since he owned the land, he believed that the trees belonged to the children. Since he did not believe he owned the trees, he could not sell them.

Difficulty: *Average*

Objective: *Essay*

19. One possible response is that Don Anselmo shows fairness and generosity when he refuses the additional money for his land. In his view, he must stick to the original price negotiated, even though it was for less land than he knew he owned. He responds with indignation, as though he were being insulted. This reaction is an example of his pride. Don Anselmo also shows pride in his family, not only by talking about them at length but also by bringing a young relative along with him to the meeting. He is generous with his time as well as his money. He agrees to meet and hear the Americans' complaints, and he has bought many trees as gifts for his descendants.

Difficulty: *Average*

Objective: *Essay*

"Cub Pilot on the Mississippi" by Mark Twain

Vocabulary Warm-up Exercises, p. 70

A. 1. apprenticeship
2. employment
3. varieties
4. tyrant
5. stingy
6. criticized
7. vigorous
8. costly

B. Sample Answers
1. I always keep <u>abreast</u> of the news, so I know *a lot* about current events.
2. When it rains, the American flag should *not* be hoisted <u>aloft</u>.
3. A terrible <u>blunder</u> made things *worse* for everyone.
4. When she recognized the *familiar* <u>dialect</u>, she realized how <u>homesick</u> she was for *her hometown*.
5. If you want to *help* the <u>environment</u>, concern yourself with the loss of habitats.
6. A <u>steamboat</u> was a great improvement over the slow-moving *flatboat*.

Reading Warm-up A, p. 71

Words that students are to circle appear in parentheses.

Sample Answers
1. <u>a common way for a boy to learn a trade</u>; I would like to serve an *apprenticeship* to a clockmaker.
2. (the last year of service); The master had to provide room and board for the apprentice and take time away from work for lessons.
3. (gentle); A person who listens to others and considers their needs before acting is the opposite of a *tyrant*.
4. (generous); A master might have been *stingy* with the food he gave an apprentice.

5. Some masters *found fault* with their apprentices constantly.

6. (his own business); A journeyman had to find *employment* because he no longer was with the master.

7. (baker), (blacksmith); Two other *varieties* of trades that an apprentice might train for include barrel making or candle making.

8. Those trades required *vigorous* health because they demanded hard manual labor and strength.

Reading Warm-up B, p. 72

Words that students are to circle appear in parentheses.

Sample Answers

1. Boats that used burning fuel to create steam power; The first *steamboat* began operating on the Hudson River in New York in 1807.

2. A steamboat would chug *strikingly* downriver at eight miles an hour, sending billows of smoke *into the air*.

3. (rough), (lively); My school *environment* is bustling, friendly, and usually cheerful.

4. northern and southern; A *dialect* is the way a language is spoken in a particular area.

5. Crews and passengers helped keep folks *up to date* on the news up and down the river.

6. gather around to hear word from their native towns; River workers might be *homesick* because they're working in a strange city or traveling up and down the river.

7. The results of a *blunder* aboard a steamboat might be an explosion that could threaten people's lives and the boat's cargo. A *blunder* is a big mistake.

"Cub Pilot on the Mississippi" by Mark Twain

Reading: Make Predictions and Read Ahead to Confirm or Correct Them, p. 73

Sample Answers

1. Brown will make Twain's apprenticeship on the steamboat miserable. / Brown is cruel and intolerant and does make Twain's apprenticeship miserable.

2. Twain will eventually strike Brown. / Twain does get into a physical fight with Brown.

3. The captain will not punish Twain. / The captain does not punish Twain.

Literary Analysis: Conflict, p. 74

Sample Answers

1. The external conflict is the struggle between Brown and Twain. Brown is Twain's boss, so Twain cannot answer back, but Brown is cruel to Twain and tries his patience.

2. Twain's internal conflict is the struggle to hold his temper when Brown treats him cruelly.

3. Brown aims a ten-pound lump of coal at Twain's brother Henry. Twain stops the coal from hitting Henry and then starts beating Brown. Later the captain tells Twain that he has done the right thing and that he should beat Brown even more thoroughly when they reach the shore. In the end, Brown asks the captain to make Twain leave the boat, and the captain instead suggests that Brown leave the boat.

Vocabulary Builder, p. 75

Sample Answers

A. 1. Because his motives were unsound, Brown needed a pretext to find fault with Twain.

2. By attacking Brown, Twain showed that he was not judicious.

3. The captain was indulgent in his treatment of the boat's crew.

B. 1. No, a *pretext* is an unsound reason used to hide real intentions. If someone has irritated you, you have a sound reason to argue with him or her, so you do not need a pretext.

2. Yes, being *judicious* means being careful and showing good judgment, so you would be judicious if you considered the consequences of your actions.

3. No, being *indulgent* means being uncritical and tolerant, so when you point out every mistake that someone has made, you are not being indulgent.

C. 1. A; 2. C; 3. B

Enrichment: Conflict Resolution, p. 78

Sample Answers

2. Brown is a bully, and because Brown is Twain's boss, Twain does not feel he can speak up for himself.

3. Twain could tell Brown that Brown's treatment of him is hurtful and interferes with his ability to learn the job of steamboat piloting.

4. Brown feels angry because his subordinate has challenged him. He acts meaner.

5. Twain tells Brown that he will discuss the problem with Captain Klinefelter.

"Gentleman of Río en Medio" by Juan A. A. Sedillo
"Cub Pilot on the Mississippi" by Mark Twain

Build Language Skills: Vocabulary, p. 79

A. Sample Answers

1. My sister took apart the engine of her car, and now she cannot *reassemble* the parts.

2. The toaster came with a five-dollar *rebate*, so we got money back.

3. Many nutritionists recommend that people *reduce* their consumption of carbohydrates.

Unit 1 Resources: Fiction and Nonfiction
© Pearson Education, Inc., publishing as Pearson Prentice Hall. All rights reserved.
214

4. Mirrors *reflect* us as we truly are.
5. In Spanish class, we *repeat* each sentence until we can say it fluently.

B. Sample Answers Follow the *Yes* or *No*.

1. Yes. Astronomers have the instruments and the knowledge that allow them to know when lunar eclipses will take place.
2. No. If I plan to attend a popular event, I expect many people will be there.
3. No. If an architect were asked to formulate a plan, he would invent a new plan.
4. No. If an architect were asked to modify a plan, she would make changes in a plan she already had.
5. Yes. *Revise* means "to look back at and change or modify," so if an architect were asked to revise a plan, he would look again at a plan he had already made.

Build Language Skills: Grammar, p. 80

A. 1. friends
2. oxen
3. fossils, teeth
4. bushes
5. stars

B. Students should write cohesive, grammatically correct paragraphs. They should include and correctly spell five irregularly formed plural nouns, and they should underline all the nouns (common and proper) in the paragraph.

"Cub Pilot on the Mississippi" by Mark Twain

Selection Test A, p. 81

Critical Reading

1. ANS: A	DIF: Easy	OBJ: Comprehension
2. ANS: B	DIF: Easy	OBJ: Reading
3. ANS: C	DIF: Easy	OBJ: Interpretation
4. ANS: D	DIF: Easy	OBJ: Comprehension
5. ANS: B	DIF: Easy	OBJ: Comprehension
6. ANS: B	DIF: Easy	OBJ: Literary Analysis
7. ANS: C	DIF: Easy	OBJ: Interpretation
8. ANS: D	DIF: Easy	OBJ: Comprehension
9. ANS: A	DIF: Easy	OBJ: Interpretation
10. ANS: A	DIF: Easy	OBJ: Literary Analysis
11. ANS: C	DIF: Easy	OBJ: Reading

Vocabulary and Grammar

12. ANS: B	DIF: Easy	OBJ: Vocabulary
13. ANS: A	DIF: Easy	OBJ: Vocabulary
14. ANS: B	DIF: Easy	OBJ: Grammar
15. ANS: A	DIF: Easy	OBJ: Grammar

Essay

16. Many students probably will agree with Twain's decision to fight Brown in order to prevent Brown from attacking Henry. Some students may think that attacking Brown with a heavy stool is going too far, while others will feel that drastic action of that sort is necessary to make sure that Brown doesn't hurt Henry. Some students will support Twain's beating of Brown, given the cruelty Twain suffered. Other students might feel that Twain should have backed off and not allowed his rage against Brown to take over. Students who support Twain's attack might point to the captain's approval as evidence that Brown got what was coming to him.

Difficulty: *Easy*
Objective: *Essay*

17. Students should describe the differences between Brown's and Twain's physical appearance, pointing out that Brown is older and larger than the younger Twain. Brown is loud and speaks with poor grammar, whereas Twain has had more formal education and speaks grammatically. Brown is quick to anger and has a negative attitude toward the people around him. Twain holds in his anger and is generally curious, positive, and eager to learn. Brown is dishonest and lacks integrity; he would rather Henry take the blame for a mistake he himself made on the river. Although Twain considers running away from the boat to avoid confronting the captain, he ends up facing the captain and being truthful about the incident. He has a sense of honesty and fairness.

Difficulty: *Easy*
Objective: *Essay*

Selection Test B, p. 84

Critical Reading

1. ANS: A	DIF: Average	OBJ: Interpretation
2. ANS: A	DIF: Average	OBJ: Reading
3. ANS: A	DIF: Average	OBJ: Interpretation
4. ANS: D	DIF: Challenging	OBJ: Literary Analysis
5. ANS: B	DIF: Average	OBJ: Comprehension
6. ANS: A	DIF: Challenging	OBJ: Interpretation
7. ANS: D	DIF: Average	OBJ: Comprehension
8. ANS: B	DIF: Average	OBJ: Literary Analysis
9. ANS: A	DIF: Average	OBJ: Interpretation
10. ANS: A	DIF: Average	OBJ: Literary Analysis
11. ANS: C	DIF: Average	OBJ: Reading

Vocabulary and Grammar

12. ANS: C	DIF: Average	OBJ: Vocabulary
13. ANS: A	DIF: Average	OBJ: Vocabulary
14. ANS: B	DIF: Challenging	OBJ: Grammar
15. ANS: A	DIF: Average	OBJ: Grammar

Essay

16. Students should describe the differences between Brown's and Twain's physical appearance, pointing out that Brown is older and larger than the younger Twain. Brown is loud and speaks with poor grammar, whereas Twain has had more formal education and speaks grammatically. Brown is quick to anger and has a negative attitude toward the people around him. Twain holds his anger in and is generally curious, positive, and eager to learn. Brown is dishonest and lacks integrity; he would rather Henry take the blame for a mistake he himself made on the river. Although Twain considers running away from the boat to avoid confronting the captain, he ends up facing the captain and being truthful about the incident. He has a sense of honesty and fairness.

Difficulty: *Average*

Objective: *Essay*

17. Students might note that Brown is such a bitter and negative person that Twain could have avoided conflict with him only by giving in to him completely. Even though Twain is afraid of Brown, he maintains his sense of self by imagining scenes of killing Brown every night. When Brown goes after Twain's younger brother with a heavy lump of coal, Twain quickly drops his fears. He not only defends his brother by attacking Brown with a stool but also releases his pent-up rage by giving Brown a thorough beating. This outburst brings their conflict to a head.

Difficulty: *Average*

Objective: *Essay*

"Old Ben" by Jesse Stuart
"Fox Hunt" by Lensey Namioka

Vocabulary Warm-up Exercises, p. 88

A.
1. vivid
2. attractive
3. charmer
4. unbelievingly
5. fascinating
6. occurred
7. tamed
8. mischievous

B. Sample Answers

1. *Competitors* aren't likely to be *affectionate* because they're out to beat you.
2. No. When people *eavesdrop* on conversations, they listen in secret.
3. Yes, because a *scholarship* awards a student who works hard in school—an *outstanding*, or good, student!
4. Yes, if you are *ambitious* and *really want to win*, it's a good idea to let people know your *qualifications*, or

why your *experience and character* make you a good candidate.

5. You want to avoid any *paralyzing* situation because then you wouldn't be able to move.

Reading Warm-up A, p. 89

Words that students are to circle appear in parentheses.

Sample Answers

1. (creature) If you want an *interesting* creature to marvel at, though, you might enjoy one of the slinky, slithery reptiles.
2. if you suggest the idea of a snake as a pet; I looked *unbelievingly* at the coach when she said I made the track team.
3. (manage these reptiles); A *charmer* is someone with a good personality. He or she usually can get people to do things by charming them or engaging them.
4. Through the ages, situations have *happened* in which people have kept tamed snakes as pets.
5. keeping a snake at home; My brother *tamed* an iguana to eat out of his hand.
6. bands of red, yellow, and black; My sister has *vivid* pink curtains in her room.
7. (colorful); I find snakes *attractive* because of their graceful movements, their bright colors, and their patterns.
8. If you are *mischievous* around snakes, you could get bitten, poisoned, and possibly killed. *Mischievous* means "being playful in a way that might cause harm."

Reading Warm-up B, p. 90

Words that students are to circle appear in parentheses.

Sample Answers

1. (all-expenses-paid tuition, room, and board); The narrator might want a *scholarship* because he or she cannot afford to pay for a prep school.
2. I enjoy working hard to invent and build; An *ambitious* person probably works hard to succeed at whatever he or she wants to do.
3. A person can *eavesdrop* by hanging around doors, listening in at keyholes, or overhearing a conversation from the next table.
4. An *outstanding* student has proved his or her ability to succeed in school.
5. (high grades, an interesting and fully-functional project, and a winning personal interview) Three *qualifications* for being a good baseball player are batting, throwing, and catching well.
6. rivals; I have played soccer against a team of *competitors* from another school.
7. (the big test); A *paralyzing* fear is one that keeps you from taking action.
8. (went to hug me); Someone can be *affectionate* by hugging, kissing, or saying nice things to another person.

Literary Analysis: Narrative Structure, p. 91

1. "He drew his head back in a friendly way." "He didn't want trouble."
2. "My father had always told me there was only one good snake—a dead one."
3. The detail given as the answer to question 2 helps the author to create suspense by making the reader wonder whether or how the snake will die in the story.
4. The passage is a flashback because it tells about events that happened before the events of the story about Andy.
5. The flashback reveals that Andy is very much like his ancestor: He is driven to succeed on an exam, and he is also attracted to a mysterious girl with slanted eyes.
6. The passage foreshadows how the mysterious girl will help Andy study for the PSAT.

Vocabulary Builder, p. 92

Sample Answers
A. 1. The <u>decadent</u> nobleman was dishonest and lazy.
   2. The <u>affectionate</u> little girl hugged her cousin.
   3. Carmen was <u>tantalized</u> by the beautiful bracelet in the shop window.
   4. With the help of a <u>partition</u>, the twins created two smaller rooms out of one large room.
   5. Mom has a hard time convincing my <u>studious</u> brother to go outside and play.
B. 1. A; 2. D; 3. B; 4. C; 5. C; 6. C

Selection Test A, p. 94

Critical Reading

1. ANS: C	DIF: Easy	OBJ: Interpretation
2. ANS: C	DIF: Easy	OBJ: Comprehension
3. ANS: B	DIF: Easy	OBJ: Interpretation
4. ANS: D	DIF: Easy	OBJ: Comprehension
5. ANS: A	DIF: Easy	OBJ: Literary Analysis
6. ANS: B	DIF: Easy	OBJ: Comprehension
7. ANS: A	DIF: Easy	OBJ: Interpretation
8. ANS: D	DIF: Easy	OBJ: Comprehension
9. ANS: C	DIF: Easy	OBJ: Literary Analysis
10. ANS: B	DIF: Easy	OBJ: Interpretation
11. ANS: D	DIF: Easy	OBJ: Comprehension
12. ANS: A	DIF: Easy	OBJ: Literary Analysis
13. ANS: A	DIF: Easy	OBJ: Literary Analysis

Vocabulary

14. ANS: C	DIF: Easy	OBJ: Vocabulary
15. ANS: B	DIF: Easy	OBJ: Vocabulary

Essay

16. Students should note that Old Ben dies in the hogpen at the end of "Old Ben" and that Andy discovers that both he and Lee are part fox. Students may say that the title "Old Ben" does not give any clues about the story's ending. Students will likely note that the title of "Fox Hunt" suggests Lee's true identity as well as Andy's, and may therefore conclude that it is the better title; alternatively, students may not like titles that can be construed as giving away a story's ending.
    Difficulty: *Easy*
    Objective: *Essay*
17. The story element that takes the reader back in time is *flashback*, and the story element that points forward in time is *foreshadowing*. Students should note that the author of "Old Ben" uses foreshadowing. Incidents and details such as Blackie's pursuit of Ben, the disappearance of Ben in the winter, Ben's close call with Fred the horse, and the untouched milk on the day of his disappearance help the author build suspense and keep the reader guessing about Ben's fate. Students should note that the author of "Fox Hunt" uses both flashback and foreshadowing. Flashbacks such as the story about Andy's ancestor and the story about Andy's previous tutoring experience with a girl give the reader insight into Andy's character, and foreshadowing such as Lee's slanting eyes and the barking German shepherd builds suspense and gives clues about Lee's identity.
    Difficulty: *Easy*
    Objective: *Essay*

Selection Test B, p. 97

Critical Reading

1. ANS: D	DIF: Average	OBJ: Interpretation
2. ANS: A	DIF: Average	OBJ: Interpretation
3. ANS: C	DIF: Average	OBJ: Comprehension
4. ANS: C	DIF: Challenging	OBJ: Literary Analysis
5. ANS: B	DIF: Average	OBJ: Literary Analysis
6. ANS: D	DIF: Average	OBJ: Comprehension
7. ANS: C	DIF: Average	OBJ: Comprehension
8. ANS: A	DIF: Challenging	OBJ: Literary Analysis
9. ANS: D	DIF: Average	OBJ: Literary Analysis
10. ANS: A	DIF: Challenging	OBJ: Comprehension
11. ANS: B	DIF: Average	OBJ: Interpretation
12. ANS: D	DIF: Challenging	OBJ: Literary Analysis
13. ANS: B	DIF: Average	OBJ: Comprehension
14. ANS: D	DIF: Challenging	OBJ: Literary Analysis
15. ANS: A	DIF: Average	OBJ: Comprehension
16. ANS: A	DIF: Average	OBJ: Interpretation

Vocabulary

17. ANS: C	DIF: Average	OBJ: Vocabulary
18. ANS: B	DIF: Challenging	OBJ: Vocabulary
19. ANS: C	DIF: Average	OBJ: Vocabulary

Essay

20. Students should recall that the outcome of "Old Ben" is the snake's death in the hogpen, and that the outcome of "Fox Hunt" is Andy's discovery that he and Lee are part fox. Students are likely to conclude that the title "Old Ben" reveals less about the story's outcome than the title "Fox Hunt," which hints at both Lee's and Andy's identity. (In the title, the term *fox* can be understood both as the hunter and the hunted.) Other students, however, may say that the title "Old Ben" is more effective for the very reason that the title does *not* undercut the story by giving away its outcome.

Difficulty: *Average*

Objective: *Essay*

21. Lee in "Fox Hunt" and the snake in "Old Ben" are similar in several ways. They both befriend a human character in the story, and they both grow to be very important to that character. The snake brings out the trusting side of the narrator, just as Lee brings out the trusting side of Andy. Both characters also appear at first to be something they are not—the snake, a dangerous creature, and Lee, a human being—and both characters come and go in mysterious ways. But Lee and the snake are very different, too. Lee is a magical character who can transform her actual appearance. She has a plan to help and later marry Andy, whereas the snake has no ulterior motive other than being himself. Old Ben and the narrator become instant friends, while the friendship between Lee and Andy develops more slowly. Finally, because he is a real character, Old Ben dies; but Lee, as a magical character, seems to live forever.

Difficulty: *Average*

Objective: *Essay*

22. The narrative structures of both "Old Ben" and "Fox Hunt" are basically chronological, but both authors also use foreshadowing and/or flashbacks to break the time sequences. In "Old Ben" the departure from strict chronology is accomplished mainly through foreshadowing. For example, at the beginning of the story, the narrator notes his father's belief that the only good snake is a dead one. Later, Old Ben's narrow escape from the horse in the barn foreshadows his later death in the hogpen. Further, Old Ben's disappearance from the corncrib in the wintertime foreshadows his disappearance at the end of the story. The author of "Old Ben" uses these foreshadowing to build suspense and to keep the reader guessing about Old Ben's fate. The author of "Fox Hunt," on the other hand, relies on both flashback and foreshadowing. Through flashback we learn about Andy's experiences with girls; about his brother's great success on the PSAT; and about the family's ancestral history. These flash-

backs give the reader important information about Andy's insecurities and motives. Through foreshadowing, such as the barking German shepherd, Lee's reddish hair and slanting eyes, and Andy's dreams of a fox hunt, we are given clues about Lee's identity. These clues help build suspense and make the reader wonder whether magic is really at work.

Difficulty: *Challenging*

Objective: *Essay*

Writing Workshop—Unit 1, Part 1

Description of a Person: Integrating Grammar Skills, p. 101

A. 1. B; 2. A; 3. A; 4. A; 5. C

B.
1. At the picnic, we will have a girls' relay race.
2. Two men's teams will have a tug-of-war.
3. The biggest tree's limb is a good place to hang the swing.
4. Mr. and Mrs. Hodges are coming with their dogs, known as "The Hodges' Three."
5. Mom is taking her book, Honesty's Reward, to read in the shade.

Unit 1, Part 1 Answers

Benchmark Test 1, p. 102

MULTIPLE CHOICE

1. ANS: D
2. ANS: A
3. ANS: D
4. ANS: B
5. ANS: B
6. ANS: C
7. ANS: D
8. ANS: B
9. ANS: A
10. ANS: C
11. ANS: A
12. ANS: C
13. ANS: D
14. ANS: D
15. ANS: A
16. ANS: B
17. ANS: A
18. ANS: B
19. ANS: C
20. ANS: C

21. ANS: B
22. ANS: A
23. ANS: B
24. ANS: D
25. ANS: A
26. ANS: B
27. ANS: A
28. ANS: D
29. ANS: B
30. ANS: C
31. ANS: B
32. ANS: A

ESSAY

33. Students may recount the story or retell it in summarized form. They may include details that point to the new ending or can make it a surprise ending, but the ending should still be in keeping with events and characterizations that come before.

34. Students should use a casual, friendly tone that sounds as if they are speaking to their friend. They should not include background information about themselves that a close friend would do but should instead focus on the situation, giving only sufficient background to explain the new experience.

35. Students should state a main impression of the person and support it with concrete examples and/or personal anecdotes. They should include sensory details about the person's appearance, behavior, and perhaps speech. In giving their thoughts on why the person has made such a strong impression, they may discuss the person's unusual qualities or his or her interaction with others.

Unit 1, Part 2 Answers

Diagnostic Test 2, p. 109

MULTIPLE CHOICE

1. ANS: C
2. ANS: B
3. ANS: A
4. ANS: D
5. ANS: D
6. ANS: C
7. ANS: B
8. ANS: B
9. ANS: A
10. ANS: B
11. ANS: B

12. ANS: D
13. ANS: B
14. ANS: A
15. ANS: D

"The Adventure of the Speckled Band"
by Sir Arthur Conan Doyle

Vocabulary Warm-up Exercises, p. 113

A.
1. beloved
2. unfortunate
3. hastening
4. withdraw
5. fate
6. Clad
7. objections
8. satisfying

B. Sample Answers

1. A father would want you to move *noiselessly* so that you wouldn't awaken his baby.
2. My father and my Uncle Scott have a strong *resemblance* to each other.
3. The best *residence* I've had is the small town I now live in.
4. I cried at the *tragic* ending of *Old Yeller*.
5. If I saw a sick person with *speckled* skin, I would keep my distance, since it could be a sign of chicken pox.
6. A bank safe has a *massive* door to try to prevent robbers from breaking into it.
7. People must admire the beauty and power of *ferocious* animals.
8. My favorite family *excursion* was to Yosemite.

Reading Warm-up A, p. 114

Words that students are to circle appear in parentheses.

Sample Answers

1. A life on the move; *Beloved* means "dearly loved."
2. (to travel); *Satisfying* needs like those for food, clothing, and shelter, is fundamental to our existence.
3. India; *Withdraw* means "to go away from a place or leave it."
4. (the different looks and way of life); I think *objections* to people's differences are ridiculous and unfair.
5. death in prison camps; The saying "a *fate* worse than death" refers to things that can happen to you in life that are so horrible you might think you'd rather die than keep experiencing them.
6. An *unfortunate* event in our town was a big flood that caused many people to lose their homes.

7. I picture a Gypsy woman with dark, curly hair, who is *clad* in layers of beautiful fabrics like lace and wearing lots of big jewelry.

8. (a more modern way of life); *Hastening* means "moving quickly."

Reading Warm-up B, p. 115

Words that students are to circle appear in parentheses.

Sample Answers

1. *Ferocious* means "fierce." All of the breeds of wild cats, bears, wolves, are *ferocious* animals.

2. traveling all around this vast country, visit one wildlife area; The *excursion* I want to take is a train ride across the whole country

3. The *massive* Himalayas must be huge mountains towering over India.

4. (thousands of plant and animal species); My place of *residence* is a big, bustling city with lots of noise and traffic.

5. Crocodiles move *noiselessly* so that they can sneak up on their prey.

6. (dole); Except for the shape of their ears, Indian and African elephants are almost identical in their *resemblance* to each other.

7. (wiping out of species); A meaningless attack by one human on another is always a *tragic* event.

8. *Speckled* means "spotted," like a face that is *speckled* with freckles.

"The Adventure of the Speckled Band"
by Sir Arthur Conan Doyle

Reading: Recognize Details That Indicate the Author's Purpose, p. 116

Sample Answers
A. 1. to frighten readers; to make readers curious
   2. to make readers curious
   3. to frighten readers
   4. to give readers a sense of relief

Literary Analysis: Mood, p. 117

Sample Answers
A. 1. thrill, terror, terrible, silence, night, low whistle, death, sprang up, too shaken
   2. seared, burned, evil passion, bile-shot, fleshless, fierce, prey
   3. dreadful, open-eyed, nervous tension, absolute darkness

Vocabulary Builder, p. 118

A. 1. threatening
   2. put the hat in her locker
   3. understandable

B. Sample Answers
1. One tangible reason someone catches the flu is exposure to someone else who has the flu.
2. One student considered wearing a sinister costume—maybe a devil's suit—to the masquerade party.
3. The proposal was rejected because the building was not in compliance with the zoning code.

C. 1. C; 2. B; 3. D

Enrichment: Consider a Career as a Detective, p. 121

Sample Answers
A. 1. He first used his skill of logical reasoning when he claimed that Helen Stoner traveled by train to London.
   2. He conducted a lengthy interview with useful questions.
   3. He first examined the window shutters in Helen's room.
   4. He made a thorough visual examination of the entire room as he looked for information.
B. 1. honesty, intelligence, knowledge of people, not jumping to conclusions
   2. science: to understand modern techniques for collecting evidence; psychology or history: to understand how people act in particular situations

Selection Test A, p. 122

Critical Reading

1. ANS: C	DIF: Easy	OBJ: Comprehension
2. ANS: D	DIF: Easy	OBJ: Comprehension
3. ANS: B	DIF: Easy	OBJ: Interpretation
4. ANS: C	DIF: Easy	OBJ: Reading
5. ANS: B	DIF: Easy	OBJ: Comprehension
6. ANS: A	DIF: Easy	OBJ: Literary Analysis
7. ANS: D	DIF: Easy	OBJ: Interpretation
8. ANS: C	DIF: Easy	OBJ: Comprehension
9. ANS: B	DIF: Easy	OBJ: Literary Analysis
10. ANS: D	DIF: Easy	OBJ: Reading

Vocabulary and Grammar

11. ANS: B	DIF: Easy	OBJ: Grammar
12. ANS: D	DIF: Easy	OBJ: Grammar
13. ANS: A	DIF: Easy	OBJ: Vocabulary
14. ANS: C	DIF: Easy	OBJ: Grammar
15. ANS: B	DIF: Easy	OBJ: Vocabulary

Essay

16. Students who evaluate the story as a good mystery may say they were intrigued by Holmes's powers of deduction and calm persistence, and that the clues presented were a tantalizing puzzle that built to a scary conclusion. Students who say they did not like the story may say they found Holmes an unbelievable character or too unemotional to get to know.

    Difficulty: *Easy*

    Objective: *Essay*

17. Students should point out that the author sets up Roylett as the prime suspect by giving him a violent personality. He has been known to lose his temper easily and had been to police court for getting into fights. In addition, Roylett keeps wild animals on his estate.

    Difficulty: *Easy*

    Objective: *Essay*

Selection Test B, p. 125

Critical Reading

1. ANS: A	DIF: Average	OBJ: Reading
2. ANS: B	DIF: Challenging	OBJ: Interpretation
3. ANS: D	DIF: Challenging	OBJ: Reading
4. ANS: B	DIF: Average	OBJ: Reading
5. ANS: C	DIF: Average	OBJ: Comprehension
6. ANS: B	DIF: Average	OBJ: Comprehension
7. ANS: A	DIF: Average	OBJ: Comprehension
8. ANS: C	DIF: Average	OBJ: Interpretation
9. ANS: B	DIF: Challenging	OBJ: Literary Analysis
10. ANS: C	DIF: Challenging	OBJ: Comprehension
11. ANS: A	DIF: Average	OBJ: Interpretation
12. ANS: D	DIF: Average	OBJ: Literary Analysis
13. ANS: B	DIF: Average	OBJ: Interpretation
14. ANS: C	DIF: Average	OBJ: Interpretation
15. ANS: B	DIF: Average	OBJ: Literary Analysis

Vocabulary and Grammar

16. ANS: A	DIF: Average	OBJ: Vocabulary
17. ANS: C	DIF: Average	OBJ: Vocabulary
18. ANS: B	DIF: Average	OBJ: Vocabulary and Grammar
19. ANS: A	DIF: Average	OBJ: Vocabulary and Grammar
20. ANS: C	DIF: Challenging	OBJ: Vocabulary and Grammar

Essay

21. Students' essays should explain the relevant clues that led them to solve the mystery, such as Helen Stoner's story of her sister's death, the Indian animals, her uncle's violent background, and so on. They should also tell which clues led them away from the eventual solution, such as the title, the gypsy camp near the estate, the cheetah, and so on.

    Difficulty: *Average*

    Objective: *Essay*

22. Students should refer to specific words and phrases, such as "thrill of terror," "terrible fate," "low whistle," and "herald of her own death." They might also mention that Helen's memory of her sister's death reminds readers of the terrifying details of the night Julia Stoner died.

    Difficulty: *Average*

    Objective: *Essay*

from *An American Childhood* by Annie Dillard

Vocabulary Warm-up Exercises, p. 129

A.
1. item
2. extent
3. sensations
4. depths
5. comparison
6. transparent
7. precisely
8. deliberately

B. Sample Answers

1. T; Scientists, after much research, might *conceivably* be able to find cures for all diseases in the future.
2. T; Race car drivers like to go fast so they can pass cars to win a race, and not being able to go at full speed would make them *restless.*
3. T; To capture the details of a person in a portrait, the artist must look at the person *posing* for long periods of time.
4. T; Mucous *membrane* is an important part of the human body and helps with the breathing process.
5. F; Because biographies are true stories, not works of *fiction*, they would not be on these shelves.
6. F; When people are in a *serene* mood, they want to be in a calm and quiet place.
7. T; People have fear and prejudice about things they do not understand, and this becomes the *basis* for their feelings.
8. T; Some flowers, like roses, have *petals* so soft that they feel like velvet.

Reading Warm-up A, p. 130

Words that students are to circle appear in parentheses.

Sample Answers

1. Fears of the dark, of monsters under the bed, being separated from parents, and loud noises are all common; *Extent* means "a range of things."

2. (imagined, very real); I do not like the *sensations* of my skin crawling and fingers tingling when my hand falls asleep.

3. object; The *item* that scared me the most as a child was a wooden mask hanging in the hallway by my bedroom.

4. (who knows where); The *depths* are a very deep part of something.

5. Parents should work *deliberately* to talk with children about their fears. When you do something *deliberately*, you do it carefully and on purpose.

6. *Precisely*, a parent wearing a green, slimy looking monster mask at Halloween could easily scare a child. A synonym for *precisely* is *exactly*.

7. help the child understand the fear; understand clearly; *Transparent* means "being able to see through something or that it is clear."

8. (one child's fears to another's); A *comparison* is a way of looking at what is the same and different between things.

Reading Warm-up B, p. 131

Words that students are to circle appear in parentheses.

Sample Answers

1. Children with too much time on their hands can *conceivably* get into trouble.

2. interesting events; A work of *fiction* is a story with made-up people and events.

3. figured out some decent ways to fill my time; When I feel *restless*, I turn to a good book.

4. (plant, four-leaf clover); My favorite flower is the winter pansy, with its colorful *petals* that look like velvet.

5. smooth, still; The still, smooth surface of the *serene* water looked like glass.

6. The writer has no *basis* for knowing how to entertain herself because she has never before been on her own for so much of the day.

7. I was nervous to start middle school, so at the beginning of sixth grade, I found myself *posing* as a super-athlete.

8. A lie is usually an attempt to cover up the truth and could be seen as a *membrane*, or thin layer of skin, that keeps the world from seeing the truth.

from *An American Childhood* by Annie Dillard

Reading: Author's Purpose, p. 132

Sample Answers

A. 1. to make readers curious
2. to frighten readers
3. to give readers a sense of relief

B. When I was in kindergarten, my next-door neighbor had a pet whose huge, box-shaped head loomed above my entire body. I always tried to keep my distance from that menacing animal.

Literary Analysis: Mood, p. 133

Sample Answers

A. 1. hit, shrank, vanished, cobra
2. labored, burst, loud, thrashed, froze
3. raced, bumped, slithered elongate, shrank, flew, vanished, wail

B. The hawk burst through the air toward its prey. The mouse slithered along the ground, then shrank and froze.

Vocabulary Builder, p. 134

A. 1. flat
2. glowing
3. it is imaginable

B. Sample Answers
1. If numbers on a watch are luminous, you can read them in a dark room.
2. When things go my way, I might feel serene.
3. Scientists say that conceivably temperatures will rise.

Enrichment: Origins of Shadow Puppets, p. 137

Sample Answers

1. The shows pass on important stories of the culture to each generation. Additionally, the shows may be very entertaining.

2. The audience's imagination responds much more readily to night shadows than to those in bright sunlight.

3. The *dalang* is the shadow puppeteer. He controls the puppets, speaks all the dialogue, and sings songs during the long performance.

4. Answers might indicate that students would want to tell stories of serious epic proportion or stories of more simple design.

"The Adventure of the Speckled Band"
by Sir Arthur Conan Doyle
from *An American Childhood* by Annie Dillard

Build Language Skills: Vocabulary, p. 138

A. apology: apologize
memory: memorize
emphasis: emphasize
1. memorize
2. apologize
3. emphasize

B. Sample Answers
1. James began to analyze the contents of the beaker.
2. It is my intention to shop for shoes this weekend.

3. Hannah used many examples from the text to establish her position.

4. Joe used an encyclopedia to determine the year the war ended.

Build Language Skills: Grammar, p. 139

A. 1. I, my; 2. they, their; 3. it, our; 4. he, his; 5. you, your

B. 1. When Paula was younger, *she* was afraid of dogs.

2. Even though dogs usually liked Paula, *she* found *them* frightening.

3. Paula's brother Ray had always wanted a dog of *his* own.

4. Paula and Ray visited a pet store where *they* watched a puppy playing.

5. After Paula held a puppy on *her* lap, *she* began to lose *her* fear of dogs.

from *An American Childhood* by Annie Dillard

Selection Test A, p. 140

Critical Reading

1. ANS: C	DIF: Easy	OBJ: Comprehension
2. ANS: B	DIF: Easy	OBJ: Interpretation
3. ANS: C	DIF: Easy	OBJ: Comprehension
4. ANS: B	DIF: Easy	OBJ: Comprehension
5. ANS: D	DIF: Easy	OBJ: Literary Analysis
6. ANS: C	DIF: Easy	OBJ: Interpretation
7. ANS: A	DIF: Easy	OBJ: Comprehension
8. ANS: C	DIF: Easy	OBJ: Literary Analysis
9. ANS: B	DIF: Easy	OBJ: Reading
10. ANS: A	DIF: Easy	OBJ: Interpretation

Vocabulary and Grammar

11. ANS: D	DIF: Easy	OBJ: Vocabulary
12. ANS: A	DIF: Easy	OBJ: Grammar
13. ANS: C	DIF: Easy	OBJ: Grammar
14. ANS: B	DIF: Easy	OBJ: Vocabulary
15. ANS: C	DIF: Easy	OBJ: Vocabulary

Essay

16. Students should describe the author's initial experience with the car lights with details that convey the fear and anxiety she felt. They might include the fact that the author calls the light a spirit or makes it sound ghostlike. They might mention that the light moves quickly toward her in bed and then disappears inexplicably.

Students may say that once the girl figures out where the lights are coming from, she can relax and enjoy the thrill of how scary they still look.

Difficulty: *Easy*

Objective: *Essay*

17. Students should identify several details that Dillard uses to bring the scene to life, including the movement of the light around the room, its similarity to a Chinese dragon and a cobra, and so on. Students will have varying answers about how effective Dillard's piece is in creating fear in readers. They might remember being afraid at night themselves, so they might identify with Dillard's experience.

Difficulty: *Easy*

Objective: *Essay*

Selection Test B, p. 143

Critical Reading

1. ANS: A	DIF: Average	OBJ: Comprehension
2. ANS: C	DIF: Average	OBJ: Comprehension
3. ANS: B	DIF: Average	OBJ: Reading
4. ANS: B	DIF: Average	OBJ: Literary Analysis
5. ANS: B	DIF: Challenging	OBJ: Reading
6. ANS: C	DIF: Challenging	OBJ: Comprehension
7. ANS: C	DIF: Average	OBJ: Comprehension
8. ANS: B	DIF: Challenging	OBJ: Reading
9. ANS: D	DIF: Challenging	OBJ: Reading
10. ANS: B	DIF: Average	OBJ: Literary Analysis
11. ANS: D	DIF: Average	OBJ: Interpretation
12. ANS: A	DIF: Challenging	OBJ: Interpretation
13. ANS: B	DIF: Average	OBJ: Interpretation
14. ANS: A	DIF: Average	OBJ: Interpretation
15. ANS: A	DIF: Average	OBJ: Reading

Vocabulary and Grammar

16. ANS: B	DIF: Average	OBJ: Vocabulary
17. ANS: B	DIF: Average	OBJ: Grammar
18. ANS: B	DIF: Average	OBJ: Vocabulary
19. ANS: D	DIF: Average	OBJ: Grammar

Essay

20. Students should identify details such as the comparisons of the lights to a dragon and a cobra, or the descriptions of the accompanying sound as a roar and a wail. They also might mention that the author refers to

the light as "it," which suggests it is a something cryptic, and therefore, scary. They should reach the conclusion that the details convey feelings such as fear, anxiety, and panic.

Difficulty: *Average*
Objective: *Essay*

21. Students should cite descriptive details about the lights moving around the narrator's room toward her bed, but stopping and disappearing just short of reaching her. They might say that the contrast with the author's peacefully sleeping younger sister adds to the feelings of fear and helplessness Dillard conveys. Anxiety increases further because young Dillard knows that the lights will most likely appear more than once. In presenting such details, students may conclude, Dillard creates a buildup of tension that is suddenly gone when she realizes that the lights result from something normal—a passing car. Her purpose, then, may be to explain how a child's mind works.

Difficulty: *Average*
Objective: *Essay*

from *Travels With Charley* by John Steinbeck

Vocabulary Warm-up Exercises, p. 147

A. 1. typical
2. prefers
3. powerful
4. creation
5. reluctance
6. conceal
7. landscape
8. genuine

B. Sample Answers
1. T; Funnel clouds, which can be seen as *omens*, signal bad weather and could fill people with *foreboding*.
2. F; *Publicity* about movie stars is sometimes exaggerated and cannot always be believed.
3. F; There should be evidence that a person has caused a *commotion* before any punishment is given.
4. T; Toddlers are curious, and because they often don't sense danger, they need *restrictions*.
5. F; Both poles are *desolate*, or empty, places.
6. T; *Suspicions* are often correct, so you should probably check on your pet's health.
7. F; When you have *clarity*, you understand a problem better and can work out a solution more easily.

Reading Warm-up A, p. 148

Words that students are to circle appear in parentheses.

Sample Answers
1. Two-lane roads with traffic lights are too slow for busy lives. I *prefer* camping in a tent in a park to visiting my cousins in the hectic city.

2. (like most drivers); A *typical* event in my day is playing soccer after school.
3. take the modern road; I have no *reluctance* to doing my chores so that I get my allowance.
4. (smoothly, forcefully) A *powerful* engine is suited to the interstate because it helps a car go fast.
5. The *landscape* I'd see includes trees, hills, houses, and rest stops along the interstate.
6. (real); Traveling on an older road is *genuine* because it offers a particular style that the interstate lacks.
7. Motels with rooms shaped liked tepees, theme diners, and streamlined service stations; The superhighway can *conceal* treasures because it goes around them and prevents people from seeing them.
8. (a certain hotel in Winslow, Arizona); A treasure in all of *creation* is my cuddly cat Paws.

Reading Warm-up B, p. 149

Words that students are to circle appear in parentheses.

Sample Answers
1. Just hearing their names—the Badlands and the Black-Hills; I've had a *suspicion* that my brother has been practicing to try out for the school play.
2. (deserted); I wouldn't expect to find many people in a *desolate* place because it's deserted and lonely.
3. (look for signs of bad things to come); Once I was home alone, and suddenly, the sky grew dark and the wind began to blow hard, creating a sense of *foreboding*.
4. (a dead bird, a sudden whirlwind); People might look for *omens* because they are worried about the future and they think that *omens* will tell them what to expect.
5. The fossils of ancient animals help us look into the past. Someone would want to look into the past with greater *clarity* to understand it better.
6. The *restrictions* I have at home are not staying out too late, no television before finishing my homework, and not spending too much time playing games on the Internet.
7. (attempted to reach the top of the monument); *Seeking publicity* means "calling attention to yourself by providing lots of interesting, and maybe exaggerated, information."
8. I wouldn't get much sleep because a *commotion* would create lots of noise.

from *Travels With Charley*
by John Steinbeck

Reading: Evaluate Whether the Author Achieves His or Her Purpose, p. 150

Sample Answers
A. 1. Steinbeck sounds honest in this passage when he admits not wanting to feel lonely. That statement makes me want to trust what he writes in the rest of

the piece. In other words, I do believe that he wants to inform me about America as he informs himself about the country.

2. Again, Steinbeck's honesty about himself—admitting that he is afraid—makes me inclined to trust the information he is giving me about this woman.

Literary Analysis: Author's Style, p. 151

Sample Answers

A. 1. *Mostly, the vocabulary of an educated person, but lots of informal, conversational words and phrases, including unusual, homey modifiers:* "warpy reservoir"; "rattler" (referring to the bakery wagon); "monster land"; "rabbity wind"; "telescopically clear"; "shaley road"; "little button things"

2. *A lot of mature sentences, but once in a while short, conversational-sounding sentences pop up to give the piece an informal feel:* "My plan was clear, concise, and reasonable"; "One sharp difficulty presented itself"; "I was not recognized even once"; "The night was loaded with omens"; "I'll tell you what then"; "I vote to stay. You vote to go"; "They [the Bad Lands] deserve their name."

3. *Personal, modest, open:* "my own shortcomings"; "I had reluctance to drive on that amounted to fear"; ". . . I hadn't paid attention"; "I came on it in amazement"; "As I was not prepared for the Missouri boundary, so I was not prepared for the Bad Lands"; "with a shyness as though I crashed a party"; ". . . I felt unwanted in this land . . ."; "I went into a state of flight, running to get away from the unearthly landscape" "And I thought how every safe generality I gathered in my travels was canceled by another."

B. Although Steinbeck seems to have the ability to write in a sophisticated way, in this excerpt, he keeps getting back to straightforward, unpretentious prose.

Vocabulary Builder, p. 152

A. 1. *synonym:* weakened; *antonym:* strengthened
2. *synonym:* difficult; *antonym:* easy
3. *synonym:* unexplainable; *antonym:* comprehensible
4. *synonym:* heavenly; *antonym:* earthbound

B. Sample Answers

1. His health was impaired by smoking cigarettes for many years.
2. Rigorous training all summer prepared me for the fall marathon.
3. Sam found it inexplicable that Sharon wanted pie instead of cake on her birthday.
4. The newlyweds were living and breathing examples of celestial bliss.

Enrichment: Travel Writing Career, p. 155

1. Answers will vary.
2. Possible answers: General research into the city should cover population size and diversity, geography/climate, language(s), major tourist sights, political and economic issues, transportation, and so on.
3. Possible answers: I could locate teenagers at schools and at popular culture events such as concerts.
4. Possible answer: I will need to hire a translator through an agency, or maybe I can find bilingual teenagers through the department of education.
5. Possible answers: My readers may want to know (a) how much freedom teenagers in that city have; (b) whether teenagers have to work or have a lot of leisure time; (c) whether schools in that city are more or less demanding than their own schools; (d) what opportunities teenagers have after they finish their formal schooling; (e) how well (or not) teenagers in that city get along with older generations.

Selection Test A, p. 156

Critical Reading

1. ANS: C	DIF: Easy	OBJ: Comprehension
2. ANS: B	DIF: Easy	OBJ: Comprehension
3. ANS: A	DIF: Easy	OBJ: Comprehension
4. ANS: D	DIF: Easy	OBJ: Interpretation
5. ANS: B	DIF: Easy	OBJ: Literary Analysis
6. ANS: C	DIF: Easy	OBJ: Reading
7. ANS: C	DIF: Easy	OBJ: Interpretation
8. ANS: A	DIF: Easy	OBJ: Comprehension
9. ANS: C	DIF: Easy	OBJ: Literary Analysis
10. ANS: D	DIF: Easy	OBJ: Reading
11. ANS: D	DIF: Easy	OBJ: Interpretation

Vocabulary and Grammar

12. ANS: B	DIF: Easy	OBJ: Vocabulary
13. ANS: A	DIF: Easy	OBJ: Vocabulary
14. ANS: D	DIF: Easy	OBJ: Grammar

Essay

15. Students should mention that on first seeing the Bad Lands, Steinbeck feels afraid because the area looks barren, desolate, and dangerous. He does not feel welcome. The first person he meets does not have much to say, and later a woman talks as though she dislikes living there. However, in the late afternoon, the sun

causes the land to look beautiful. Students might note that the colors are magnificent and the night becomes welcoming and pleasant.

Difficulty: *Easy*

Objective: *Essay*

16. Students' responses describing the Bad Lands should include such details as the vastness and loneliness of the land, the scarcity of people, the harsh and sparse vegetation and wildlife, and the colors of the landscape. Students' personal reactions to the area will vary, but students should provide reasons for their opinions.

Difficulty: *Easy*

Objective: *Essay*

Selection Test B, p. 159

Critical Reading

1. ANS: C	DIF: Average	OBJ: Comprehension
2. ANS: A	DIF: Average	OBJ: Comprehension
3. ANS: C	DIF: Challenging	OBJ: Comprehension
4. ANS: A	DIF: Average	OBJ: Comprehension
5. ANS: A	DIF: Average	OBJ: Reading
6. ANS: C	DIF: Challenging	OBJ: Interpretation
7. ANS: B	DIF: Average	OBJ: Interpretation
8. ANS: D	DIF: Average	OBJ: Interpretation
9. ANS: A	DIF: Challenging	OBJ: Interpretation
10. ANS: B	DIF: Average	OBJ: Literary Analysis
11. ANS: D	DIF: Average	OBJ: Interpretation
12. ANS: C	DIF: Challenging	OBJ: Reading
13. ANS: C	DIF: Average	OBJ: Literary Analysis
14. ANS: B	DIF: Challenging	OBJ: Literary Analysis
15. ANS: B	DIF: Challenging	OBJ: Reading

Vocabulary and Grammar

16. ANS: C	DIF: Average	OBJ: Vocabulary
17. ANS: A	DIF: Average	OBJ: Grammar
18. ANS: D	DIF: Challenging	OBJ: Grammar
19. ANS: C	DIF: Average	OBJ: Vocabulary

Essay

20. Students may say that Steinbeck's truck seems to be well outfitted, and he has prepared himself emotionally by bringing Charley as a companion and safety measure. Some students, though, may find ways in which Steinbeck might have done less or could have done more, before his trip. For example, he could have planned to contact his friends often by phone so that they would not worry about him.

Difficulty: *Average*

Objective: *Essay*

21. Among the things that Steinbeck discovers about America, students might mention the following: people were not as curious about him as he had expected; the roads were not as dangerous as he had feared; landscapes were startlingly diverse, as illustrated by the difference between the areas east and west of the Missouri River; a landscape that appears barren and desolate during the day can become beautiful at night. Students might mention that Steinbeck's discoveries about America cause him to look inward, allowing him to discover new things about himself.

Difficulty: *Average*

Objective: *Essay*

"The American Dream"
by Martin Luther King, Jr.

Vocabulary Warm-up Exercises, p. 163

A. 1. slavery
2. individual
3. democracy
4. equal
5. segregation
6. destruction
7. perspective
8. emerge

B. Sample Answers

1. During the *pursuit* of the *moral* thing to do, I have sometimes found myself in a *dilemma*.
2. The *legacy* I might receive from my grandparents is believing it's important to help others.
3. I do believe that people are *essentially* good.
4. The *development* of a business requires money and hard work.
5. I believe that my success is *ultimately* up to me.
6. A child is often the *heir* to his or her parents' possessions.

Reading Warm-up A, p. 164

Words that students are to circle appear in parentheses.

Sample Answers

1. The board wouldn't allow his daughter to attend an all-white school in his neighborhood; Another form of *segregation* is making African Americans live in separate housing.
2. (way of looking at the situation); My *perspective* on an open campus is that it is OK for high school but not for middle school.
3. of the same quality; Getting a bike is *equal* to getting a skateboard.

4. From a lawsuit brought by just one *person*, the movement to allow black children into white schools grew. The *individual* I admire is my basketball coach who teaches us all what being fair means.

5. opening doors from which blacks had been barred; Brown winning his case helped bring on *destruction* of unfair practices and opened opportunities for African Americans.

6. Finally, they could start to emerge as full citizens and enjoy the same rights as other Americans, such as voting.; When someone is freed from *slavery*, he or she doesn't belong to anyone anymore.

7. To *emerge* as a citizen means to begin participating in the voting process.

8. people vote for representatives who make the laws of the land; Living in a *democracy* means having freedom of speech.

Reading Warm-up B, p. 165

Words that students are to circle appear in parentheses.

Sample Answers

1. turn of events; If I found a lost ring and got a reward, it would be an unexpected *development*.

2. (What was right and what was wrong?); I have faced a *moral dilemma* when I made plans with one friend, then was asked to go somewhere better with another friend.

3. my goal to be elected to City Council; I was in *pursuit* of a lead role in the spring musical.

4. (inheritance); There is more than one kind of *legacy* because you can inherit wealth, and you can also inherit attitudes and feelings.

5. (at heart); I feel that *essentially* most people would rather do good things than bad things.

6. someone who would follow in their footsteps; I might be *heir* to my family's sense of humor.

7. finally; *In the end*, we would all be better off if we conserved natural resources.

"The American Dream"
by Martin Luther King, Jr.

Reading: Evaluate Whether the Author Achieves His or Her Purpose, p. 166

Sample Answers

A. 1. This passage cites slavery and segregation as support for calling America "a dream as yet unfulfilled." The historical facts make me agree with King.

   2. In this passage, King makes America's situation sound urgent—as if time is running out. Since the passage scares me a bit, I guess it helps King achieve his purpose of getting me to agree with him.

3. This passage contains both a compliment and a warning—sort of like "tough love." It makes me want to be on King's side.

B. King's specific purpose seems to be to remind readers of continuing unequal, prejudicial practices in America and to inspire readers to act in ways that will promote universal brotherhood. He seems to make those points very clearly, so I think he accomplishes his purpose.

Literary Analysis: Author's Style, p. 167

Sample Answers

A. 1. *Many formal, sophisticated words and phrases:* universalism, noble, schizophrenic personality, sociopolitical document, tragically divided, world perspective

   2. *Repetition:* "It does not say some men. . . . It does not say all white men. . . . It does not say all Gentiles. . . . It does not say all Protestants"; "Through our scientific genius . . . now through our moral and spiritual development . . ."; "we must learn . . . we must come to see. . . . We must all live together; we must all be concerned about each other." *Some long, complicated but smooth, even sentences:* "Very seldom . . . the worth of human personality"; "Now, more than ever before . . . true saviors of democracy."

   3. *Mostly serious, urgent, authoritative, preaching:* "the clock of destiny is ticking out"; "she can no longer have second-class citizens"; "Now, more than ever before"; "Now may I suggest some of the things we must do."

B. In long but direct sentences, King balances two ideas, often conflicting. This balance is not only rhythmically pleasing but also effective in getting his point across memorably. So I would say King's style is forthright and formal, but he is not above a little joke (the Bob Hope story).

Vocabulary Builder, p. 168

A. 1. *synonym:* opposite; *antonym:* same

   2. *synonym:* contradictions; *antonym:* agreement

   3. *synonym:* sure; *antonym:* doubtful

   4. *synonym:* abuse; *antonym:* respect

B. **Sample Answers**

   1. The short sister was the antithesis of the tall sister in all respects—not just in height.

   2. One of several paradoxes of life is that the human heart can be filled with love and with hate at the same time.

   3. When my brother has a strong opinion, he comes across as unequivocal.

   4. In certain cases, making employees work overtime without paying them is exploitation.

Enrichment: Delivering a Speech Effectively, p. 171

The paragraph by Martin Luther King, Jr., marked up with words and symbols to represent one possible delivery:

Man's specific genius | and technological ingenu-

ity | has **dwarfed** distance | and placed time in

chains. | Jet planes have compressed into minutes |

Drag out "days and months."
distances that once took days and months to cover. |

It is not common for a preacher to be quoting Bob

Hope, | but I think he has aptly described this jet age

in which we live. || If, on taking off on a nonstop flight

from Los Angeles to New York City, | you develop

hiccups, | he said, | you will hic in Los Angeles | and

cup in New York City. | **That** is really *moving*. || If

you take a flight from Tokyo, Japan, on Sunday

morning, | you will arrive in Seattle, Washington, on

the **preceding** Saturday night. | When your friends

meet you at the airport and ask you when you left

Tokyo, | you will have to say, "I left tomorrow." ||

speed up
This is the kind of world in which we live. Now this is

a bit humorous but I am trying to laugh a basic fact

slow way down
into all of us: || the world in which we live | has

become a single neighborhood.

from *Travels With Charley*
by John Steinbeck
"The American Dream"
by Martin Luther King, Jr.

Build Language Skills: Vocabulary, p. 172

A. 1. creation; 2. decision; 3. solution; 4. conclusion;
5. decoration

B. 1. intention; 2. analyze; 3. achieve; 4. determine;
5. establish

Build Language Skills: Grammar, p. 173

A. 1. herself; 2. themselves; 3. himself; 4. itself (*accept himself* or *herself*); 5. yourself; 6. himself;
7. ourselves; 8. herself

B. Sample Answers
1. I asked myself whether or not I wanted to run the long race.
2. Beverly told a funny story about herself.
3. We congratulated ourselves for completing the project.
4. The puppy found its way home by itself.
5. You can teach yourself to speak a foreign language.

"The American Dream"
by Martin Luther King, Jr.

Selection Test A, p. 174

Critical Reading

1. ANS: B	DIF: Easy	OBJ: Comprehension
2. ANS: C	DIF: Easy	OBJ: Interpretation
3. ANS: C	DIF: Easy	OBJ: Reading
4. ANS: D	DIF: Easy	OBJ: Literary Analysis
5. ANS: A	DIF: Easy	OBJ: Literary Analysis
6. ANS: C	DIF: Easy	OBJ: Reading
7. ANS: C	DIF: Easy	OBJ: Comprehension
8. ANS: A	DIF: Easy	OBJ: Comprehension
9. ANS: D	DIF: Easy	OBJ: Interpretation
10. ANS: B	DIF: Easy	OBJ: Comprehension
11. ANS: D	DIF: Easy	OBJ: Literary Analysis

Vocabulary and Grammar

12. ANS: C	DIF: Easy	OBJ: Vocabulary
13. ANS: B	DIF: Easy	OBJ: Vocabulary
14. ANS: A	DIF: Easy	OBJ: Grammar
15. ANS: B	DIF: Easy	OBJ: Grammar

Essay

16. Students should explain that King wants readers to accept the equality of all men. Students who think King accomplished his purpose may note that he cites the basic premise of the Declaration of Independence to support his view and warns that America will not survive as a leading nation if it does not put the declaration into practice.
Difficulty: *Easy*
Objective: *Essay*

17. Students should explain that with technological advancements, airplanes have become faster. As a result, people can cross the world in hours and days rather than weeks and months. Some students may agree with King that this pace allows more opportunities for communication and understanding among people in different countries. Others will argue that making the world smaller has done nothing to improve world brotherhood.

Difficulty: *Easy*
Objective: *Essay*

Selection Test B, p. 177

Critical Reading

1. ANS: A	DIF: Average	OBJ: Comprehension
2. ANS: C	DIF: Challenging	OBJ: Interpretation
3. ANS: D	DIF: Average	OBJ: Comprehension
4. ANS: B	DIF: Average	OBJ: Reading
5. ANS: C	DIF: Challenging	OBJ: Interpretation
6. ANS: C	DIF: Average	OBJ: Interpretation
7. ANS: A	DIF: Average	OBJ: Reading
8. ANS: D	DIF: Average	OBJ: Interpretation
9. ANS: A	DIF: Average	OBJ: Literary Analysis
10. ANS: B	DIF: Challenging	OBJ: Reading
11. ANS: B	DIF: Average	OBJ: Literary Analysis
12. ANS: C	DIF: Average	OBJ: Literary Analysis
13. ANS: A	DIF: Average	OBJ: Comprehension
14. ANS: B	DIF: Challenging	OBJ: Interpretation
15. ANS: C	DIF: Challenging	OBJ: Comprehension

Vocabulary and Grammar

16. ANS: C	DIF: Average	OBJ: Vocabulary
17. ANS: B	DIF: Average	OBJ: Grammar
18. ANS: D	DIF: Average	OBJ: Vocabulary
19. ANS: A	DIF: Average	OBJ: Grammar

Essay

20. Student responses might include some of the following ideas: King argues that America is not living up to its ideal of equality and is instead a nation divided against itself. This division, he argues, will ultimately weaken the country and its credibility among other nations. His conclusion that "we must all live together as brothers, or we will all perish together as fools" is logical because it follows that if technology has made the world a single neighborhood, then the actions of any one member of that neighborhood will affect all the others. If we allow disharmony to continue, it will spread and destroy our nation and others.

Difficulty: *Average*
Objective: *Essay*

21. Students' answers should center on King's main directive, that people need to see the world as one, and all people should treat one another as equals. This is a moral and ethical stance that can be acted out in the ways one chooses to live every day. Students might point out that treating other people with more kindness, respect, and care would be a start toward accomplishing what King is talking about.

Difficulty: *Challenging*
Objective: *Essay*

"Up the Slide" by Jack London
"A Glow in the Dark" from *Woodsong*
by Gary Paulsen

Vocabulary Warm-up Exercises, p. 181

A. 1. rig
2. barren
3. firewood
4. pose
5. ascent
6. gully
7. ebbed
8. pulse

B. Sample Answers
1. F. Even though my homework *consumed* only ten minutes, I may have spent enough time on it because that may be all that was needed to do a good job on it.
2. T. Mountain climbers need handholds and footholds and an *outcropping* of rock provides a *favorable* place for the climbers to find them.
3. F. A nightlight with an *eerie* glow could scare a young child.
4. T. When you have *nausea*, you usually throw up *convulsively*, which means that you cannot control it.
5. T. Driving in a snowstorm can be very *treacherous* because you cannot see and the road is probably very slippery.
6. F. A sign that is *upright* is not one that has fallen over but one that is standing straight up.

Reading Warm-up A, p. 182

Words that students are to circle appear in parentheses.

Sample Answers
1. (People before them had already staked their claim to most of the gold fields.); Something that might *pose* a problem to me would be having a test in every subject on the same day.
2. driving a team of dogs, hooked up; I'd like to drive a dog *rig* because it would be fun to travel over the frozen ground at high speed.

3. (frozen); The Sahara is a <u>barren</u> desert.

4. <u>descent</u>; Going up twenty flights of stairs would be a difficult *ascent*.

5. <u>falling down into</u>; Near my house there is a *gully* that is filled with jagged rocks.

6. (fire, wood); My family has used *firewood* when we're out camping and built a fire for roasting marshmallows.

7. (bright stars); A secondhand on a watch would *pulse* with each second.

8. <u>brilliance of the lights</u>; *Ebbed* means "got dimmer or faded."

Reading Warm-up B, p. 183

Words that students are to circle appear in parentheses.

Sample Answers

1. (haunted); At the haunted house, many *eerie* faces stared out at me.

2. As you draw closer, you will be able to see mushrooms <u>sticking out</u> on the surface of a tree that is <u>standing tall and straight</u>.

3. (can help out); Good weather is *favorable* to my weekend soccer game.

4. <u>poisonous</u>; When we went white-water rafting, we came upon *treacherous* rapids.

5. (become very sick); Having the flu might make someone feel *nausea* and throw up *convulsively*.

6. (time); Waiting in line to check out in the busy stores at the mall <u>consumed</u> a lot of my time.

"Up the Slide" by Jack London
"A Glow in the Dark" from *Woodsong*
by Gary Paulsen

Literary Analysis: Fictional and Nonfictional Narratives, p. 184

1. the characters of Clay and Swanson; Clay's discovery of the dead pine; Clay's plan to retrieve the pine in 30 minutes

2. the landscape, the Siwash village, the Yukon River, Moosehide Mountain, Lieutenant Schwatka

3. the explanation of the glowing log; a scientific, informational, or factual detail

4. the details describing Paulsen's and the dogs' approach of the glowing form; the description creates suspense

Vocabulary Builder, p. 185

Sample Answers

A. 1. When we completed our *ascent*, <u>we sat down to rest on the hilltop</u>.

2. <u>Pulling a wagon full of bricks</u> requires great *exertion*.

3. It is difficult to *sustain* <u>anger toward a friend</u>.

4. The upward-facing lampshade *diffused* <u>the light onto the ceiling and walls</u>.

5. Before our *descent*, <u>we cleaned up our mountaintop campsite</u>.

6. Using a careful *maneuver*, <u>the skater lifted his partner over his head</u>.

B. 1. C; 2. A; 3. D; 4. B

Selection Test A, p. 187
Critical Reading

1. ANS: B	DIF: Easy	OBJ: Interpretation
2. ANS: C	DIF: Easy	OBJ: Interpretation
3. ANS: A	DIF: Easy	OBJ: Literary Analysis
4. ANS: D	DIF: Easy	OBJ: Comprehension
5. ANS: B	DIF: Easy	OBJ: Comprehension
6. ANS: C	DIF: Easy	OBJ: Comprehension
7. ANS: A	DIF: Easy	OBJ: Interpretation
8. ANS: D	DIF: Easy	OBJ: Comprehension
9. ANS: D	DIF: Easy	OBJ: Literary Analysis
10. ANS: B	DIF: Easy	OBJ: Interpretation
11. ANS: C	DIF: Easy	OBJ: Comprehension
12. ANS: A	DIF: Easy	OBJ: Literary Analysis
13. ANS: C	DIF: Easy	OBJ: Literary Analysis

Vocabulary

14. ANS: D	DIF: Easy	OBJ: Vocabulary
15. ANS: B	DIF: Easy	OBJ: Vocabulary

Essay

16. In "Up the Slide," Clay Dilham's decision to take the journey in thirty minutes shows great self-confidence . . . or conceit; his attempt to get to the fallen tree shows courage and determination. In "A Glow in the Dark," Gary Paulsen's decision to run the dogs without a lamp may show either bravery or foolishness; his actons toward his dogs show that he is affectionate and good-natured; and his decision to approach the light shows that he is courageous. Students' preferences for one character over another will vary, but should be supported with reasons.

Difficulty: *Easy*

Objective: *Essay*

17. A fictional narrative tells a story about made-up characters or events. For example, in "Up the Slide," the character of Clay Dilham and the events of his journey are all imaginary. However, the author of a fictional narrative can borrow details from real life, such as the Yukon River and the town of Dawson. A nonfictional narrative, on the other hand, tells *only* about events and people from real-life. Nothing in a nonfictional narrative can be

made up. For example, the author of "A Glow in the Dark" describes something that actually happened to him. Even though he tells the story in an exciting way that makes it *sound* fictional, every detail in the story is actually true.

Difficulty: *Easy*
Objective: *Essay*

Selection Test B, p. 190

Critical Reading

1. ANS: A	DIF: Average	OBJ: Interpretation	
2. ANS: D	DIF: Challenging	OBJ: Comprehension	
3. ANS: C	DIF: Average	OBJ: Interpretation	
4. ANS: D	DIF: Average	OBJ: Literary Analysis	
5. ANS: B	DIF: Average	OBJ: Comprehension	
6. ANS: A	DIF: Challenging	OBJ: Literary Analysis	
7. ANS: C	DIF: Challenging	OBJ: Comprehension	
8. ANS: B	DIF: Average	OBJ: Interpretation	
9. ANS: D	DIF: Average	OBJ: Comprehension	
10. ANS: A	DIF: Challenging	OBJ: Literary Analysis	
11. ANS: C	DIF: Challenging	OBJ: Literary Analysis	
12. ANS: D	DIF: Challenging	OBJ: Interpretation	
13. ANS: D	DIF: Average	OBJ: Literary Analysis	
14. ANS: C	DIF: Average	OBJ: Literary Analysis	
15. ANS: A	DIF: Average	OBJ: Literary Analysis	

Vocabulary

16. ANS: A	DIF: Average	OBJ: Vocabulary
17. ANS: B	DIF: Average	OBJ: Vocabulary
18. ANS: C	DIF: Challenging	OBJ: Vocabulary
19. ANS: A	DIF: Average	OBJ: Vocabulary

Essay

20. Students should note that the details of each story reveal a great deal about each character. In "Up the Slide," Clay's expedition shows that he loves a challenge; his reaction to each problem along the way shows intelligence and determination; and his underestimation of the time required for the outing and its risks shows his great self-confidence or his recklessness and youth. In "A Glow in the Dark," Gary Paulsen's choice to run the dogs without a light may show either his bravery or his foolishness; his reactions to his dogs show that he is affectionate and good-natured; his reaction to the light shows that he has an active imagination; and his investigation of the light shows his courage and curiosity.

Difficulty: *Average*
Objective: *Essay*

21. Students should define *narrative* as any type of writing that tells a story; they may mention that most narratives are told in chronological order. "Up the Slide" is a fictional narrative. Its characters and events are invented, although it borrows some details (such as the Yukon River and Moosehead Mountain) from real life. "A Glow in the Dark" is a nonfictional narrative. Everything in the story actually exists or occurred in real life. Some of the details that Paulsen includes, though, give the story the excitement of fiction. For example, his slow approach to the strange glow adds drama and suspense to the narrative.

Difficulty: *Challenging*
Objective: *Essay*

Writing Workshop—Unit 1, Part 2

Autobiographical Essay: Integrating Grammar Skills, p. 194

A.
1. he; arrow to *Raul*
2. his; arrow to *Daniel*
3. I, our, arrow from *our* to *Bethany and I*
4. some, their, others; arrow from *their* to *some*

B.
1. Several are running in their first marathon.
2. Lilianna said she would bring her own water.
3. One of the boys left his towel on the ground.
4. All of the runners had to turn in their registration forms last week.
5. Both girls sprained their ankles sprinting for the finish line.

Spelling Workshop—Unit 1

Commonly Misspelled Words, p. 195

A. 1. really; 2. happened; 3. favorite; 4. caught; 5. we're; 6. beginning; 7. weird; 8. friends; 9. they're; 10. especially

B. **Sample Answers**
1. At the beginning of "The Sound of Music," Maria is on the top of a mountain singing. The movie is based on actual events that happened during Von Trapp family's escape from Austria in World War II. "My Favorite Things" is the title of a song in the movie.
2. The weird glow in the forest at night caught the attention of many of the town's residents. Friends and neighbors could not really believe they had seen something so mysterious. They were especially frightened when it began to float up to the night sky.
3. My friends and I enjoy many of the same activities. We're always playing soccer and riding bikes. My mother always reminds me that they're very special people.

Unit 1, Part 2 Answers

Benchmark Test 2, p. 198

MULTIPLE CHOICE

1. ANS: A
2. ANS: C
3. ANS: D
4. ANS: A
5. ANS: B
6. ANS: C
7. ANS: D
8. ANS: B
9. ANS: B
10. ANS: A
11. ANS: D
12. ANS: A
13. ANS: C
14. ANS: B
15. ANS: A
16. ANS: D
17. ANS: B
18. ANS: A
19. ANS: B
20. ANS: C
21. ANS: C
22. ANS: A
23. ANS: D
24. ANS: B
25. ANS: C
26. ANS: C
27. ANS: A
28. ANS: C
29. ANS: D
30. ANS: C
31. ANS: A

ESSAY

32. Students' narratives should recount events in chronological order. They should make the situation clear and clearly state the change that took place in their outlook.

33. Students should clearly state the situation and give some indication of why they feel it needs improving. They should then suggest the actions to take and/or the change in attitude that they feel would improve the situation or solve the problem entirely.

34. Students should use a consistent first-person point of view. They should present a clear sequence of events that centers around a particular conflict or problem. They should include their feelings about the incident and make clear why the incident is significant for them.